Sudan

Sudan

Race, Religion and Violence

JOK MADUT JOK

ONEWORLD

OXFORD

SUDAN: RACE, RELIGION AND VIOLENCE

A Oneworld Book
Published by Oneworld Publications 2007

Copyright © Jok Madut Jok 2007

ISBN-13:978–1–85168–366–6

Typeset by Jayvee, Trivandrum, India
Cover design by Design Deluxe
Printed and bound by Thomson-Shore Inc., USA

Oneworld Publications
185 Banbury Road
Oxford OX2 7AR
England
www.oneworld-publications.com

CONTENTS

ACKNOWLEDGEMENTS

Many people and institutions have helped make this book possible. I am particularly grateful to a large number of Sudanese, many of whom I cannot mention here by name for their own safety. I am thankful to the United States Institute of Peace for their financial support of research in Sudan (Grant number SG-31-00) and to the Woodrow Wilson International Center for Scholars for a year-long fellowship, which provided a wonderful environment to do research, think and interact with a cohort of other fellows. Much of this book was written during my tenure at the Wilson Center and I cannot give enough thanks to the staff of the center for their assistance with various research questions, colleagueship, and support. I also want to thank Duana Fullwiley for reading parts of this book. I am particularly indebted to John Ryle, Chair of the Rift Valley Institute and all the staff of the institute for facilitating my trips to Sudan. Coordinating flights, logistical requirements, and obtaining travel permits would have all been beyond my capacity without the institute's support. My special gratitude goes to the publisher and the editorial staff of Oneworld Publications, and to the anonymous readers, whose comments have greatly helped improve the manuscript. But I must quickly add that any enduring mistakes and weaknesses of the book are entirely mine.

ABBREVIATIONS

AMIS   African Union Mission in Sudan
AU   African Union
DUP   Democratic Unionist Party
ECOS   European Coalition on Oil in Sudan
EDF   Equatoria Defense Forces
GNOC   Greater Nile Petroleum Operation Company
ICC   International Criminal Court
IDP   Internally Displaced Persons
IGAD   Inter-Governmental Agency for Development
JEM   Justice and Equality Movement
LRA   Lord's Resistance Army
MSF   Medecins Sans Frontieres
NCP   National Congress Party
NDA   National Democratic Alliance
NGO   Non-Governmental Organization
NIF   National Islamic Front
NUP   National Unionist Party
OLS   Operation Lifeline Sudan
PDF   Popular Defense Forces
SAF   Sudan Alliance Forces
SANU   Sudan African Nationalist Union
SLA   Sudan Liberation Army
SOAT   Sudan Organization Against Torture
SPLA/M   Sudan People's Liberation Army/Movement
SSDF   South Sudan Defense Force
SSLM   Southern Sudan Liberation Movement

INTRODUCTION

RACIAL AND RELIGIOUS POLARIZATION AND THE POLITICS OF DISUNITY

In the summer of 2003, I chanced upon a meeting between Lazaro Sumbeiywo and a Dinka community in the town of Malualkon in the Bahr el-Ghazal region of southern Sudan. Sumbeiywo is a retired Kenyan army general who was the chief mediator in the Sudanese peace negotiations under the auspices of the Inter-Governmental Agency for Development (IGAD). He had landed in the town during a tour aimed at acquainting himself with the popular opinion from a cross-section of Sudanese communities and civil society groups regarding the peace process. At this meeting, I was particularly struck by a speech given by one of the tribal chiefs, Makwec Kuol Makwec of the Malwal section of Dinka. In passionate remarks addressed to General Sumbeiywo, the chief enumerated, with a noticeable anger, the 'racial differences' that set southern and northern Sudanese apart and the reasons why he thinks they cannot belong to a single polity. His reasons, which were received with applause from the crowd, included such practices as ritual female genital cutting prevalent in northern Sudan and Islamic ritual ablutions that the 'Arabs do after they defecate,'[1] all of which he took to be markers of what he called 'racial differences,' and that these racial differences are evident in the peoples' moral attributes, conduct and in the way the Arab-dominated government has treated the south. He went on:

> When you visited the north, you must have noticed the differences between the Arabs in the north and us here in the south ... they are red-skinned and we are black ... their names were Ali, Muhamed, Osman, etc. and our names here are Deng, Akol, Lual, etc., we have no shared ancestry, they pray differently but they want to force us to believe in their gods, they try to impose their language upon us

and they have killed our people in the process over the years. They chop off women's breasts during the raids; they have taken our people and forced them into slavery. Their climate is arid and hot and ours is cooler and vegetated, and they want our land. Their economy is more advanced and we have nothing here because they have extracted our resources for their own use, their entire way of life is different from ours, they are dishonest, they have no respect for kinship, they take their own cousins in marriage, and now you are asking us if we can live together with the Arabs as one people in a country where we, the black people, do not have a voice? If you really want to bring peace and you have the support of people from other countries in this mission, my suggestion to you is that you treat this country like a piece of cloth, have John Garang grab one end of it and Omer al-Bashir the other, and you take a knife and cut it in the middle. I assure you, the Arabs are not people we want to share anything with and history speaks for us. We have never been one, we will never be one ... They have done terrible things to us. We are not one race.[2]

The northeast African nation of Sudan is a country where relationships between ethnic and regional groups are ravaged by violence and the country is now on the verge of disintegration – both literally in terms of some of its regions seeking to break away from the polity, and figuratively in terms of the state lacking legitimacy in the eyes of the citizens. The purpose of this book is to use ethnographic and historical methods to explain how the wars and subsequent humanitarian catastrophes have threatened the unity of the country. It examines the intersection of race and religion as sites for the violent contestation of identity of the Sudanese nation. The book argues that the state, largely controlled by groups that self-identify as Arabs, has sought to forge the Sudanese national identity as 'Arab' and 'Islamic' while the majority of the population increasingly prefer to identify themselves by their specific ethnic/tribal names or simply 'African' or 'Black.' The problem is that, as the above quote has shown, these categories, which are clearly cultural and experiential identities, are taken by the Sudanese as the markers of racial identities, and they have become the basis for racial alignment as the state targets the non-Arab and non-Muslim groups for violent absorption into the 'Arab race,' or for exclusion from state services if they insist on asserting their perceived racial or chosen religious identity. These categories are also part of the model used by the politically excluded groups to explain and historicize the structures of inequality that marginalize them. They use this explanation as part of their effort to forge forms of resistance on the basis that all the non-Arabs who feel excluded from the vital structures of the state share a common platform in opposition to racial and religious politics in the country.

While various Sudanese communities may categorize each other in the same way that racial groups are popularly categorized in the Western world, i.e. in terms of physical characteristics (Hannaford, 1996; Omi and Winant, 1994), the Sudanese popular notions of race are not based on phenotypes alone, and they are not fixed. They are also pegged to a host of practices such as religion, economic activities, material conditions, the naming of people and other cultural practices. The geographic distance between groups, the natural environment in which each group lives and their language are also considered part of the racial schema. In other words, these characteristics, which are not always part of the definition of race in contemporary social sciences, but are aspects of social relations, become the lines separating racial identities. This means that racial boundaries are very fluid in Sudan, and there are many ways in which people who may be classed as blacks could also pass as Arabs, while those who have been known to be Arabs could decide to label themselves as African or black if their political circumstance demanded and allowed it. For example religion, particularly Islam, is taken by those who self-identify as Arabs as a way to relate more closely to Arabian tribes of the Middle East because of the origins of the faith. The more learned in Islamic theology, the closer to being Arab a person becomes. This means that a non-Arab who wants to become one could racially 'pass' through expressed devotion to Islam. Some northern Sudanese even try to trace their genealogy to the Prophet Muhammad as a way to claim both piety and Arab origins. Others choose to be Arabs on the basis of how good their knowledge of the Arabic language is, and having a native

Sudanese tongue other than Arabic counts against one's pure Arabness. In other contexts, people who have become native speakers of Arabic or devout Muslims as a ladder to advancement of their status and expected to be socially and politically included as Arabs, have had the disappointment of being rejected from the Arab category due to their blackness, no matter how culturally Arab or learned in Islamic religion they had become. Interviews with many Sudanese Muslims have revealed a variety of ways in which race and religion meet to influence social relations. The political confrontations that have plagued the country are a manifestation of such racially and religiously based relations. One Darfurian informant said:

> Because Islam says that there is no distinction between Arab and non-Arab, we the non-Arab Muslims believe that we are brothers with all the rest of the world's Muslims, but our Arab brothers in the north do not see it this way. They think that they are better Muslims because their race brings them closer to the Prophet, and that blacks can never make good Muslims.

While it is possible that racial identity can be conferred upon a group by others, it is also evident that in many contexts identity – racial, religious or otherwise – depends on what people think their own identity is, and not what others think one ought to be. In this regard, Wole Soyinka says that 'race is an act of will,' meaning that in a situation like Sudan, where race cannot be attributed to physical characteristics, an individual or a group can choose their racial identity.* The problem arises when one group attempts to impose its notion of identity on others. Because the group that endeavors to promote its racial concepts normally does so from the position of political and economic power, it creates extreme reactions from the other groups as they try to distance themselves from the identity of the politically dominant group. In Sudan, this creates two types of reactions from the marginalized populations. There are

* Due to lack of clarity of race, many Sudanese use the terms 'Arab-African', 'Black-Arab', or 'Arab-non-Arab' dichotomies interchangeably. They are used in the same way throughout this book.

those who seek to be included in the power structures by submitting to the notion of Arabism and in the process risk losing their indigenous identity; but still become something like second-class Arabs in the eyes of those who regard themselves as more Arab. Then there is a common thrust among other excluded people to assert more strongly the very characteristics of difference that had been the basis for their exclusion and victimization. This is what has made the wrangling over the nation's identity in Sudan so deadly, as non-Arabs fight not only for political inclusion but also to prevent the country, whose population is over 70 percent non-Arab according to recent estimates, from being labeled an Arab country.[3] A further problem with concepts of race in Sudan is that it becomes closely associated not only with economic and political exclusion if one refuses to be incorporated into the Arab race, but also with everyday experiences of derision, contempt and harassment. In other words, if ethnic groups insist on asserting their non-Arab identity, they could suffer exclusion, but if they accept the cultural incorporation, it also makes them a second-degree Arab. 'You are damned if you become an Arab and you are damned if you don't,' said a man from the Nuba mountains in central Sudan, 'and that is why I think people should just be what they want to be rather than the country imposing a rigid system of racial classification.' One of the results of this racial confusion in Sudan has been the tragic conflicts that have plagued the country for over fifty years. The causes of these wars are many, but race and religion have proved divisive and powerful separators invoked by both sides of the conflict, although in a fluid manner, and dependent on specific political circumstances that may necessitate assertion of Arabness in one context and blackness in another. By focusing on race as an important factor in the conflicts, however, I do not ignore the other factors such as resource competition, 'criminalization of the state' (Ferguson, 2006) or the political economic and benefits of war. Rather, I mean to show that these factors are not mutually exclusive. Notions of racial inequality give rise to unequal distribution, and resource competition is thus conducted through the prism of race.

Although this transient nature of racial concepts is not unique to Sudan, the Sudanese citizens racially perceive of themselves and of each other in ways that differ drastically from the way race is popularly perceived and talked about in the Western world, something that is intriguing to outside observers. While the Sudanese have an elaborate vocabulary of racial identification that classifies people into racial groups on the basis of physical characteristics, mainly phenotypic such as complexion – they use an array of skin colors like blue, black, brown and red, which are all in essence types of black and to a lesser extent, genotypic, race is also marked by a host of cultural, political and economic relations.[4] Although the Sudanese are continually engaged in construction and reconstruction of their racial identity, these classificatory systems seem well understood by the Sudanese but far less obvious to outsiders given the evident physical similarities between all the groups. ('They all look black to me,' is the reaction that I have heard from many Westerners.) The racial boundaries are continually made and unmade. Thus, the broad categories of 'Arab' and 'African' have come to be the easiest way to speak of race in Sudan, as they are thought to encompass both the outer characteristics of people and the inner, unobservable attributes such as mental capacities, morality, and other cultural values. The term 'African' does not mean much at all, at least for the majority of the rural population. The term has come to be part of the Arabs and to gain sympathy from the outside world by reducing the conflict and the massacres of their people to events defined by race. The term 'African' is also one that the authorities and elites of the north use, but selectively. The state strives it build an Arab state, and the more Sudanese people they can persuade to take on the 'Arab' label, the more proudly the ruling elite would pronounce Sudan as an Arab country. But the elite are also quick to point out that they are also African, especially when they are speaking to foreigners. In this way they deflect the claim that their actions are racist. How can they be racist against 'Africans' when they are themselves African, they reason. That the Arabs in Sudan are also clearly African, at least by residence, and that there could be black Arabs, is a fact that adds more confusion to the racial lines but is immaterial in Sudanese daily life. Although there is no agreement as to what they really mean, these Arab-African/Black categories are used both by Sudanese and outsiders to explain some of the root causes of the Sudanese conflicts, such as the ongoing Darfur conflicts that place the Arab-run government in Khartoum and its allied militias on one side, and the African people of Darfur and their opposition armies on the other. These conflicts have escalated into genocide since 2003.

Furthermore, racial lines and the degree to which Sudanese people are bounded by them are magnified and concretized by confrontations over resources as the wars in Darfur have demonstrated. As Arab cattle herders lose much of their grazing land to drought and desertification, and therefore seek pastures in the areas occupied by settled farming African communities, the non-Arab Darfurians stick more strictly to the racial category African or black (and African lands) in order to deny the herders grazing rights on the basis of a local history of demarcation of tribal territories.[5] The narrative production of this history ranged from descriptions of the non-Arabs as original inhabitants (the Fur, from whose name the term Darfur is derived, the Masalit, the Zaghawa), to the coming of the Arabs supported by the state, to Arab attempts to steal the land from the rightful owners by trickery, and, finally to the attacks that have culminated in the 2003–2006 genocide. In these narratives the Arabs are depicted as outsiders and the Blacks as an indigenous people under occupation, and therefore the insurgency, in addition to being waged in order to attain the region's share of national resources and political power, is also a strategy to defend the region against the marauding Arabs. The central government, having always faced political as well as security pressures from the Arab groups that want access to better grazing lands and services, decided in 1983 and again in 2003 to offer military support to these Arab groups in the name of fighting regional insurgencies, and in the process used counterinsurgency claims as a pretext for reconfiguring territory allocation and land use.[6] So although the genocide in Darfur is being waged in the name of racial and religious domination, it is safe to say that it is also for the survival of Arab cattle, which in turn is intrinsic to the survival of the Arab race and way of life in the region. In turn, the African Darfurians began to emphasize their African identity and increasingly described the confrontation as a racial one, for the conduct of war, once underway, began to show racial projects operating in everyday military activities. Of course, it is possible that the Darfurians began to emphasize the racial aspects of this confrontation in the same way southerners had done for years, as such depiction of the North–South conflict was beginning to draw international efforts to negotiate a settlement and yielding results, perhaps partly because of the 'race card.' A Western diplomat involved in the peace talks said, 'If Arab-African racial explanation of the North–South conflict has worked to get southerners a chance for self-determination, why would the others not expect it to work for them as well?' If it is indeed true that the black Darfurians had begun to rationalize this way, one begins to see the debates on the concept of race in Sudan as falling into two categories. One is that a group's racial identity is ideological, forged as a discourse for self-assertion, and is historically contingent. The other is that racial identification is primarily a structural phenomenon, i.e. a response to economic marginalization, exclusion from power, and other forms of inequality.

These racial dichotomies have also been used for decades as part of the southern local historical narrative to explain the five decades-long North–South civil wars as setting Arab northerners against African southerners. Southern advocacy groups and political parties which seek to represent the south as a racially defined population frequently use this North–South divide to mean the same thing as Black-Arab or African-Arab divides. Thus race in Sudan, although clearly a perceived construct with vague Arab and African racial categories, has become a battleground in which the nation's identity is contested. The marginalized populations use it as a part of their liberation discourse: the dominant groups use it to emphasize their supposedly superior status and to raise their supporters to defend their privileged position. The violent expression of exclusionary policies by the state, the violent attempts by the indigenous political movements to gain autonomy, and local activist networks advocating human rights have all used this interpretation of race to justify their actions. In other words, the

Arab-African divide has not only functioned as an important factor in the Sudanese wars, at least as a pretext, but also as a defining factor in political and military alliances. For example, all the Sudanese governments since independence have made a concerted effort to make the country primarily Arab, with numerous biases in allocation of resources favoring the groups that have accepted this Arab identity. The rest of the populations that feel marginalized have also used race to explain why they think that they have been excluded from political gains and the fruits of economic development. For instance, in the late 1970s and early 1980s, the government of Ja'afer Nimeiri conducted a massive campaign to forcibly repatriate rural migrants – those coming from the south, the west and the Nuba mountains – from Khartoum, as a way to deal with overcrowding in the city, unemployment, and crime. To carry out this program, the police used racial profiling to identify who was to be arrested. Those arrested were detained or loaded onto lorries and transported back to their regions or other more rural areas that the detainee chooses to be taken to, usually the agricultural schemes in southern Blue Nile, Kordofan or south Darfur. Because this program, known as *Kasha* in Sudanese colloquial Arabic, was based on using perceived racial appearances of people to identify who is to be repatriated from the national capital, it was carried out against all Nuba and southerners in such an arbitrary and indiscriminate fashion that it was decried as racist. Black university students, government officials and other long-term residents who had jobs and families in the city were often arrested and forced into *Kasha* trucks or jails, without examining their identity cards, and from where they were frequently released only after paying bribes.

Clearly the lack of employment and the disproportionate concentration of services and jobs in the capital and other northern cities was one of the reasons why the people living in remote regions were increasingly migrating to the north. Yet, during this same period, the government constantly altered a number of development plans such as the building of manufacturing plants in the south – for example, they diverted the equipments initially intended for a number of industrial projects in the south. The fruit canning factory in Wau, the Melut sugar factory in Upper Nile, and Tonj twine-making facility all lost their equipments and technicians, which were diverted to similar projects in the north even though the planning and foreign development aid had designated the projects to these southern towns by name. Some of these development plans had in fact been marketed to donor countries specifically as part of a postwar effort to rehabilitate the southern economy and to help southern Sudanese catch up with their northern counterparts. However, once the projects were funded, some of the funds were immediately diverted to northern projects. Such programs were taken by the local populations in these areas as evidence of blatant Arab racism toward non-Arabs and the state's racialized development policies favoring the Arabs. They argue that, if we are to take the non-Arab experience of citizenship in the Sudanese state seriously, any discussion of national unity must first of all be about social relations of citizenship and inequality on a nationwide basis. The debate goes something like this: to speak of racial difference the way non-Arabs do is to uncover the otherwise disguised relations of inequality, but when the Arab elites talk of equality, they do so in order to deflect claims of the state's recognition and responsibility for all citizens.

Furthermore, the anthropological understanding that race is the product of social circumstances rather than anything natural or essential about people's physical attributes does not make it less real for everyday Sudanese, as will become clear in the chapters that follow. In fact, it demonstrates the notion that while race cannot be pinned down in genetic terms it continues to be very important in everyday life. There is a big difference between what Sudanese people take to be their common sense about racial groups, i.e. the way racial programs operate at the level of everyday experience, and what science has to say about racial differences being unfounded on a biological level. The classification Arab vs. African is an example of racial formation as a state practice in the Sudanese context, despite official rhetoric which denies the significance of race. The Sudanese state often speaks of the non-existence of racial inequality by pointing at the constitution and the concept of equal opportunity encoded in it, but the social circumstances of non-Arabs reveal clear evidence pointing to incongruity between the equality of opportunity that the constitution speaks of and its outcome in terms of everyday experience and actual access to services. A non-racial constitution enables the state to get away with racial discrimination.

A Muslim Dinka who had lived in Khartoum observed:

> They tell us that we are all citizens of Sudan and that we are equal in front of the law, but any southerner will tell you that this is not true ... The police, the Arab merchant, and many other types of northerners show you in so many ways that you are expected to be a member of a servant class.

For decades scholars in the social sciences have articulated the social construction of race as both culturally and historically contingent, where traits are read off bodies as those bodies come to signify place and power, or lack thereof, in a given society (Omi and Winant, 1994; Bowker and Star, 2000). There are clear parallels between Sudan and other countries in the West in terms of how race is made. The classifications Arab and African, despite their shortcomings as a meaningful way to pin down people's racial identity, are as real as the way they operate in the form of stereotypes that people encounter in their daily lives. For example, in the northern cities, there are a host of preconceived notions about Blacks that inform the manner with which the state, the individual Arab, and northern communities deal with them – the Black student at Khartoum University who is taken for a servant looking for domestic work, a non-Arab businessman who gets harassed by the police on the assumption that he may be a thief, the common slurs hurled at non-Arabs as being lazy, uncivilized, unintelligent, prone to crime, the caricature of southerners or Nuba in everyday northern humor etc. – are all among the many ways in which race is experienced in Sudan. At the national level, race and racialization of social structure manifest themselves in the conflicts and destruction that they have incited in Sudan. Although this racial divide has no scientific relevance, we cannot deny its role as a trigger for political and social behavior. As Michael Omi and Howard Winant demonstrated, race should be seen 'as a dimension of human representation rather than an illusion' (Omi and Winant,

1994: 55). The state-supported racialization of social relations has been a deadly project in Sudan and has prompted people to carry out terrible acts of violence, to deny services, and to determine a person's status in the nation. Because those dominating the political power are included in the category Arab, the Arabs occupy the top of the ladder in the socioeconomic hierarchy and that racial hierarchy is therefore also reflected in the governing process, the control of state power and resources. I no longer see the impact of race as being limited to what people think of one another or to the racial slurs mentioned above, but as a mechanism for allocation of rights, resources and social standing. It has to be seen as a reality built into the structures of government, the social and political institutions of the state.

As successive Khartoum governments seek to assert their authority, and the ruling Arab groups seek to consolidate their hold on power, they apply some of these racial and religious differences as the criteria for choosing to ally themselves with some groups against others. Some of these alliances have encouraged bloodshed and much of the suffering that has gone on since the mid-1950s, making violence the predominant method to enforce the unity of the country, and making Sudan a country that faces the threat of disintegration. This threat has become increasingly visible and demonstrable over the last twenty years as more and more non-Arab and non-Muslims who feel excluded from the centers of power move further away from Sudanese citizenship and instead offer loyalty to racial, regional or ethnic citizenship. Along with the increasing politicization of Islam and consequential economic and political exclusion of the vast majority of people, these racial concepts are the crux of the Sudanese conflicts. At the very least, even if race is not the initial cause of the violent conflicts (I have already mentioned confrontation over natural resources) the racialized social structure is deployed as a weapon and ideology with which these resource wars are fought.

In religious terms, Sudan has been developing an extremist branch of Islam that has not only created a religiously intolerant society but also promoted a strain of Islamic militancy that has provoked accusations of international terrorism, an image that many

Sudanese living in the peripheries have attempted to distance themselves from. Like race, the role of religion in these conflicts cannot be divorced from other factors, but rather shows that religion in Sudan merely provides the lens through which the world is seen. The rise of militant and political Islam in Sudan dates back to 1965, but has increased dramatically since the National Islamic Front's (NIF) ascent to power in June 1989. Since then the NIF, which has changed its name to the National Congress Party, has become widely known as a regime that has successfully used civilian atrocities, ethnic cleansing, and genocide as instruments of domestic political repression with impunity. It has ruled with an iron fist and critics have been tortured, detained indefinitely without trial, or exiled: it goes without saying that the NIF has a dismal human rights record. The use of Arab militias, the Popular Defense Force, to effect indiscriminate attacks on civilians accused of abetting opposition forces in the south, slave raiding, the summary execution of twenty-eight high-ranking army officers without trial in 1989 on trumped-up charges of disloyalty, the execution of business executives on charges of illegal currency dealing under the revamped Islamic law (shari'a), the imprisonment of political leaders and exile of others like Sadiq al-Mahdi of the Umma Party and Muhamed Osman al-Mirghani, the denial of food aid to displaced persons due to allegations that they were supporters of the opposition armies, and suppression of basic civil liberties like freedom of association, freedom of the press and the persecution of critics who pointed out the state's failure to provide services, were all abuses decried by the Sudanese public. They prompted the US to impose economic sanctions on Sudan, primarily as a state sponsor of international terrorism such as the hosting of Osama bin Laden and the assassination attempt on Egyptian president Hosni Mubarak at the Organization of African Unity summit in Addis Ababa in 1995. The United Nations Commission for Human Rights has appointed a series of special rapporteurs to investigate the distressing reports and allegations of deliberate civilian displacement, torture of political opponents, massacres, slavery, and genocide, mainly in the south of the country and in the Nuba mountains.

Because this strife is driven by politicized Islam, the area of the country most affected by it has been the south, as Islamists have stated in various forums that the insurgency in the south is driven by anti-Islamic sentiments held by southerners, and therefore a war against it is not only legitimate, but also sanctioned by Islamic Jihad, or holy war. The Nuba mountains, the southern Blue Nile, and currently the western region of Darfur have also been severely affected by the war in terms of civilian atrocities, destruction of assets, the denial of food aid as a weapon of war, persecution of their political leaders and the destruction of their social and cultural institutions, or ethnocide. Although they have historically been part of the north in the old North–South dichotomy which characterized earlier conflicts, since 1983 they have been drawn into the war alongside the south, particularly because of the southern leaders' revised discourse about the conflict. The leaders of the south-based opposition Sudan People's Liberation Army (SPLA), especially its inspirational leader, the late John Garang, pitched the conflict as being more about cultural, economic, and political marginalization of the peripheries than race and religion. This appealed to a large northern population who began to either join the south or set up their own regional rebellions against the Arab-run state. The result was that some regions within the traditional north, such as Darfur, used the concept of marginalization in their war against the government, even though Darfur had been the strongest support base for successive Khartoum governments in the wars against the south for over half a century. This revised view, setting the regions against the central elite, has caused many Sudanese citizens to constantly reimagine their relationship with the nation state. The new discourse had the potential to develop class differences over race and religion as the basis for periphery vs. center and the elite vs. the marginalized confrontations, but the ruthless racialized reaction and declaration of holy war by Khartoum against these rebellious regions has renewed and strengthened racial and religious adherence in the regions as well as tying the inhabitants more strongly to their geographical regions in disfavor of their citizenship in the nation. Note the words of Amal, a Darfurian woman who was raped: 'I hate Arabs, I even hate my Arabic name and I wish I could get rid of it ... I hate having thought of myself as a citizen of Sudan all my life ... if Darfur was an independent nation, this would not happen.'

The race-based and religiously inspired military reactions to regional opposition have gained much international attention due to the ghastliness of the atrocities carried out, and have made Sudan a pariah state in the eyes of many countries, especially in the West. It has also created a stronger desire for autonomy in the peripheral regions. This book explains this development by describing and tracing contemporary histories of Sudan's many conflicts, which have raged on and off since 1955. These protracted internal conflicts have caused the death of over 2.5 million Sudanese since 1983 and the displacement of more than five million others. The wars have also resulted in the destruction of infrastructure and people's livelihoods, especially in the peripheries, and disastrously reduced living standards for the bulk of the Sudanese population.

Since 1998, Sudan has also plunged into an abyss *vis-à-vis* national unity due to its oil industry in the south. The oil industry, instead of becoming a panacea for Sudan's economic woes as many Sudanese say they had hoped it would, has come under fire in international circles and from within. No sooner did oil revenues begin to flow into the hands of the government in Khartoum in 1999 than the NIF government used them to arm itself and fight the southern-based opposition Sudan People's Liberation Army (SPLA) with more brutality, to target for eviction the Nuer and Dinka civilian populations that occupied the oil region, and to augment its economic, political and social support base within the northern part of the country. As a Nuer man who was displaced during a government attack on his village said, 'Again, typical of Sudan, even a development that could have been good news [enormous oil profits] turned out to be an omen for the ordinary people'. Oil-related atrocities were so devastating that they prompted lengthy and distressing reports from every major human rights group in the Western world,[7] government policy agencies, especially in the US,[8] major think tanks and research institutes,[9] and non-governmental organizations[10] around the world.

The scramble for Sudanese oil reserves and prospects by such disparate countries as Canada, China, Malaysia, Sweden and others sharpened the clear rift between international market interests and the micro-level politics of indigenous groups' claim to ownership of resources. These countries were quickly accused of putting their financial interests before human security in Sudan, especially as those who live in the oil regions were quick to use race and religion as the loci for the contest over oil revenues. The foreign oil companies and their mother countries were implicated in facilitating the government's war machinery because they allowed Khartoum to use oil-related facilities such as the all-weather roads and aircraft landing fields they had constructed to stage attacks, against both the civilian population in the oil areas – in order to make way for these foreign oil companies – and the opposition forces operating within the oil region of Upper Nile.[11] Oil exploration has exposed another layer of violent racial and religious politics. Because economic development and concentration of resources has been racially defined, the Arabs would be the first to benefit from the southern oil resources in line with what had historically been regarded as a racially based state discrimination. This was absolutely unacceptable to southerners: Western countries such as Canada and Sweden were accused of 'making the looting of our oil possible on behalf of the Arab north' (as described by one informant), and regarded as having let down their Christian brethren at a time when they were expected to back up the south. The involvement of the Chinese in the Sudanese oil industry was viewed as a result of pure greed: 'the Chinese got blinded to human suffering by their hunger for energy sources,' one informant stated. The involvement of the Malaysians was read in the south as a form of Islamic alliance with Khartoum, and many voices could be heard calling for the US and other Western Christian countries to come to the rescue of south Sudan in the name of their shared faith. The reports by the British charity Christian Aid[12] and by an alliance of Canadian churches and faith-based NGOs uncovering the oil-related atrocities,[13] which brought a great deal of international attention to the role of oil in the destruction of south Sudan, were met with considerable gratitude in the south. The way local communities perceived themselves in relation to a wider Christian world was heightened by these reports, which raised hopes for an international intervention: but the complaints from a few diplomatic circles did not translate into concerted action for a long while.[14] As will be explained later, there were a number of attempts to force the Sudan government to suspend oil activities until it had reached a peaceful settlement with the south. NGOs, human rights groups, and Sudan activists in the West called for foreign companies that conduct business in Sudan to be delisted on the US stock markets as a way to force them into abandoning their deadly alliance with the Sudan government. Talisman, a Canadian company, withdrew from Sudan in 2002 and was forced to sell its stake in Sudanese oil to an Indian oil company when the Sudan controversy became a liability in terms of its stock performance on the Western capital markets, especially when the company was sued in New York by Sudanese communities affected by the oil–military complex.

Gruesome state violence, oil-related and otherwise, continued unabated and revealed the racial and religious classification in the conduct of war itself. The mechanisms with which violence is carried out in Sudan, its resultant social and economic dynamics, and the manner in which it is locally embodied, have garnered local and international human rights concern because of the obvious racist and religious fanaticism exhibited by Muslim soldiers serving in the non-Arab areas in the south and in the non-Muslim regions of the west. Where Islam could function as a tool for the training of a soldier to shed his remorse for his victims, as is the case for soldiers who are sent to the south, the Muslim soldier is imbued with the belief that he does not have to adhere to any boundaries because the enemy is not a co-religionist. In those areas where government soldiers and the local population in a war zone are both Muslim, the race factor becomes instrumental in the formation of the soldier's character. This explains the shocking incidents of mass rape that have been carried out by both the Janjaweed Arab militia and the regular armed forces in Darfur. In view of the way Arab soldiers behaved toward southern women throughout the North–South war – often justifying sexual assault on grounds that they did not share the same faith – that a Muslim soldier should violate the bodily integrity of a Muslim woman, as they did in Darfur, reveals not only the manipulation of the soldiers but also the intersection of religion and race as the state's tools of suppression, alternating between race and religion according to the prevailing political and military situation in a given region. It also reveals another differential in the experience of violence, especially the gendered aspects of it, no matter which region, racial or religious group is at war. Violence in Sudan can be characterized as both conjunctural, where there are definite actors who commit violence at the behest of state institutions or other powerful agents within the state, and structural, where poverty, inequality, gender bias, racism, religious bigotry, and inadequate services form a less visible but equally pernicious violence that is a part of the social fabric of Sudanese society. For example, in addition to reports of mass rape, the use of women as war trophies and other forms of sexual violence, Sudan has attracted attention for the use of child soldiers, unpaid militias who consider rape and abduction of women and girls as forms of payment, the conditioning of young soldiers to violence over many years, violent humiliation of the enemy's female population, and the reproduction of such violence within the soldiers' families and communities, all of which reveal gender differentials and hierarchies in the war experience.

In the meantime, international attention did little to inspire concerted international efforts to help Sudan come to its own internal settlement or to pressure it into an internationally mediated one. The so-called international community was able to muster sympathy for the war victims, however, and poured aid money into funding the humanitarian programs which became the subject of international human rights and research scrutiny in their own right. Debates ensued as to whether or not the agencies themselves were actually exacerbating the conflict by allowing the international community to avoid any real political solution to Sudan's crises, whether aid was functioning as an alibi for the failure of the international community to seek solutions to the root causes of Sudan's conflicts by instead throwing money at the crisis; and by permitting the local authorities to neglect the welfare of their own people, or worse, to deny certain citizens, in this case those understood to be both Black and non-Muslim, such basic human rights as access to humanitarian aid.[15] At the same time other populations – Arabs and certain types of Muslims – in this two-tiered system of citizenship, were deemed superior and worthy of the riches and resources extracted from the peripheries, or more deserving of foreign relief.

Among the many problems of humanitarian aid is its distributive role in exacerbating the politics of the conflict in Sudan: as it feeds the victims of the conflicts it also frees the victimizers to continue to feed themselves lavishly while the violence persists. In other words, the government of Sudan has often used humanitarian aid to negotiate political space as it traded humanitarian access for diplomatic leniency on human rights abuses. It also taxed humanitarian agencies so heavily that much of the government's war effort was underwritten by these taxes for a number of years before the oil funds came into the pipeline. It continues to do this in reference to the humanitarian efforts in Darfur. For example, the Office for the Coordination of Humanitarian Affairs in Khartoum reported that its effort to assist some 3.5 million people who were in need of humanitarian assistance in Darfur was encumbered by government machinations to drain relief efforts of their ability to save lives. For example, since December 2005, the government has required 'three extensions to stay visas,' and each time all visas and travel permits for some 800 international NGO staff working in Darfur must be renewed. 'Until granted, international staff cannot move freely and do their work. In addition, each renewal costs US$240 per person, thus the two recent renewals of Darfur visas cost the humanitarian community over US$380,000; funds that otherwise could have been spent on the provision of humanitarian assistance.'[16] An exercise in international goodwill turned out to have tremendous potential for harm at the national level due to the racialized politics of conflict.

Since the latter part of 2002, two issues at opposite extremes have made Sudan a country that arouses conflicting emotions and judgments. The first was the peace negotiations between the government and the south-based SPLA, which had been taking place intermittently for years. Under the auspices of the Inter-Governmental Agency for Development (IGAD) the peace negotiations had reached a promising level by July 2002, when the Machakos Protocol was agreed upon in the Kenyan town of that name. That framework became the basis for the eventual 'comprehensive peace agreement' signed on January 9, 2005. Both ordinary Sudanese, who were desperate for peace, and the mediators who so much desired to see their labors bear fruits, found great optimism in the Machakos accord, and there was hope for Sudan once again. But this peace process was still beset by challenges. The interested parties in the international community who brokered this deal were still concerned as to how to make it inclusive of all Sudanese political forces in order to increase its chances of long-term stability. Many smaller parties and military groups had been excluded from the negotiations and these were posing a threat to the peace process.[17] In addition, there had already been a lot of talk throughout the process about postwar reconstruction, the cost of which was predictably enormous, and the sources of the money for it uncertain. Reconstruction efforts were likely to be daunting given the war-induced destruction and the extreme underdevelopment in the south. Other difficult issues of postwar rehabilitation included the prospects of the return of internally displaced persons (IDPs) – estimated at 4.5 million – and refugees from neighboring countries – said to number about 640,000 – the restoration of what little was left of the infrastructure, and how to implement the agreement itself and hold the parties to honoring their commitments.[18] All these issues continued to pose a threat as potential spoilers of the peace agreement.

The second issue was that as the south was entering into a brokered peace, the western region of Darfur plunged into yet another chaotic war in which the Arab-led government and its allied Arab militias, the Janjaweed, fought local opposition forces and the African population thought to be the support base for the opposition. As the world community prepared to celebrate the hard-won peace which ended the twenty-two-year-long North–South conflict, a new but not so different violation of rights and assumption of lands and goods with racial ideologies and identities at stake sprang up. As mentioned earlier, the conflict in Darfur arose from a series of political disputes between two groups: the Arabs who make up the government-backed Janjaweed militia and the region's non-Arab farmers. In 2002 some Arab herders, reportedly at the behest of a growing Arab alliance, engaged in particularly bloody massacres against the settled farmers. This triggered a rebellion against the dictatorship in Khartoum launched by the non-Arab tribes, as the massacres added to the tensions that had been growing over a long period of time. As we will see in the chapter on Darfur, the region had been experiencing turmoil for some time due to droughts and scarcity of resources, recurrent famines in the 1980s (to which the government had responded half-heartedly due to the racial politics outlined earlier), proliferation of firearms due to wars in neighboring Chad, and general exclusion from service provision, which had triggered sporadic violence against Arab traders. In any case, when the Darfurians formed opposition armies – the Sudan Liberation Army (SLA) and the Justice and Equality Movement (JEM) – in their attempt to register the region's unhappiness with this situation and to change it, the government responded by unleashing the Janjaweed against the entire non-Arab civilian population living in the rural areas. These Arab militias have since engaged in mass killings, rapes, lootings and burning of villages, to a degree never witnessed anywhere in Muslim regions of the country in recorded history. The government was, however, quick to announce that the attacks were triggered by tribal hatreds and that it had no role in the violence, but many citizens of Darfur hold Khartoum responsible for the atrocities. 'The government of Sudan has taken advantage of local economic rivalries and political divisions in order to effect its racialized reallocation of resources ... and is perpetrating crimes against humanity,' said Mudawi Ibrahim Adam, a human rights activist who monitors the abuses in Darfur. Due to its speed and the extent of its violence, the Darfur conflict quickly replicated the horrors of the NIF's genocidal efforts in the Nuba mountains in 1992, the southern oil regions between 1998 and 2004, the militia raids in Bahr el-Ghazal since 1983 and the aerial bombing of villages. These actions had been the characteristics of the regime's war conduct for the previous two decades. In fact, many people in the south wonder how northerners can be surprised at what the NIF is doing in Darfur, as southerners had lived under such circumstances for decades. One informant said:

> We sure did not see so many northern Sudanese protesting Khartoum's atrocities in the south in the manner they now do regarding Darfur. Could it be that northerners find themselves closer to Darfurians in the racial and religious hierarchy in this country?

The Darfur crisis attracted international attention because of the humanitarian tragedy that defined it and the gruesome manner in which the government-backed Arab Janjaweed militias killed and displaced the African people of the region. Other factors, such as the debates on the role of the international community when faced with acts of genocide, also increased its visibility. As the reports of mass killings continued to emerge from Darfur, a debate ensued as to whether or not to characterize it as genocide. Many major newspapers in the Western world published front page stories of one aspect of the crisis or another and the debate became very much a public affair, prompting the creation of some of very active student organizations and other anti-genocide activist groups in the US condemning the mass killings, looting, destruction and rape in Darfur. After much debate in the European Union, the United Nations, and the indecisiveness of the African Union – mainly over the definitions of genocide and whether the international conventions on genocide apply to the situation in Darfur – the US sent a special genocide verification team to Chad to interview the refugees, and the State Department finally determined that genocide was indeed being perpetrated by the government and its allied Arab militias. Colin Powell, then the highest ranking African-American in the Bush White House, told the world that genocide was and still is being committed.

Nevertheless, the Darfur crisis prompted some of the most puzzling contradictions in the ways in which international relations work. For example, some countries and organizations, including both the African Union and the UN, preferred the phrase 'ethnic cleansing' over 'genocide,' while the US described it as genocide, but contrary to what had been assumed – that declaring genocide was being committed would force these countries into action as the instruments of the international conventions on genocide call for – the declaration did not translate into action to stop the killing, and it seems it was made without the intent to do so. There are many explanations for this inaction in the face of such tragedy, most of which are beyond the scope of this book, but most important for our purposes here are the geopolitical interests of Western countries, local racial politics, and the politics of a Christian conservative White House. For example, while the US was condemning genocide and describing it as 'the worst humanitarian disaster in the world today,' as Colin Powell put it, there were concurrent clandestine dealings between many countries and the very regime that was annihilating a section of its own citizens. At a time when the US was regarded as the only country with the resources, political will, and clout in the international community to intervene, the US government invited Salah Gosh, head of Sudan's intelligence and a man many reports had implicated in the execution of genocide, to Washington. The invitation outraged many groups within Sudan and the US, highlighting as it did Washington's dual interest in enlisting Khartoum's help with the war on terrorism.[19] As the atrocities were being carried out even during Gosh's visit, it was clear that he was not in Washington to discuss how to end the violence, but more likely to hammer out mutual national security concerns. Such dealings reduce the credibility of the US and other countries that acted in this manner as genuine mediators. Inside Sudan, the local politics of racial divide manifested themselves in this environment. In the south and Darfur, for example, the involvement of the US Secretary of State, who was a 'Black man,' was greeted with jubilation because of the hope that he might favor their position over that of the Arabs, but local people quickly became suspicious of him when it transpired that he appeared phenotypically closer to the Arabs, especially in view of the inaction of the US government with regard to stopping the massacres. In terms of religion, the government of Sudan had been suspicious or outright critical of the George W. Bush presidency because of the involvement of the Christian right in electing Bush and in criticizing the Khartoum government for its persecution of Christians in Sudan. At times this suspicion translated into fear of invasion by the US, especially in the wake of the US invasions of Afghanistan and Iraq, both of which led many Muslim societies to accuse Bush of an anti-Islam crusade. These myths were used to boost local radical Islamic support and financial and diplomatic support from other Islamic countries.

The Darfur crisis was covered more regularly in the Western media from 2004 when the ten-year anniversary of the 1994 Rwanda genocide was commemorated in various forums around the world. The pronouncements made at that time by world leaders that 'We will never again allow genocide to be perpetrated,' came back to haunt them when it looked as if genocide was being allowed to take place once again, and no one had the will to give 'never again' meaning. The question of what to do with the perpetrators of genocide, whether there was a strong international political will to bring them to book, and what to do in order to restore normality to the lives of Darfurians, now added to the issues that made Sudan a continuous concern for many in the world community. The deployment of a peace-keeping force by the African Union, the demands by many Sudanese and some foreign agencies to involve the European Union, NATO, and the UN, have all been the subject of international and national debate. When the US became head of the UN Security Council in February 2006 John Bolton, the US ambassador to the UN, pushed for deployment of UN peace-keeping troops to replace the African Union peacekeepers, as the latter was proving ineffectual in protecting civilians. The final outcome of these debates was still awaited when this book was in its final stages of writing, but the massacres were still going on in Darfur. In September 2006, the UN Security Council passed a resolution to send UN peace keeping troops to replace the African Union force, but the government of Sudan objected to such a force and President Omer Al-Bashir described the resoultion as an attempt to 'recolonize Sudan'.

The escalation of violence in Darfur while the southern peace processes were underway also led to a dilemma among diplomats and countries that sponsored the southern peace deal: the crisis was threatening the viability of that peace – was it not more sensible to seek a resolution that joined resolving aspects of each conflict in one accord? To attempt to bring Darfur into the southern peace initiative, which had already made unprecedented progress, was to risk slowing down or losing that progress, in addition to the difficulty of actually combining issues of two conflicts that were inherently distinct in their histories and in their root causes. Yet to focus solely on the southern peace while Darfur burnt risked the continuation of the Darfur crisis with its attendant humanitarian catastrophe and its potential to slow down the implementation of the southern peace accord.[20] In the end, the mediators made a crucial decision to concentrate on seeing the southern peace agreement through, in the hope that once the SPLA became a partner with the NIF in what was to become known as the 'government of national unity,' as the agreement stipulated, attention would then be turned to Darfur. It was hoped that the SPLA would use its position as a partner in the government of national unity to tackle the war in Darfur. There was a presumption that the SPLA had better relationships with the Darfur opposition forces because they had been allies at one time against the NIF regime, and that once it became part of the government of national unity it would be in a better position to bring the two sides in the Darfur conflict together.[21] Since that agreement, the world and more specifically the people of Darfur who continue to reside in IDP camps within Darfur and refugee settlements across the border in Chad, are still waiting for the SPLA to take up this mediating role, with little prospect of it happening. Meanwhile in the rural areas of Darfur, violence continues unabated and mortality rates remain alarmingly high. Sudan remains in the ignominious company of nations such as Turkey where during World War I close to a million Armenians were massacred by the Young Turks; Hitler's Germany during World War II; and many other genocidal governments such as the Ethiopian communist regime of Mengistu Hailie Mariam, and the Cambodian Khmer Rouge regime with its 'killing fields.'

Furthermore, Sudan continues to be a source of international diplomatic speculation and of worry for the ordinary Sudanese in terms of how to bring peace to Darfur, sustain southern peace, influence the Khartoum government to relax its Islamic militant project and give up its sponsorship of terrorist groups, the future of the oil industry, and also what the fate of this giant country will be, especially in light of the continuing commitment to Arabism at the center matched against the rising commitment to other ethnic and racial identities in the peripheries. Of particular uncertainty, both among the Sudanese themselves and outside observers, is whether the country can really remain a unified state, given the possibility that the south will break away after the interim period stipulated by the comprehensive peace agreement,[22] and that many regions of the country peripheral to the centers of power might follow the path of the south over the coming decade. In this book, I argue that the history of conflicts in the Nuba mountains, the southern Blue Nile and other contested territories reveals that the populations of these regions seeking autonomy share common points of opposition that transcend any traditional notion of the state. In their quest to form independent states or to join in union with the south, these contested territories all define their will to secede by the neglect shown them and the blatant racial and religious discrimination that underpins it. This study also shows the extent to which any optimism that mass discourses of unity could have sewn is increasingly hopeless. Many Sudanese feel that the longer the conflicts in the northeast, the western region of Darfur and the Nubian north drag on, the more likely it is that these regions will also seek to opt out of the union.

This book is about the ways that Sudan's various regional conflicts cannot be analyzed independently of each other. It is my view that these violent conflicts can only be understood as strands of one interrelated story in which happenings in one geographical region of the country have triggered events in all others. Such an approach is taken as an attempt to break away from the usual fashion in which the contemporary histories of Sudan have been written. All too often, Sudan is depicted as a homogenous country. Especially in the area of political science, law, history, women and gender, and religious studies, a book about a specific region assumes that its arguments hold for the whole nation. Following from that, such scholarship assumed that national unity appeared *sui generis* from the drawing of the borders.[23] Such works have presented an all too coherent picture that portrays Sudan's experience as a logical predictable progression toward a unified cultural character (al-Affendi, 1991; Bleuchot and Hopwood, 1991; el-Bakri and el-Wathig, 1983).[24]

Despite the existence of extensive works of scholarship on the recent history of Sudan, or perhaps because of them, there are three reasons for writing a book on its contemporary political and social history. One is that Sudan's national identity is far from achieved – on the contrary, the country is moving toward disintegration and ethnic-based armed struggles have arisen everywhere since 1983. The southern war of liberation, the Nuba revolts, southern Blue Nile, the Beja rebellions in the Eastern region, Nubian opposition in the far north, and the Zaghawa, the Masalit, and the Fur in Darfur, all paint a picture of a nation falling apart. Moreover, the death and destruction that have accompanied political dissent, and which have left jarring wounds in the hearts and minds of the Sudanese people, spread disunity beyond the places in question and sow the seeds for future unrest.

Like race, religion, and a seemingly natural affinity to one's land, ideas of national unity appear to have a geographical basis in this troubled country. Many Sudanese living in the areas peripheral to the centers of power often say that Sudan has never existed as a unified state, except nominally. The nation has never secured legitimate authority for most of the marginalized groups. This is largely because the state has proved to be more of an extractive power than a provider of services, and has extracted resources from the people through extreme forms of state violence.[25] Although there has never been a country-wide survey to ascertain popular opinion, my conversations and interviews with Sudanese from different walks of life have revealed that this sentiment is widespread. As an informant from the south said: 'This country of ours is like a highwayman, it robs our resources and never gives anything back, it says "give me your money, your loyalty, your identity, or you will lose your life".'

Given the violent history of Sudan, it is not surprising that war and its consequences have become the most important subjects of social science and humanities research in the country, notably in the south and the west where wars have been endemic for over five decades, and more recently in the northeastern province where the Beja, the majority ethnic group in the region, have armed themselves against what they see as a state-supported racial discrimination against them. This research interest in war is indicated by the numerous studies sponsored by the UN,[26] foreign governments (especially the donor countries that provide funds for humanitarian programs),[27] the high volume of reports on human rights violations,[28] reports commissioned by private NGOs,[29] and by the large amount of academic literature amassed by individual researchers (Keen, 1994; Harir and Tvedt, 1994; de Waal, 1997; Nyaba, 1997; Hutchinson, 1996). The hope that research into the causes and consequences of war, whether such research is purely academic or action-oriented, may benefit from a historical perspective is one reason for the attempt in this study to provide such a perspective.

A second reason for writing this book is that Sudan has been depicted in international circles as a weak or failing state: in fact it is not necessarily a weak state, but rather one where the racially and religiously inspired ruling elite have capitalized on the threats of fragmentation and disintegration to consolidate their legitimacy through further violence. The state has increasingly become a monopoly of a few who have entrenched themselves by increasingly promoting and strengthening the political and military position of their narrow but well-funded support base. It is therefore important to describe some of the reasons why Sudan has gained the attention of the international news media from the 1980s to 2000s, with a view to pointing out some of the misrepresentation of the basic issues. One of the main reasons for this attention, beside the obvious humanitarian tragedies sparked by prolonged conflicts, is that journalism usually sets itself up to be pandered to by the warring factions, as each side vies for the sympathy of the audience – reader, viewer, and listener. Journalism seeks to capture the stories of suffering from a perspective that looks for shock effect and entertainment aspects over informative ones. The result is that the depth of the story is often missed in favor of spectacle, and the potential for misrepresentation is frequently present. Applying this view to a context such as Sudan, where racial and religious sensitivities inform the local discourse about the conflict, means that there is a danger of superficial coverage, which could lead to a misinformed policy-making process in the areas of peace-making, humanitarian aid, and diplomacy. Of course there is a flipside to this, which is that media reporting of crises, when done properly, can be extremely useful in raising international awareness, which in turn can caution international actors about how their roles might exacerbate the crisis or help to design best practices that could ease the tragedies. Media coverage of Sudan has described it as a country defined by famines and a procession of benevolent foreign aid workers, with huge amounts of money donated by Western countries being spent on delivering humanitarian assistance to the starving Sudanese. The resurgence of slavery and the rise of militant Islam along with its role in international terrorism in the 1990s have also taken up much media space. More recently, specifically since 1998, the representation of Sudan's woes in the international media has been dominated by oil-related government atrocities in the Upper Nile region, and by the distressing reports of genocide perpetrated by the government and its allied militias in the western region of Darfur since early 2003. While all these descriptions reflect the realities of life in Sudan and merit attention whether independently of each other or as interrelated factors, what is absent from this picture, especially for those who have been observing events in Sudan from a distance, is a clear connecting thread between these media images on the one hand and state terrorism, human rights violating militias, slavery and genocide on the other. In other words, what has gripped the attention of the world community about Sudan may be read as the usual problems of failing states, corruption, ethnic rivalry, and resource mismanagement that have come to characterize Africa in the post-colonial period, but there are also man-made problems of a different kind. Such depiction of Sudan's conflicts has disproportionately focused on the humanitarian tragedies that have resulted from the events above, but it has done little by way of explicating racial and religious nuances of the conflict, the victims' stories about their war experience, and the local perceptions about the causes of the crisis itself.

While media attention has resulted in some criticism of the government of Sudan, in half-hearted international economic sanctions, and international vilification of the government over human rights violations and accusations of sponsorship of terrorism for the last two decades, locally they have produced little else. Such criticism has actually strengthened the state because very little meaningful action is taken by way of a concerted international action that could force the Sudanese regime to desist from rogue behavior. The ruling elites have manipulated the weaknesses of the international system that criticizes them and turned it into a stronger force against the Sudanese people, playing to their more militant domestic constituency by darkly warning of an Anglo-American invasion (something neither the British nor the Americans have threatened in recent history) and promising to kill the infidels in the same way they are being killed in Iraq should an American invasion of yet another Muslim nation come to pass. In other words, the government has used international criticism to its advantage by forging a narrow but very strong local support on the basis that the country is being targeted unfairly by the Western world. The government appeals to these privileged few, whose egos are massaged by being described as more nationalist, that they must protect their nation against the West, which the current Islamist government has described as the enemies of Islam.[30] Protecting the country means targeting certain population groups, such as those who have complained about poverty in their areas and were therefore suspected of being the local arm of foreign antagonistic countries such as the US or Israel, for elimination. It is therefore important to point out how the international community, while it has spoken out against the government's human rights record, did little more than talk between 1983 and 2003, something that has given the core elite in the successive governments of Sudan a sense that international threats without action are business as usual. For the ordinary Sudanese, international geopolitics has created a twisted logic. Many Sudanese seek international attention because it gives them the hope of possible outside intervention against the regime, but at the same time international criticism of the regime, if it is not followed by action, gives the government in Khartoum the pretext it needs to clamp down on basic liberties on the basis of alleged looming foreign aggression. To many in all the dissenting regions I mentioned earlier – the south, Nubia, the Nuba mountains, the Blue Nile, Beja, Darfur – it seems that international criticism only weakens the opposition and the politically excluded groups. One opposition leader said:

> There were times during the second term of Bill Clinton as president of the United States when we wished the Americans would either shut up completely or back up their criticism with some action, because any threatening remark they made against Khartoum was enough to guarantee the Islamists a lot of support from Iran and Iraq and other Middle Eastern countries.

The reverse may also be true – such outside criticism gives the opposition groups false hope for international intervention, and thus prevents them from seeking peaceful settlement. To the credit of the international community, however, while it has failed to stop the killing, there is no denying the humanitarian commitment to relieve the suffering of the war's displaced. The establishment of Operation Lifeline Sudan (OLS), an umbrella group comprised of UN agencies and NGOs, brought much-needed aid to the large number of internally displaced persons (IDPs) that make Sudan home to the biggest IDP population in the world. OLS has also provided much support to many communities that were host to the IDPs, especially in the south where it functions as the only source of supplies in lieu of the government.[31]

While the international community has exhibited contradictory behavior – oscillating between sanctions against Sudan on one extreme and what some Western countries have called constructive engagement on the other – it has given the international human rights groups a chance to critique the process of such engagement. Despite its limited effectiveness in saving lives, the presence of the world community through aid programs has enabled many groups and organizations to maintain contacts with ordinary Sudanese people in their darkest hour. The daily struggles of the people of Sudan during the many years of turmoil came to the attention of the world community because of the humanitarian presence in Sudan. It gave the ordinary people of Sudan the conviction that their voice would be heard as long as foreign aid groups were active in their country. Both the aid community and the Sudanese people have lived and continue to live with the horrors of state terror. Such heroism lies behind the struggle by the ordinary Sudanese to lead relatively normal lives despite the aforementioned horrors and death: to describe this struggle is to suggest that there is a historical, cultural, resource and environmental context to the anguish in Sudan that has so engaged the world.

The history of post-colonial Sudan and contemporary political developments, especially research on Sudan's civil wars that have threatened the unity of the country, has mainly been written by a northern elite who have defined the question of Sudan's unity or fragmentation as the 'southern problem.'[32] Thus the third reason for this book is a reckoning with the particular means of history-telling that have prevailed in the works of these writers (Beshir, 1974, 1975; Fadlalla, 2004; Hasan, 1971, 1973; Abd al-Rahim, 1969; Abdin, 1985; al-Safi, 1986, 1989; Khalid, 1990). Their fields span history, law and political science: they argue that the south has consistently sought ways to opt out of a unified state, and that the north must maintain the nation's territorial integrity (Beshir, 1975).[33] This is a moral story where race and religion put Arabs and Muslims in the place of the good citizens who have made a social and political contract for unity. In popular discourse and in certain versions of this story, the south's will to secede is framed as a for-eign-instigated desire rather than an independent one. Contrary to what the historical record shows, the common view among north-ern academics and policy-makers is that the British colonial administration created the division between north and south. To this day, and despite the scars of protracted conflicts, there is still much talk among northern intelligentsia of a foreign conspiracy to divide the people of Sudan. Rarely, if ever, do they acknowledge that there has never been any historical oneness between the 'two parts,' or many parts for that matter. The fact that Sudan's history has been rife with if not defined by hostility, whether in disguised forms or outright military action, has become a peripheral view-point in such visions. Few writers and politicians in the north acknowledge that the current onward march to subsume the southern populace and appropriate their cultural and ethnic iden-tity into whatever the northern elite desired, which began with the Turkiyya in 1821, has been central to the southern aspiration to secede. It is now the reason why other peripheral regions within the 'traditional' north like Darfur and the northeast have followed the same dissenting path taken by the south. Northern academic dis-course on the so-called southern problem goes as far as chastising the ruling elite for not doing enough to make southerners feel a sense of belonging, but never acknowledges the connections between southern grievances and the developments in other regions of the nation.[34] There is little, if any, recognition of the his-torical trajectories and political processes (for example the attitude of the Muslim populations of the north toward non-Muslims) which has culminated in the south moving toward the path of secession. A similar dismissal of regional grievances was recently applied regarding the emerging threats of disintegration posed by the eastern province, from Darfur in the west, and from the Nubian far north.[35] Such a mythico-historical approach – writing the histories of each regional conflict as 'problems' arising from within the region and on their own, unrelated to the actions of the center and separate from the events occurring in other regions – has proved deficient at best in providing an integrated history, and has at worst been degenerating into ethnic, regional and racial history; a kind of academic discourse informed by political loyalties and cultural nationalism.[36]

Likewise, the few works of social science and historical research that are undertaken by southerners have come as a response to the northern discourse on the conflict; a kind of grievance approach to history by both academics such as Francis Deng, the late Dunstan Wai, Leek Mawut, Deng Akol Ruay, and politicians like Bona Malwal, John Garang, and Abel Alier.[37] Outstanding works on Sudan's conflicts and their histories written by non-Sudanese are also available, but many of them also fall into these North–South categories.[38] Either they tend to be about the north, while claiming 'Sudan' in their titles,[39] or are exclusively about the north or the south (for example the instructive works of Douglas Johnson in both history and ethnography),[40] or specifically about any of the new conflicts in the other regions of the country.[41] To provide a balanced history is to avoid falling into these categories, and that requires a comprehensive look at the social and cultural diversity of Sudan and how such diversity shapes the reactions of each region to the pressing issues facing the country. To address developments in the south as entirely independent of what occurs in the north as a means of explaining the various conflicts of Sudan is, in my view, a deficient approach. In other words, Sudan's conflicts have always been regarded as a product of northern-centric bias, but need to be viewed as having gradually become periphery-centric as well. How the events in the south, the north and the other parts of the country feed each other is, again, the point of this book.

In what follows, my approach focuses on the heroism of the ordinary Sudanese people in their day to day reckoning with state power. I have made a conscious choice to present the lives of everyday people rather than the usual focus on the elite who, during their struggle for power, may claim to represent the aspirations of everyday citizens but who actually rarely involve 'the people' in decisions as to what courses of action should be taken in response to a particular political situation. This is not a story of war heroes, political elite, sectarian parties, military dictators, and policy-makers at the national level: it is a story of what is common and different between the various peoples of Sudan, regardless of the region or ethnicity to which they belong. It is a story of how the people of Sudan have managed to live through the wars for such long periods, and a description of the attempts by the Sudanese people to come to grips with the realities of these wars and of state-sponsored violence. Their resilience or domination in the face of tragedy depends on the causes of a region-specific conflict and how long the conflict has persisted.

THE SOURCES

Most of the material for this study was derived from interviews with a variety of Sudanese people. Interviews were conducted over many years, sometimes directly related to this project and at other times in the contexts of other research programs. In addition to secondary sources, a great deal of material was gleaned from unpublished NGO reports, human rights reports, and UN news networks. Select journalistic material from both international and local print media has also been consulted in reference to specific factual issues and events. Listening to so many Sudanese who are not men or women of political power, those whom one might characterize as 'ordinary people,' I rarely hear them discussing the causes or the histories of the conflicts. Their discussions, heated as they may be, are rarely about the issues of wealth and power-sharing that are usually identified as the root causes of the conflicts: these are focused on by the leadership and without popular discussions. Where they do discuss national politics, wealth and power-sharing at the center, it is easy to see that the interviewees have merely adopted the discourse handed down to them by their political leaders, rather than thinking independently about these issues. For example, during the interviews with Sudanese in the south, when I asked individuals why in their opinion the south was at war with the north, the response referred to recent wartime incidents of slave raiding, aerial bombing, or the killing of a prominent person by government security agents, but not any specific reasons that had prompted the south as a whole to revolt against the government in the first place. Most southerners offer the abstract answer, 'So we can be free from Arab domination.' In fact many people, including some rebel soldiers, wondered aloud why they had initially decided to join the rebellion. When one probes, one finds most ordinary Sudanese talking about how families and communities could best live with the realities of the war, because they usually have very little control over the making of the decisions leading to war. What emerges from these interviews is that war takes on its own dynamics once it has started. For example, if a group of soldiers who hail from a particular geographical location or ethnic group mutinied, and the government retaliated against the entire population of that region, this government's action becomes a more important cause of populist protest than the initial grievance that had prompted the mutiny. It was this government's act of indiscriminate retaliation and collective punishment of the population in areas of revolt that drew everybody into the war. As we will see below, this was clearly the case when the Darfur conflict erupted in February 2003. The size of the current Darfur opposition armies has increased many times since the start of the war, largely because youths were forced into the arms of the opposition by policies that rushed to stigmatize the entire non-Arab population in the region. It was also the case when the Beja of the eastern region, the Nuba mountains and the southern Blue Nile all were drawn into the war as a result of their leaders being targeted for political persecution. These reveal two levels of thinking about the conflicts: the political organizational level dominated by the leaders, and the war experience as lived by everyday people. There is clear demarcation and a strong debate between those who make war decisions and those who do the fighting on the one hand, and the people who live under difficult war-induced conditions on the other.[42]

The only issues that I have found commonly discussed, especially in the south, were those of race and racism and religion, particularly how they relate to the politics of inclusion or exclusion from power and resources. In reference to race and racism, it was argued repeatedly that the Arab and non-Arab divide upon which the relationships between the state and the people are built, and which has led to the domination of government by the Arabs, were among the major factors influencing the attitudes of the state toward the remote regions and in return causing resentment in the peripheries toward the state. Areas of the country inhabited by people who can relate to the ruling elite, as in the case of the northern province, even in some minute way, were more likely to dismiss race as a factor in the crises of the state. Regions occupied by people who self-identified as non-Arabs were more likely to complain of racial segregation in access to jobs, promotion, contracts, and social services, or emphasize the role of race as the most important factor in state violence toward them. With regard to religion, the use of Islam by some northern political parties as a basis for their claim to power was also discussed in the interviews as the cause for the rift between both Muslims and non-Muslims, and between the radical Islamists who are accused of politicizing religion and the more liberal parties and individuals who argue that a multi-religious and multicultural society like Sudan cannot afford to favor specific belief systems.

This study will focus on the south, the Nuba mountains, the southern Blue Nile region and Darfur, where war and all its attendant and tragic consequences have been endemic for nearly two decades. It will also look at Nubia in the far north and the Beja in the northeast, specifically in the Red Sea hills. In these regions, war has increasingly become a part of life. The civilian rural population is drawn into the conflicts in ways that disempower them because the decision-making process regarding going to war does not involve them, but their leaders expect that they will support the war. The result of this impasse is that the national army class entire communities in the dissenting regions as enemies of the state, and these communities have to make difficult decisions on a daily basis as to whether or not to support the opposition armies: to openly support their local opposition movement is to provoke indiscriminate state wrath, but to express skepticism toward the local movement is to risk weakening their only voice in these racial and religious confrontations. Many of them like to think that the decision as to how to deal with the consequences of the war – whether to participate in it, relocate, or remain passive – is still within their scope of power. Therefore, although this study will undoubtedly make references to the factors and root causes of these wars, as articulated by the leaders of the competing factions, if only to provide the context, its main concern will be the connections between the regions in terms of people's reactions to the state as well as the various efforts to live with the wars.[43] As such, this is a story about the everyday relations between the people and the state, between the civilians and the various armies involved in Sudan's conflicts, and between the peoples of different ethnic groups and regions, including the interaction between those who were internally displaced by the wars and those who became their hosts.[44]

It is also important to point out here what this book does *not* cover. The analysis focuses on the fifty-year period since independence, therefore any reference to political developments before 1956 will only be dealt with in passing. The reason for this summary reference to the pre-1956 period is that both central government and the peripheral regions have blamed colonialism for the root causes of the turmoil in Sudan, but from entirely different perspectives. Each of the Khartoum regimes, as represented by the northern elite, has asserted that colonialism was responsible for sowing the seeds of dissent in the peripheries.[45] The populations of the marginalized peripheries, or at least their leaders, have also always blamed the colonial powers. For them, the British imposed this polity upon them in a fashion that victimized them and the existence of Sudan as a unified state was not achieved through a legitimate process. If their stakes for autonomy, equitable distribution of power and wealth cannot be achieved in a unified state, complete independence becomes a viable option.[46] These two contentious viewpoints define the majority of works on Sudan's colonial history. It is my goal to go beyond such facile accounts to better engage with the complex picture that defines Sudan's stability, or lack thereof, in the post-colonial period.

HISTORY AND IDENTITY POLITICS: THE FATE OF THE UNION

Sudan's past is replete with independent, successive or concurrent states ranging from Kush, Meroe, Napata, Funj, Darfur, the Mahdist state, and Dar Masalit, to name a few. It has also had plenty of experience with localized state formation, for example the many tribal kingdoms throughout the south, some of which remain as nations within a nation to this day – for example the Zande, the Shilluk, the Anyua, and the Lotuho. The process of encompassing the current territories as a nation state began with the Ottoman Empire's occupation and control of the northern territories in 1821 and was completed during British colonial rule (1898–1956). However, since Sudan became a self-governing nation state in 1956, it has faced many significant political challenges in its effort to maintain its territorial unity. Like most sub-Saharan African nations, it has been hard to convince the Sudanese people of various nationalities that they belong to this post-colonial structure. Although the assigning of ethnic groups to bounded regions was an effect of previous colonial strategy, groups in question came to be intensely loyal to these ethnic regions, more so than they are to the state, and the state has had to use harsh measures to bring the various peoples into its fold. The result is that many ethnic territories have serious grievances with central government, and the government has responded to these with extreme violence in order to subdue this dissent. The combination of these grievances, the militarized responses by Khartoum to the bitter anger in the peripheries, lack of national unity, and the government's brutal methods to achieve such unity have all proved lethal to Sudan's unified existence.[47] They have dragged the nation into protracted and costly civil wars for the better part of its five decades of independence. Its religious, racial, ethnic and economic diversity have made it difficult for Africa's largest country to achieve a strong national identity that incorporates and embraces its various population groups. As we saw earlier, the insistence of the ruling elite on giving the whole country an Arab identity has given rise to a situation where many ethnic groups do not regard themselves as part of this identity and, to say the least, are not proud of their citizenship in such a polity.[48] These challenges threaten its existence as a unified nation state and manifest themselves in as many ways as there are ethnic regions.

As it is about to enter into its sixth decade as an independent nation, Sudan is currently unable to avoid recognizing its ethnic and religious multiplicity, but the challenges threatening its existence as a unified nation and setting it on the path to a possibility of disintegration continue to magnify, if only due to the racial and religious ideologies of its ruling elites. Some of the most important issues that have challenged its existence since independence have included, in no particular order of importance, first, the rise of militant Islam and the insistence of this class of Muslims on the establishment of a theocratic state based on the full application of the Islamic law (shari'a), despite the presence of non-Muslim citizens in the country. Insisting on Islamic law without a clear conception as to how non-Muslims and moderate Muslims fit into the polity has been one of the most difficult political challenges facing Muslim extremists in Sudan. This insistence on the application of Islamic law all over the country jeopardizes North–South unity, because the south would not accept such laws and could use this as grounds for demands to secede. To exempt the south and set up two constitutional systems also allows the regions to develop parallel political entities, which again could lead the south to secession. The current North–South peace agreement exempts the south and the capital Khartoum from shari'a but it remains to be seen how its implementation works as radical Islamists reject the idea of a secular capital.

Second, the ruling elite, comprised of riverine Arab tribes of middle Sudan occupying the region that extends from Dongola north of Khartoum to Kosti, has pursued a national unity based on widespread institution of the Arabic language and the domination of Arabized racial groups. Many of the grievances of those in the peripheries emerge in this context.[49] However, beyond these complaints Arab domination has also been evident in the political and economic hegemony of the sectarian political parties, the Umma Party and the Democratic Unionist Party (DUP).[50] It is also seen in the Islamic and Arabic-oriented educational system, the government-run media, the disproportionate financial backing of Islamic institutions such as Islamic banks and other businesses controlled by self-professed radical Muslims, the legal and judicial systems that are clearly without specific regard for non-Muslims, and the monopoly of the political process by the ruling National Islamic Front since 1989.[51]

The third challenge is the effort by these ruling tribes and elite to muzzle the voices of the peripheral and the politically excluded areas through the use of repressive measures such as the massacres of civilian populations in the dissenting regions. Eye-witnesses interviewed in recent years have spoken of slave raids, rape, looting, and destruction of assets: all because the entire population of a region is stigmatized as anti-Arab and against the government or its Islamic ideology. One woman interviewed in 2001 in Aweil West County in south Sudan offered her views on the reasons why government agents were engaging in these actions:

> They want to silence us, and if we refuse to be silenced, they will try to destroy us, to eliminate us ... This does not work of course because they will never finish us off ... Human beings are like groundnuts, just as you cannot extract all the nuts from the earth, nothing can ever deplete human beings. They avoid our guerrilla armies because they know they can't defeat them, so they turn their guns and bombs towards the women and children as the only way to weaken our resolve. But on the contrary, they make our people angry and less malleable to the image that the government wants to form ... their attacks only cause more youth to challenge their racist policies by joining the rebels.[52]

Such mass murder, usually carried out by a combination of the Sudan armed forces and government-recruited tribal militias, has been either in the name of counterinsurgency or military escalation of a situation that could have been resolved in other ways.[53] These policies have also included arbitrary detention of leaders of these communities, torture of detainees, and the use of some of the marginalized groups against the others in what has escalated into chaotic ethnic wars. The latter has been increasingly observed and articulated by the leaders of the peripheral groups and documented in recent years by researchers and human rights and humanitarian agencies, both local and international (Human Rights Watch, 1995, 1996; UN Human Rights Commission, 1999, 2000, 2001; Ryle and Gagnon, 2003; Prunier, 2005; Flint and de Waal, 2005). The local Sudanese human rights movement has also grown and become increasingly sophisticated in critiquing the situation.[54] The ongoing conflict and disaster that began in 2003 in Darfur, the Dinka-Nuer conflicts between 1991 and 1998 and the outbreak of violent conflicts in the areas inhabited by the Beja tribes of the Red Sea region since 1995 are a few examples of extreme cases of ethnic polarization.

These three challenges have been represented in various ways in different regions. How each of them manifests itself depends on the political environment and the cultures of each region. For example, south Sudan's reaction to the propagation of Arab culture and the increasing Islamization of the politics of state building is different from the way the other regions of the country have reacted to similar issues (for example the Fur, the Tunjur, the Zaghawa, and the Masalit in the west, the Nubians in the north, the Beja in the east, the Nuba in central Sudan, and the Funj in southern Blue Nile).

Even within the region that is home to what is considered dominant groups, i.e. the riverine region predominantly inhabited by the Shaigiyya, the Danagala, and the Ja'aleen, running from Dongola north of the capital down to the southern edges of al-Jazira province, the question of politicization of Islam has been as divisive among Muslims as the traditional North–South conflict. For instance, although all are Sunni Muslims the politically dominant groups belong to various Sufi orders or *tariqas*, whereby the *shaykhs* who lead them are influential in people's interpretation of Islam. On the basis of these orders, Sudanese Muslims often disagree on the question of which party is more suitable to apply the Islamic law, as some groups claim to uphold Islamic ideals better than the others. Many within the Muslim regions, although in the minority, flatly reject a theocratic state, because they are aware that such a state allows only certain regions and specific political parties and families to monopolize the state power in the name of Islam.[55] As a result, each of the various regions of the country has had different responses to centralized state power which practices political and economic exclusion on the basis of race or religion. The state – or more correctly the Khartoum governments that have ruled since independence – has increasingly been deemed autocratic and heavy-handed in its dealing with the disenchanted regions and murderous and genocidal toward the ethnic groups that try to challenge the government on the issues of national identity and on the question of inequitable distribution of development and service projects and political power (Garang, 1987).

The challenges facing the nation also present themselves in the form of disenchantment with central government for its failure to respond to specific needs of the regions. Most remote regions have not received a quick response from Khartoum when famines induced by floods or droughts occur (Cater, 1986; de Waal, 1985; Kebbede, 1999; Burr and Collins, 1995), and the lack of response is often viewed locally as a sign of racism. Frustration with insecurity caused by the proliferation of assault weapons from the wars of neighboring countries (Prunier, 2005), economic stagnation (Johnson, 1994; Kok, 1996) or the decline of social services (Harir, 1992, 1993) have all triggered criticism of the government, particularly the Arab elite who run it. Unsurprisingly the government in Khartoum, whether it is controlled by a militant Islamic group as it has been since 1989 or in the hands of one of the sectarian political parties as was the case during the last three postcolonial democratic interludes, does not respond well to criticism.[56] Such critiques have often provoked a government response that is heavily politicized and militarized, leading to prolonged and deadly confrontations as the wars in Darfur, the south and other peripheries have demonstrated. Each regional or ethnic response to state power depends on the point in history at which a trigger to a confrontation presented itself and a rallying point was finally articulated by an emerging leader within the disgruntled group, and on the ideological framing of grievances. Military conflict between a specific ethnic region and the Khartoum government usually simmers for a while, waiting either for another major event to start the fight or for a local leader to articulate its difficulties and unify the voices that challenge the government.

If a leader is to unify the voices and urge the people to rise in coordinated political dissent, the issues of immediate concern to the group have to be presented in the form of ideological explanation for the everyday experiences of deprivation. Complaints about uneven economic development, inequitable distribution of resources and provision of services that falls short of reaching each region are usually explained locally from an ideological standpoint. In the last five decades since independence, such explanation has come in the form of alleged marginalization from the centers of power, i.e. a kind of exclusionary political process in which the elite at the center are said to connive against ethnic regions at the periphery. The ideological explanation has also taken the form of claims of religious persecution, racial discrimination, cultural suppression, or the increasing social class gaps as the root causes of marginalization and exclusion. This is how local leaders find justification for a populist protest and confrontation in order to rectify the situation. Many Sudanese I interviewed often insist that such confrontations could have been avoided and disagreements settled more peacefully if successive Khartoum governments had been less defensive and more confident that the people merely wish for good governance.[57] Instead, the ruling elite tend to dismiss complaints from the peripheries as triggered by politically misguided tribalism, ethnic loyalty, racial inferiority and lack of patriotism on the part of regional leaders.[58] Local leaders who speak on behalf of their regions are often regarded by power-brokers in Khartoum as driven by greed for power.

Abdel Aziz, a fighter from Darfur, asked:

> Why do the Arab leaders in the government always equate criticism with disloyalty? Instead of addressing citizen's concerns to restore their confidence in state institutions, answering questions about how to improve the relationships between the people and the state, how to benefit from constructive criticism, Khartoum always responds by shooting down the critics ... this is really why people choose to take up arms.[59]

Clearly Khartoum's militarized responses to local grievances lead to militarization of local politics and the reproduction of violence, even within the dissenting communities.

THE ORGANIZATION OF THIS BOOK

This study is divided into eight chapters. Chapter 1 traces some aspects of the rise of militant Islam by describing the actions of two of Sudan's most autocratic military regimes – those of Ibrahim Abbud (1958–1964) and Ja'afer Nimeiri (1969–1985). These two regimes oscillated between secular military rule and establishing an Islamic state. They also responded to the international geopolitics of the Cold War in ways that suggested lack of commitment to any concrete national policy that could promote racial and religious coexistence, justice, and national unity.

Chapter 2 describes the different regional or ethnic reactions to the actions of central government *vis-à-vis* the demands for services by the peripheries. It focuses on the southern responses to racial and religious ideologies that attempt to build national unity on the basis of a racially and religiously tiered society. It also addresses the Nubian protests regarding the destruction of their traditional livelihoods and ancient heritage, most palpably disregarded as a national heritage through the building of the hydroelectric dam at Aswan in the 1960s, which resulted in relocation of the people from Halfa to Buttana and the submerging of many villages. A second project which threatens to repeat the same tragedy of the Aswan dam is now underway at Merowe, and the Nubians are engaged in what is clearly a losing campaign against the project. This chapter also examines the crisis in the eastern province, the Nuba mountains, and the southern Blue Nile, and their own grievances toward the state. Such regional remonstrations have taken the form of conscription into the SPLA and also been expressed through the setting-up of various activist groups and community associations.

Chapter 3 addresses the history and conduct of the war in Darfur as well as the international responses to the humanitarian tragedy that resulted from Khartoum's indiscriminate reactions to the uprising. I will argue that race and ethnicity have greatly influenced interactions between the various groups living in Darfur, but were never the cause of such violent confrontations until February 2003. What elevated the conflict to the level that we have witnessed since then was a combination of economic pressures, environmental strain (diminishing resources due to drought), and the deployment of racial divisions by both the government and the opposition forces – the SLA and the JEM – as a strategic tool to raise their support base for their respective causes.

Chapter 4 examines the war in the south and focuses specifically on how the government targeted civilians between 1983 and 2002 in order to deny opposition forces a local base for popular support. I show how power contains within it tools that can be used in resistance to it. For example, such attacks, which are meant to demonstrate the power of the state to coerce citizens into its fold, only inspired more youth to join the ranks of the SPLA and other opposition groups. This chapter also deals with the immediate social and economic consequences of the state's violent reaction to the south's politics of secession.

Chapter 5 looks at the government-sponsored atrocities relating to oil exploration and production. Just as environmental and resource pressures in Darfur gave rise to racially based confrontations, when oil production began in the south in 1998 the determination of the south to deny the government this resource intensified, and the issues of race and religious differences between north and south were deployed to galvanize local popular support for a continued struggle. Southern leaders were aware that access and exclusive control of the revenues by the government could tip the military balance they had maintained since 1983. Nevertheless, oil revenues streamed into Khartoum due to cooperation or collusion by major oil corporations from Canada, China, Malaysia, Sweden and other countries. This new-found wealth quickly proved ominous for the south as Khartoum refused to engage in good faith peace talks. Oil money also enabled Khartoum to revamp its military advantage. In order to secure access for foreign oil corporations, particularly in western Upper Nile, the government and its allied militias displaced the Nuer and Dinka populations inhabiting the region through raiding and indiscriminate aerial bombardment. These acts have incited accusations of genocide from both the international community and local groups. Some oil companies, for example Talisman Energy Inc. of Canada, succumbed to this criticism and withdrew from Sudan. Others from countries with less pristine human rights records remain openly complicit in what amounts to ethnic cleansing if not outright genocide in the oil regions.

Chapter 6 describes the ideological and practical backgrounds to how the peripheries resist state power and how the state has reacted to this opposition in the south, the Nuba mountains and the southern Blue Nile, specifically the actions of Arab soldiers who are armed with racial and Islamic discourse that incites them to suspend any feelings of remorse toward the people in these regions. Here I will examine Khartoum's call for Jihad, or holy war, in order to entice young militant Muslims to fight against what it calls the enemies of Islam.

Chapter 7 chronicles the regional impact of Sudan's wars, especially the threat of a spillover into neighboring countries, and how its neighbors have responded. It addresses the efforts of these countries and others in the international community to mediate peace talks and pressurize the government of Sudan to desist from using allegations of counterinsurgency to mask mass murder of innocent civilians.

The concluding chapter summarizes the entire study and reviews the implications of the book's findings in terms of the importance of including race and religion as key categories of analysis in the study of Sudanese conflicts, the direction the country is headed in terms of break up versus unity, and state building in Sudan. If the country should disintegrate, as all signs indicate, what are the possible fault-lines? If unity is preferred by most Sudanese, what does the country need to do in order to maintain that unity, equitable existence, peace and prosperity?

Although the story I tell in this book about the intersection of race and religion in the contestation of the country's national identity is particular to Sudan, I believe it makes several broader contributions. By demonstrating that Sudanese society is polarized along racial/ethnic and religious lines and that the country's territorial unity is threatened by the ruling elite's attempts to homogenize its racial and cultural identity, the book challenges the prevalent notion that like most African post-colonial states, Sudan must maintain the boundaries it inherited even at the cost of Sudanese lives. Moreover, by incorporating an analysis of the everyday war experience and how it has propelled the populations that are peripheral to the centers of political power toward stronger adherence to racial/ethnic or regional citizenship instead of a 'Sudanese citizenship,' the book complicates the dominant understandings of post-colonial states that favor the material necessity of unity over the moral demands to explore the local desires for autonomy as a viable solution to protracted internal conflicts. Finally, the book moves beyond accounts that emphasize state power to analyze how elements of its own weakness reside within that power, including how the state's use of violence to assert itself produces greater commitment among the marginalized populations to break away. It examines how the interplay of state power and the resilience of local identities, the ruling elites' racial and religious ideologies and those of the marginalized shape the form and content of the ongoing contest over Sudan's identity.

1

THE MILITARY–ISLAMIC COMPLEX AND THE NORTH–SOUTH DIVIDE

Studies of political Islam[60] in many countries claim that increasing numbers of young people, especially the very poor and the silenced among them, have been flocking to radical Islam as a result of their anger at the systems of misrule that have impoverished their countries (Manji, 2004; Burgat, 2003; Lewis, 2003; Ayubi, 1993).[61] It has been said that in countries such as Algeria and Egypt, Muslim militants choose the way of terror as the best approach in their attempts to change governments that restrict the political space and are averse to democratic political opposition. Finding themselves without a forum in which to openly engage the authorities, they fall into the hands of radical Muslim politicians who have a political ax to grind with these autocratic regimes, who are often good allies of the economically advanced Western democratic countries (Tibi, 2002; Beinin and Stork, 1996). In other words, the 'terrorist' acts that target Western countries are really an extension of the opposition to local undemocratic regimes within the Muslim world (Lewis, 2003).[62] It is argued that while some Muslim leaders with radical religious ideology may seize on these young militants, recruit them into Jihad and deploy them for whatever causes these leaders may champion, it is possible that these militants target the West primarily as an extension of their opposition to their local governments and not necessarily because they hate the West. Even if they were to express hatred toward the West, they would do so because of what they see as duplicitous Western policies that allege democracy but continue to give support to undemocratic governments in the Islamic world (Gerges, 1999). Young Muslim militants see the fact that governments in the Islamic world, especially in the Arab Middle East, are good allies of the Western democracies as evidence of hypocrisy on the side of both types of government: how could Western democratic governments support undemocratic regimes in the Muslim world, and how could a self-respecting Muslim government form alliances with the immoral Western governments? (Gerges, 1999; Pipes, 2002, 2003).[63]

This characterization of militant Islam may fit the predominant pattern in the world today, but it is incorrect with regard to Sudan. Sudanese militant Muslims who are active within Sudan are not necessarily pitted against the state. As the case of the National Islamic Front under Hassan al-Turabi has shown, the phenomenon is one in which very well-educated, politically well-placed and socially well-to-do elite manipulate the poor for their own political ends within the state (al-Affendi, 1991). They capitalize on religious sentiments to explain away their own failure and blame Western countries for their country's economic problems. The geopolitics of the Cold War era aside, when Nimeiri switched from Communism, which had kept him in power and kept Soviet support flowing in, to Islamic fundamentalism,[64] he did so in response to pressures from Islamist leaders like Hassan al-Turabi, at one time a dean of the faculty of law at the leading national university and Sudan's Attorney General, by no means a poor politically marginalized man.

Undoubtedly the goals of militant Islam are as much about the propagation of the faith as they are political, but like all things religious, it is difficult to know with certainty, beyond what my respondents say in the interviews and do in their daily lives, what the motives of those who champion political Islam and radicalism are. However, many Sudanese appear to believe that although the Islamists in Sudan stress strict and literal adherence to the basic Islamic principles, i.e. the real meaning and aspirations of Islamic fundamentalism, they are simply interested in using Islam as a vehicle for access to and control of the government rather than genuine devotion and commitment to a return to the sacred fundamentals of Islamic belief. It is equally common to hear Sudanese people insisting that the Islamists in power only pretend to behave more strictly according to Islamic teaching, while actually engaging clandestinely in un-Islamic behavior. Sudanese Islamists have been popularly referred to as *Tujjar al-Deen*, or 'merchants of religion.' Of course, in the politically charged environment of Sudan, people will always argue over issues of morality and the Sudanese Muslims, like followers of other faiths, bitterly disagree on matters relating to the role of religion in politics and governance. What cannot be denied is that the radical ideologies held by some of them in their drive to create a unified Islamic state have polarized the Sudanese people over religion and have resulted in a hierarchical society where Muslims are favored by the state system. Rather than uniting Sudan, this has driven the country to the brink of disintegration. This chapter will examine the politics and poetics of the transition from a secular constitution to an Islamic theocratic regime and describe the causes of this transformation. The chapter also deals with the many Sudanese jokes, songs, and political satire that have become common among the Sudanese as an informal way of criticizing opportunistic political leaders who oscillate between secular or socialist ideologies to market capitalist orientation to becoming Imams (an Islamic scholar or spiritual leader) according to the demands of international geopolitics. To do so, it draws on ethnographic, oral history, archival, and journalistic sources, with a view to uncovering the attitudes of Sudanese people towards their political leaders, i.e. how the Sudanese scrutinize the leaders' claims of piety despite well-known recent histories that indicate otherwise. In what follows, I will argue that the rise of political militant Islam occurred within a political grouping that was already fairly radical and as a product of a confrontation between an ill-educated Islamist military class and the more organized, student-based militant groups; and that although the end goal for this Islamic extremism was partly to achieve unity of the nation by suffusing the country's population with a uniform cultural worldview, the policies of Arabization and Islamization actually became ever more divisive and destructive to the very thing they were intended to build.

Under the Ottoman Empire when Sudan was called the Turco-Egyptian Sudan, or the Turkiyya as it is popularly known within Sudan (1821–1881/5), the country was a country in name only as the southern region (one-third of the country) was considered a mere field from which slaves were harvested (Collins, 1971, 1992). The south was not effectively controlled by the government nor did it benefit from state services, a situation which endures to this day. This meant that the populations occupying what later came to be known as the 'southern region,' when the country was finally ruled as one, had many reasons for wanting to be separate from such a polity. In addition to the bitter and negative encounters between the state and the people of the south, there has never really been a historical oneness between the people of the south and those living in the north. Although there are differences among the various ethnic nationalities within the south, there is a larger degree of cultural, linguistic, and kin affinities between them than one would find between southern and northern groups. Geographical proximity between north and south has not translated into cordial relations and a series of antagonistic encounters meant one side (the north) constantly attempted to assert its over-lordship and the other (the south) was thus reduced to a state of self-defense (Majak, 1990). Of all the occasions of encounter, slave raiding and enslavement were probably the most damaging of the relationships between the people of the two regions.[65]

Under British colonial rule the country became known as the Anglo-Egyptian Sudan (1898–1956). The seeds of the current challenges to its territorial integrity, planted in the previous era, were nurtured by various colonial policies which wavered between attempts to govern it as a single polity on the one hand and ruling the south as a separate entity on the other.[66] Finally, during the post-colonial period (1956–present), Sudan has passed through so many contested evolutionary stages that its continued existence to this day as a unified nation state, especially the fact that the south remains in union with the north, is almost a miracle. Like most sub-Saharan post-colonial African states that are plagued by sub-cultures of violence fueled by attempts to assert a unified national character, Sudan has suffered from a crisis of national identity as the government has toyed with the promotion of an Arab and Islamic disposition while trying to portray the country as Afro-Arab. The state, and its Arab ruling elite, attempts to strike a balance between appeasing the multitude of non-Arab groups within its borders and fitting into the wider black Africa for diplomatic purposes while continuing its racial and religious project. Such a project is indicated by the imposition of Arabic as the national language and the expansion of state sponsorship of Islamic-based social programs.[67] It has also tried to achieve this while it worked on converting everyone to a national outlook designed by the elite, which sparked what became a brutal contest. The first civil war in post-colonial Sudan, borne of this contestation of the character of the nation, started in 1955 and lasted for seventeen years, and was a direct reaction to the process of decolonization that had sought to replace British colonialism with another form of colonialism – Arab nationalism. It was also a result of the long history of the slave trade and slavery that had left a residue in the collective psyche of the Sudanese communities from which the slaves were taken (Jok, 2001; Johnson, 2003). The second round began in 1983 and continued unabated well into 2005: we will return to this latest round of war in the pages to come.

THE FIRST WAR: A BRIEF BACKGROUND

At the time of independence, there were two significant developments in Sudan which overshadowed the immediate nationalist euphoria that had prevailed at least within the north when colonialism ended in 1956. The first was the mutiny of southern soldiers in the Equatorial corps at Torit a few months before independence, in protest at arrangements that were being made about the future of a post-colonial Sudan. The soldiers had heard rumors that the new

Arab soldiers who had come to replace the British and Egyptian officers of the Anglo-Egyptian Condominium were to form the local army in the south and southern soldiers were to be transferred to the north. As most south Sudanese did not want to remain in the Sudanese polity, but wanted the British to set up two separate schedules for independence of two countries, the southern soldiers objected to such a transfer. The mutiny and the government's response to it were to escalate gradually into what became the first North–South civil war, which lasted seventeen years.[68] The second, the event that robbed the Sudanese of the euphoria of independence, was the 1958 military coup led by Ibrahim Abbud, which ended what was considered a promising though fledgling participatory democratic process in the north. The ascent of Abbud to power led to a heavy-handed military dictatorship for the next six years before it too was ended in a popular uprising in Khartoum in October 1964. The dominant policy of his dictatorship was that he sought the most brutal means to curb the dissent in the south and maintain the territorial unity of Sudan at all cost. This was the first time since the ending of the slave trade that a Sudanese government had unleashed such brute force in an effort to bring the multitudes of nationalities into the fold of the state. Even the British colonial authorities, arguably the only real government whose actual presence had been felt by the people in the peripheries and who were thought to be ruthless in their 'pacification' policies,[69] were considered by southerners to be even-handed in comparison to Abbud's regime. Much of this violence, although a purely military campaign to defeat a breakaway group, was pitched in religious terms, but was actually a type of political-military ambition with religious overtones which were used to justify the atrocities as sanctioned by Islam, since they were committed in the name of defending a Muslim state. In other words, if the Sudanese version of Islam did not allow separation of religion and state and that defending the nation was in essence a defense of the faith, then the suggestion that Islam was against violence was an absurd assertion since the state, by its very nature, was not only very violent but also monopolized the use of violence. There were undoubtedly many disagreements among northerners between the supporters of the government's use of violence and those objecting to such politicization of Islam.* The latter believed that Islam, at its core, was a religious faith and that putting it to such military and political uses risked portraying Islam as a political or military institution rather than a code of ethics intended to guide individual conduct. An Islamic military–political complex prevailed nevertheless. Of course, as I will show in later chapters, even the horrendous level of state violence under Abbud was to be surpassed in later years as each successive government proved more violent in its approach to dissent than its predecessors.

The increased application of force against critics of the regime, whether they were individuals such as the various leaders of the sectarian parties in northern Sudan such as the Umma Party, the National Unionist Party, or groups as was the case with the southern rebellion, became the order of the day under Abbud. His government became best known for its brutal murder of chiefs and heads of clans, setting groups against one another, promoting some groups at the expense of others and imprisonment of political opponents. The actions of Abbud's regime gave rise to the racial and ethnic cleavages that would tear apart the fabric of relative coexistence that had been characteristic of Sudan's ethnic relations five decades later. This level of violence was meant to inflict fear so that ideas of a possible breakaway would be abandoned, the more so because conflicting northern and southern opinions on the status of the south had become increasingly intense. Southerners thought that the outgoing colonial authorities had guaranteed a gradual but eventual secession for the south, or at least a federal system with the rights to self-determination: northerners believed that no such provisions were made in the processes that led to independence. From the very beginning of the independent period most, if not all, northern politicians saw the southern preference for the federal system as a step toward an eventual total secession. Political leaders regarded the south as a source of wealth for the development of the north – a

* There was no doubt in the minds of liberal northerners that, if the state could be so brutal in the south, there was nothing to prevent it from similar behavior in the north.

rationale reminiscent of the earlier times when the south was a source of slaves, ivory, timber and other resources – and could not allow its secession. It was at this time that Sudan was described as the next 'breadbasket of the Arab world.'[70]

Letters to the outgoing colonial authorities and speeches by the nationalist leaders in the north make it clear that the justification for continued unity was that of the old slave masters: unity must be maintained in the interests of the south.[71] In the years leading up to independence northerners, who were better organized as a political force and better equipped by colonial education, were deeply concerned that the British were planning to give the south a separate status that could lead eventually to southern self-government, and were keen to thwart this plan. Thus southerners were excluded from the constitutional processes and agreements between the pro-independence northern Sudanese nationalists and the British regarding self-government for Sudan. Not a single southern Sudanese leader took part in the negotiations and the agreements leading to independence, and consequently all issues that concerned the south were decided without southern participation. In the first two years after independence, all northern political parties were intent upon suppressing any southern calls for self-government or federalism. Although the situation for the leading southern politicians and their constituencies who wanted more out of independence than the government was willing to concede worsened under Abbud, an atmosphere in which a military solution to achieve the submission of southerners was preferred had been particularly characteristic of the pre-independence government of the National Unionist Party under Ismail al-Azhari and the post-independence government of the Umma Party. Both of these civilian governments feared that southern disappointment might lead to even stronger sentiments favoring self-determination. This was one of the main reasons why Abbud's military coup – which differed in essence from that of later coups by Nimeiri and al-Bashir – succeeded. The ruling Umma Party handed over power to the army in 1958 in the belief that the army had better policies and capacities for suppression of the rebellion in the south than a political party. Giving power to a military officer meant that the army could act as a mere figurehead while the real power remained with the politicians. It was also useful that any failure at this crucial hour could be blamed on someone other than the political leaders, who were always wary about losing the south during their time in power, as it would almost certainly stain the party's image in the north forever and jeopardize their future electability. The other reason for the handover of the government to Abbud was that the civilian government lacked the resolve to deal with the issues facing the nation at that time due to the intense competition for political influence that had been going on prior to independence. The political parties that had emerged at this time were typically divided in three ways, each following a religious sect – one of several Sufi orders or Tariqa as these are known in Sudan. The main ones were the Mahdiyya (of the al-Mahdi family), the Mirghaniyya (of the Mirghani family) and the amalgamation of other parties such as the Islamic Movement for Liberation, which had an association with Egypt's Muslim Brotherhood,[72] and the Al-Ashiqqa Party[73] which wanted to unite Sudan with Egypt. Realizing that they might lose power to rival Tariqas, the Umma Party of the Mahdi's family opted for a military regime that they hoped might function under their directives while they worked to regain their footing.

General Ibrahim Abbud immediately went to work to prove just what the politicians expected of him, i.e. to assert state power over the dissenting south, but showed no submission to any of them. His policy was two-pronged and aimed at quelling the demands by various ethnic regions for either total inclusion or autonomy. One was to embark on a campaign to hunt down the mutineers and their alleged civilian backers: the other was that Abbud's government took it upon itself to achieve what he thought the politicians had failed at: forging a unified national identity based on Arabic and Islamic teachings. Abbud's policies were therefore shaped by an imperative to transform the indigenous societies. He wanted Sudan to be more Arab than any previous governments had hoped. Unlike the politicians he was more open, never mincing his words about his aspiration to build an Islamic state. (Many northern politicians, including Sadiq al-Mahdi, have been caught telling their Arab brethren in the Middle East of their desire to turn south Sudan into a corridor through which Islamic and Arab culture enter Africa, but they would hesitate to make such remarks within earshot of non-Muslim and non-Arab Sudanese.) On the question of Arabization Abbud seemed to be conflicted, but because he was willing to accommodate the political leaders who were interested in promoting Arab culture and because of his own apparent conviction as to how the nature of Sudan's national identity should appear, his government pursued a policy of Arabization as a crucial aspect of his Islamization project. He pursued these ideas as two sides of the same coin, and promoted them through significant changes in the educational system.

To his credit, Abbud built more schools in the south than any other government in the past. Many of the enduring educational physical infrastructures in the south to this day were built with funds solicited from foreign countries for the express purpose of uplifting south Sudan to the level of the north. However, the policy of promoting education had many motives. First, Abbud wanted a government-run school system in order to discourage Christian missionary activity, which had been the only source of education in the south: missionaries were to be expelled from Sudan in 1964 on his orders and under the pretext that they had been encouraging southerners to seek autonomy. Second, he introduced Arabic as the medium of instruction and poured Muslim and Arab teachers into southern schools. Third, as more and more southern children joined the school system, Islamic proselytizing was carried out more vigorously to convert the southern children, and it became a requirement for non-Arab and non-Muslim school-children in some parts of the country to drop their indigenous names in favor of Arab or Muslim names before they could enrol in school. Many did so solely to secure access to the school system, only to switch back later on when they had graduated.

The 1955 Torit mutiny was progressively escalating into a southern-wide rebellion, and Abbud inherited this situation when he took power. His policy was to pursue the mutineers in the bush of south Sudan, and his army began to burn villages throughout 1958 and 1959 in an effort to confine the rebellion to the southern-most region of Equatoria. These measures were so repressive that many south Sudanese, especially the educated few who were naturally suspected of supporting the mutineers; were forced to hide in the bush. Some joined with mutineers to set up what later became full-scale guerrilla armies: others went into exile in the neighboring countries of Uganda and Kenya, which were still British-ruled. Many more went into Congo when it became independent from Belgium in 1960. The cycle of violence became increasingly vicious as the government further sought to contain this flight of the edu-cated civilians into the guerrilla movement (the guerrilla army was named Anyanya, a term that has become part of the vocabulary of all southern languages but whose etymologic origin remains a subject of disagreement). When civilians were arrested and tortured for their alleged role in the revolt, more and more of them joined the insurgency in order to escape the repression. The exiled politicians eventually organized themselves into a political movement called the Sudan African Nationalist Union (SANU), which became one of the two southern political parties contesting the autonomous par-liament and government of the south – called the High Executive Council for the south and based in Juba – after the Addis Ababa agreement that ended the war in 1972.[74]

Abbud's policies brought southern discontent to a point that threatened a breakaway and also made many northern political forces unhappy because it outlawed political parties, dismissed the parliament and set up a strong-arm rule that relied on military decrees to govern. Despite this, it was its policies toward the disap-pointed peripheries that were most dangerous for the survival of the young nation as a unitary state. From 1962, Abbud's policies of cultural homogenization of the country were in full swing. In addi-tion to the dismissal of the Christian missionaries, removal of edu-cation from the hands of missionary societies and changing schools into Islamic schools and the requirement that non-Arabic speak-ing children must learn Arabic, attempts were made to outlaw the expression of religious and cultural differences. Concurrently, the government continued to Arabize the entire country and put more pressure on the south to conform to Islamic standards. For example, there was a requirement that mosques be constructed in the most central locations in southern towns, and some of the money for these projects was to come from government coffers. There were no similar projects for other cultural beliefs or non-Islamic faiths. These developments were enforced through a bolstered military presence in the south, in Darfur and Kordofan. All the towns and sizeable rural villages in the south received a military force or a police contingent which was charged with patrolling and observing the people as a way to prevent them from joining the rebel movement. Former Anyanya fighter Akol Giir Thiik described this time:

> It was like living under foreign occupation and we knew that somebody was constantly watching us ... These soldiers were behaving like criminals ... and we had to leave for the bush to join the Anyanya as that was the only way to escape the humiliation the Arab soldiers were bringing upon us.

The military activities of Abbud's regime and the government's commitment of further resources to the army were no panacea for the country's increasing slide toward disunity. On the contrary, between 1962 and 1964, when Abbud was strengthening his Arabization and Islamization policies, the repressive military campaign caused a downward spiral in economic development and reduction in social services. It seemed that the government had not only failed to end the war, but that the insurgents were defeating the government indirectly by draining resources toward the army and away from service provision within the northern peripheries. Within the south, repression of civilians suspected as fifth columnists in support of the rebellion increased. Some of the neighboring countries – Ethiopia, the Central African Republic and Congo – were wary of Sudan's Islamic regime and supplied the Anyanya forces with guns and ammunition, marking the earliest wave of internationalization of Sudan's conflict. The gains that Abbud's regime had made in securing a relatively improved economy began to be eaten away by the military engagements in the south. This was marked by a general social unrest in the north, which over time developed into a populist protest and condemnation of the regime. Abbud was judged to have failed on many fronts. Islamists among students regarded Abbud, who was not well-educated, as ill qualified to articulate the Islamist project. Other opponents felt that he had not brought a resolution to the civil war, the issue which had gained him support (because of the notion that a military problem such as the southern rebellion required a military government). On the economic front, his success in promoting growth was short-lived. The brief period of growth during his first two to three years in office was due to a coincidentally successful cotton crop rather than to responsible fiscal planning by his regime. With regard to a host of other domestic and international issues, the image of Sudan did not improve as Abbud's 1959 Nile water treaty with Egypt submitted the country to the mercy of outsiders. These sporadic protests reached a turning point in October 1964, when secondary school and university students led a general uprising to protest the government's failure to meet the economic needs of those living in Khartoum and other northern cities. The popular protests progressively formed into a northern opposition, which began to demand Abbud's resignation. When he did resign, a transitional government was set up with Sirr al-Khatim Khalifa, a long time civil servant with no party affiliations, as Prime Minister. This was the first popular northern revolution since independence, a source of pride and often invoked by the Sudanese. Even today when they think of ways to change government during the successive periods of dictatorship that came after Abbud, northern opposition groups call for another 'October Revolution.'

However, it was the period immediately following the October Revolution that gave hope of a new era. There was euphoria over the ending of the military dictatorship, the institution of civilian rule, and the resumption of party politics. The record shows that there was hope that the October Revolution could bring resolution of the civil war so that the resources of the country could be put into development and provision of services. There seems to have been a genuine realization that the 'southern problem,' as it was known in the northern political discourse on the conflict, was not just delaying development but tearing at the fabric of the nation's unity. Political leaders, resuming the business of rivalry for office, began to speak of the necessity to 'recognize the southern grievances.' It became a subject of political campaigns as each party claimed to be best suited to bring an end to the war. Some southern political figures were enticed back into participation in the governing of the country, and many of them joined the government with the hope that the post-revolution discussions regarding a new constitution and accommodation of southern views would be realized: that they would translate into either a return to the policy of separation of religion from state with which the British had governed the country, or a referendum in the south to decide its status. Military confrontations in the south were reduced somewhat, giving a sense that the elections for the legislature that were scheduled to take place in 1965 would give the south an opportunity to participate at the center. The Round Table Conference was convened in Khartoum to try to tackle the 'southern problem.' It was intended to bridge the gulf between northern and southern politicians over the rights of the south to a referendum regarding its status in the country – what it revealed were nearly irreconcilable differences. Southern politicians, though in disagreement among themselves over many issues, had a unified position that the south should hold a plebiscite to determine once and for all the southern opinion on either unity or separation. Northern politicians did not want to discuss self-determination, federalism, or an autonomous status for the south. This rift was so bitter that the conference neither reached any agreement nor revealed by way of publication of minutes what the outcome of the talks was. Much of what is known today about the Round Table Conference was revealed in a later analysis by Muhamed Omer Bashir, a northern academic who had been the secretary of the conference.[75]

The south was denied participation in the 1965 elections due to allegations of insecurity. The Umma Party – one of the sectarian parties that had long been associated with the Mahdists – won over half of the parliamentary seats, which enabled it to form a coalition government with Muhamed Ahmed Mahjub as Prime Minister. Once again, the main task for Mahjub was to solve the 'southern problem.' The Sudanese were increasingly tired of what they regarded as bad governments: a change, no matter what uncertainties it may bring with it, was always considered better than the prevailing circumstances. Abbud's regime was so hated that the general sentiment held that anything that replaced it was an improvement. In this spirit, Mahjub's ascent to power was received with a sense of renewed hope that things might change for the better. Unfortunately, the first order of business for Mahjub's government was to send more troops to south Sudan with new instructions to break the back of the rebellion by any means. Having no legislators in the new parliament to speak for southern constituencies, except for a few that were hand-picked by the northern parties, the sense of hope evaporated as the Sudanese army set fire to homes and churches, closed schools, destroyed crops and maimed livestock throughout the southern region. The policies that had fanned the rebellion and drained the economy of the country continued as if they had never been the reasons that had brought about the October Revolution. Of the army's conduct in the south after Mahjub's coming to power, Clement Mboro, a prominent southern politician at the time, was to say in an interview conducted in Nairobi, Kenya that 'it became such a vicious cycle, the government killing more and more innocent people and destroying property, southerners becoming more angry and joining the Anyanya rebel forces, and the army killing more people under the pretext of looking for the rebels.' Hundreds of thousands of southerners fled into refugee camps in neighboring countries and hundreds of thousands more had died by the late 1960s. Estimates of lives lost in this first Sudanese civil war were put at half a million.[76]

This period, considered the second democratic interlude – the first was from 1956 to 1958 – was equally marred by serious inter- and intra-party squabbles, about power and issues threatening national unity, such as the ongoing war in the south. The rivalries were at times severe and caused a split in 1966. The ruling Umma Party, for example, broke up due to a disagreement between Mahjub and Sadiq al-Mahdi. Mahjub argued that party politics was weakening the resolve of northerners to maintain control over the south; al-Mahdi thought that a party majority was the only way forward. He gained ground and became Prime Minister for a brief period in 1968. As the political leadership continued to focus on these feuds rather than on efforts to solve the country's basic problems of food, water, and the ongoing conflict in the south, the government's moral authority declined and the Sudanese people again became tired of civilian rule. Naturally, it was both the south and the west that were most unhappy with al-Madhi's government, each having its own grievance along similar lines: either a conditional absorption or an exclusion. For example, the south was particularly outraged over Sadiq al-Mahdi's uncompromising commitment to convert it to Islam. While traveling abroad he had gone on record on several occasions saying that making the south Muslim was the quickest path to unity, stability and development. He was said to have pleaded with the Pope 'to agree with him to convert all southern Sudanese into "believers", whether Muslim or Christian':[77] but it is clear what he really wanted was to convert them to Islam. In this atmosphere of jockeying for political power, religious discourse functioned as the best way to gain support in the more distant but committed Islamic communities in the peripheries.[78] The people of Darfur were angry that the major political parties used the west of the country to bolster their hold on power, but once in power gave all the attention to their kith and kin in Arab-inhabited regions in the central and northern provinces in terms of services and other government-sponsored programs.

Given the disillusionment among the Sudanese people with the successive civilian governments, just as they had with Abbud's military dictatorship, so they were ready to instigate change again. It is the nature of a politically frustrated Sudanese public to rationalize that any change, no matter what uncertainties it may bring with it, is welcome. Change arrived on May 25, 1969 when a group of junior officers, led by a colonel named Ja'afer Muhammad Nimeiri, staged Sudan's second military coup since independence. Because the parliamentary democratic interlude had been judged to have fallen short of resolving the most pressing problems of the nation, the return of military dictatorship with an aura of stronger leadership was at first accepted with jubilation, which gradually turned into cautious optimism and, over time, into fear.

President Nimeiri ruled Sudan through a brutally uncompromising military junta called the Revolutionary Council. The group had no pretensions about its readiness to kill with impunity where they felt there were efforts to undermine their grip on power. Yet Nimeiri had to struggle to assert his authority over his many potential rivals, including some sporadic and limited revolts such as the one staged by the al-Ansar,[79] the followers of the Mahdi, on Abba Island, and the 1971 attempted regime overthrow by members of the Sudanese Communist Party and their allies in the armed forces led by Hashim al-Atta. Both of these protests by family based sectarian parties, and the attempted military coup, were speedily crushed with shocking brutality – the killing of individuals the state had accused of involvement in the risings were carried out summarily and were never fully investigated. Many Sudanese recalled these events with horror for years to come. To this day, many families, whether among the more powerful Arabs or from the remote territories, have not had their cases heard regarding the mysterious circumstances under which their loved ones were killed. The most frequently cited incident was the execution of al-Shafi'a Ahmed al-Shaikh for his involvement in the communist attempted coup. Al-Shafi'a's family, especially Fatima Ahmed Ibrahim, his wife and former president of the Sudanese Women's Union, continues to this day to call for these members of Nimeiri's clique to be tried in court for their summary execution of al-Shafi'a. A similar case is that of a southerner, Joseph Garang, who had been a prominent member of the Sudan Communist Party and was once the minister for southern affairs in the Nimeiri government, the regime that eventually executed him. One of the most well-known military persons implicated in these summary executions was Abu al-Qasim Ahmed Ibrahim, Nimeiri's right-hand man and second in command of the ruling junta. During interrogations of al-Atta's attempted coup plotters, Abu al-Qasim Ibrahim was said to have boasted that he had crushed the Ansar revolt with the speed of lightning and that he had no qualms about repeating the exercise by killing all the coup plotters and dumping their bodies in the river Nile without anyone ever questioning him. Many of them were executed, disappeared or let go on condition that they give up their political activism.[80]

In the south, given that Abbud's regime (which had only been changed a mere five years earlier) and the democratic government that Nimeiri had overthrown had both been fearsome, it was not lost on southerners that the return of a military dictatorship could be ominous for them. For the first three years of his rule, Nimeiri's government continued policies similar to those of Abbud from 1958–1964 and the 1965–1969 parliamentary governments, especially over the issue of the southern rebellion. Having been a socialist who played the geopolitical games of the Cold War era to his advantage, receiving aid from the Soviet Union throughout the first four years of his rule, Nimeiri's army received more hardware and training, which meant that the army posts in the south were rejuvenated in their plans to effect a final solution to the rebellion. Happily for the people of Sudan, Nimeiri had been in the war as a junior officer in the south some few years earlier, and had apparently hated the war.[81] While the military dynamics of the war could not be halted overnight, Nimeiri had a different approach in mind. Shortly after the coup, despite the fact that the fighting in the south had not died down, he announced that it was better to seek a political solution to the conflict in the south and declared how he intended to accomplish this. By late 1971, having been confirmed as President in a nationwide referendum, Nimeiri did an about turn, and instead of continuing his militaristic attitude to the southern opposition, began to make contact with the southern guerrilla movement with suggestions for peace negotiations. Unlike Abbud's more aggressive and single-minded search for military victory against the rebels, Nimeiri opted for a simultaneous search for a peaceful settlement while equipping his southern garrisons for self-defense. He instructed his forces to defend themselves but not to initiate aggression: by 1972 it had become easier for the government and the Anyanya movement to negotiate. The move toward a search for peaceful settlement was also pushed forward by other developments within the south. For example, the many southern opposition factions, some of which had been extremely hostile to one another, were unified under one more cohesive umbrella organization – the Southern Sudan Liberation Movement (SSLM) – led by General Joseph Lagu. As a more ingenious officer than many other guerrilla leaders, Lagu had made good use of his position as the head of the new, more powerful and strongest of all the southern rebel movements – Anyanya – to bring unity to the forces, making it easier to gather them together for peace talks with the government and presenting them as a unified and stronger voice at these peace negotiations. I have listened to General Lagu many times over the years as he narrates this history in the UK, where he has been in exile since the end of Nimeiri's rule. He has been keen to educate a younger generation of southerners about this experience.

The historic peace agreement between Nimeiri's government and the SSLM finally came in February 1972. It was signed in Addis Ababa under the auspices of the World Council of Churches. There were apparent pressures, including military considerations on both sides. Many northern leaders, military and civilian, felt that such a peace deal involved too much compromise, that a military solution was still possible, and that Nimeiri had sold out to the south. Within the south, the mistrust of northern governments caused some leaders to try to talk General Lagu out of the peace negotiations. These pressures were so strong that the whole deal to end the war was reached in three days. Many southerners who were not entirely happy with the outcome were quick to criticise Lagu and other leaders who attended the negotiations. 'How can you fight for seventeen years and reach an agreement in three days?' Barry Wanji, one of the Anyanya leaders, would lament many years later. Many southerners would later argue that the pressure brought to bear on southern negotiators and the speed with which the agreement was reached led to the south making too many serious concessions that were later responsible, if indirectly, for triggering the second round of the North–South war in 1983.

The agreement was based on a consensus that the south could function as one unit, but northern politicians had wanted it to be broken up into three disparate and rival provinces: Upper Nile, Equatoria, and Bahr el-Ghazal. The terms of the agreement also established that the south could set up its own regional government to handle local governance: more of the funds to build and support its autonomous institutions were to be provided by the national treasury. Most importantly, the southern delegations liked the commitment the government made to help repatriate and reintegrate the hundreds of thousands – perhaps as many as a million – south Sudanese who had fled the fighting and were refugees in neighboring countries. In compromising that the Sudan remained a unitary state, and to establish a mechanism to alleviate their fear of persecution once back in the country, the southern delegation demanded and received commitment from the government delegation that a sizeable number of rebel forces be gradually absorbed into the regular Sudan armed forces. I was a young boy at the time of the agreement and as I recall, the end of the war was met with a great deal of jubilation in the south, particularly because the UN and a number of European NGOs had set up various programs of rehabilitation for war-affected communities and reintegration of the refugees. I came to understand much later that the atmosphere of euphoria I witnessed was only among the general public who had been extremely tired of the war, and did not necessarily exist among the rebel fighters. For the general population, anything that could calm the fighting even for a while was desirable. This peace may not have been a perfect one, but it had achieved a period of respite. Chief Bol Malek of the Jurwir section of Dinka commented:

> We knew that we could not trust the Arabs with this agreement ... some of our educated children knew this was a bad agreement, and we knew that war could always resume, but our people were exhausted by war and by death and we wanted to rest ... Not having to run at the sound of guns or news of Arab soldiers descending on our villages was really a good thing ... We wanted peace even at the expense of our dignity ... The peace was a war tactic, we needed to regroup, rearm and resume at the right moment. Throughout the many years of calm following the

agreement, I had never forgotten the necessity of going back to war when the time was right.

The next ten years proved to be the first period of relative calm in the whole country since independence. The new government of the autonomous south and the central government began to enact some of the proposals made in the agreement and the people could be visibly happy with the limited services flowing to south Sudan, especially schools and child vaccination, veterinary services, employment, and resumption of travel and market activity.[82] As far as the former Anyanya fighters and some exiled politicians were concerned, the agreement was a sham and they expected it to crumble very quickly. Many of them did not want anything short of total independence. Indeed, in protest at this agreement many exiled nationalists such as Gordon Muortat Mayen, Mayar Ayii, and Aggrey Jaden[83] never returned to Sudan. Some of the fighters who were absorbed into the national army remained organized and on alert in the event that the south should be cheated, and sporadic revolts would be caused by them for some years to come. For example, in 1975, a group of them under the command of captain Aguet Marial from Yirol were frustrated that the arrangements stipulated by the Addis Ababa accord worked mainly in the interest of the Arabs, and returned to the bush with the intention of continuing the war. When confronted by their senior officers, they killed two of them: Abur Nhial and Gibril Makoi. This incident sent a wave of fear across south Sudan that the war had resumed, but calm prevailed and residents of the south, who had just elected the first regional assembly in 1974, began to feel the effects of a southern government exercising authority over a unified south. There was a widespread sense of stability: people could travel with relative ease between the cities and the rural areas for trade, paid work, and to seek other kinds of services. There was a pervasive feeling that the people had begun to regain trust in the government and songs praising peace were heard during this period. Until this point in the history of the relationship between the state and its citizens there had never been a cordial interaction and the past was replete with violent encounters. The government had always been an extractive one, using force to coerce the people into giving things, like paying the poll tax, which they did. In return the people expected the government to provide services, but for most of the time it failed to do so. These violent encounters were still vivid in the country's collective memory and both the violence of the war period and the ten-year hiatus between the wars are depicted in stories and songs that are still currently popular throughout the south.

THE BEGINNINGS OF DISUNITY

Nimeiri took advantage of this period of relative calm and the cautious degree of trust given him by southerners to push ahead with some development projects funded through international aid. Western multilateral financial institutions like the World Bank and the International Monetary Fund provided some of the funding and the oil-rich Arabian peninsula countries also donated. Kuwait was particularly generous toward the southern government, and had set up an office in Juba to oversee Kuwait's development contribution. The head of this office, known affectionately to southerners as Abdalla al-Kuwaiti, became the face of international goodwill in the southern Sudanese capital of Juba. However, many of the projects seemed to benefit the north more than the peripheries, and complaints were voiced over how the north was exploiting the agreement to advance itself at the expense of the south. It was the initiation of specific projects deemed unfavorable to the south that caused what was low-key grumbling to rise to the level of serious confrontation that would begin in 1983. For example, the Jonglei Canal project, which was intended to drain the swamps of the Sudd into the White Nile and increase the amount of water reaching the north and Egypt, was perceived as an indication of northern intentions to use southern resources for the benefit of the north with no immediate or foreseeable dividends for the local communities. The Jonglei project created many disagreements in the southern parliament. It was presented to the people by local politicians as a positive step for the southern economy, but others highlighted possible environmental damage to the local ecology, arguing that such damage far outweighed any economic benefits that might accrue in the future. Environmentalists and lay persons alike argued that the local Dinka, Nuer and other groups who inhabit the swamp region would lose their grazing pastures, the rich wildlife sanctuaries would be decimated, and there was a possibility of desertification of the area. Above all, opponents of the project argued that it appeared to be more beneficial to northerners, who would enjoy increased water flows down the Nile and thus a better irrigation system than southern communities. They were also angry that the project was conceived and started without consulting the inhabitants of the area. Both the government of Sudan and the Egyptian authorities had made pledges that the project would result in local development, as schools, hospitals, and transportation facilities would be set up before the project began and more such services would be provided at the time of completion. When the project began none of this had happened, and mass protests were staged by outraged student organizations across the south. The mood of the southern population was also inflamed by the discovery that the president of the High Executive Council, Abel Alier, himself a Bor Dinka from the areas to be affected by the canal, had been involved in this plot to drain the swamps. Alier was said to have once told the opponents of the project during a parliamentary debate in the Regional Assembly that 'if the canal has to pass through somebody's eye it will have to go through it.' Many accusations of this nature were made among southerners who suspected that some of their political leaders were in league with the Khartoum government to exploit the south for their own individual benefit, but in a police state with limited civil liberties no independent and reliable investigations were ever made into such allegations, and public officials were quick to dismiss them as lies concocted by their political opponents and intended to discredit their otherwise good and well-intentioned policies.

Furthermore, the decisions that Nimeiri made regarding the exploitation of oil reserves indicated to southerners that he planned to channel the southern resources north. Oil had been discovered in the Bentiu region of western Upper Nile in the south by the US-based Chevron oil company in the mid-1970s: almost immediately Nimeiri made the decision to pipe the oil to a refinery in the northern town of Kosti, instead of building a facility near the location where the oil was to be produced. This was construed locally as another attempt to deny the south the employment opportunities and other profits that would accrue from oil development. While the rationale behind such decisions and policies is always arguable, many of Nimeiri's projects never saw the light of day because of corruption and a lack of managerial skills in his government: many ministers were men of politics with little or no technical qualifications, and were more interested in attracting funds for new projects than completing those already underway. Many such projects, for example Anzara Textiles in Equatoria province, the Melut Sugar Project in Upper Nile, the Twine and Rope Factory in Tonj, and the Food Canning Factory in Wau, all of which were run from Khartoum under the ministry of energy and industry, drained the funds received as loans from foreign countries but never produced any goods. Worst of all, the budget for these southern projects was part of the whole budget intended for the south but was never sent to Juba because the factories were supposedly part of the national government. The result was a huge foreign debt, causing Nimeiri to waver ideologically in order to use Cold War geopolitics to his advantage. Having been a socialist one-party system in the initial phases of the May revolution, Nimeiri's Sudan Socialist Union government was able to receive help from the Warsaw Pact countries. However, as his projects failed and he needed funds to service his debts he switched to the US. Because Sudan is a large and strategically positioned country, it rapidly became the third largest US direct foreign aid recipient in the world after Israel and Egypt. Turning to the capitalist West meant having to abide by certain requirements to meet the terms imposed by the debtors, including an increase in the official prices of some basic consumer goods: the price of oil, bread and sugar increased vastly. These policies in turn prompted widespread riots by students and angry consumers and increased political activism among parties that had always been opposed to Nimeiri but had no open platform on which to express their grievance and present their agenda. Even Islamist groups which did not like the West were happy about the opening of the political space that accompanied Western aid. The Islamists were later to use this space to embark on a drive either to get into Nimeiri's government and change some of its policies or help overthrow it, but this would take some years to gain momentum.

However, despite the policy blunders and the criticism that followed, Nimeiri was credited and praised for a number of successes such as ending the first round of the bloody North–South war, an achievement that also renewed the possibility that Sudan might survive as a unified state. However, praise of this achievement was made during the first few years of his rule, and was largely confined to the south where the impact of the war had been most acute and where the population was most enthusiastic about the ending of hostilities. In the north there were considerable allegations that he was making the north pay a heavy price to gain unity with the south.

POLITICAL ISLAM AND DISUNITY

As Nimeiri saw his northern support diminishing, he began to enact specific policies to appease the new northern voices that were clearly becoming a threat to his government. For example, in 1982 he began to gradually dismantle the main clauses of the agreement that had ended the war because it suited him to do so, largely at the behest of Islamist groups such as the National Islamic Front led by Hassan al-Turabi. At the risk of losing his secular support base during the late 1970s, Nimeiri responded to the Islamists by enacting new legislation that he deemed more attractive to radical Muslims. This coincided with the rise of Islamic fundamentalism in Sudan and in other Muslim countries. Robert Collins observed the following during a visit to Khartoum in April 1982:

> The explanation for Nimeiri's erratic behavior is that since the inauguration of the policy of Reconciliation in 1977 elements

hitherto hostile to him on the Right, particularly Sadiq al-Mahdi, Sharif al-Hindi ... and the Muslim Brothers quite separate from any association with the Ansar and the Sharif, returned to the Sudan and in the course of the next few years became increasingly close to Nimeiri and rose in Byzantine fashion to have greater influence in his councils.[84]

The rise of political Islam and the radical movement in Sudan dates back to 1965 when Hassan al-Turabi, a Western-educated legal scholar with strong ties to the Egypt-based Islamic activist movement called the Muslim Brotherhood, returned to Sudan and began uniting the Sudan branch of the Muslim Brotherhood with the country's other like-minded groups. The group became known as the Islamic Charter Front and eventually changed its name to the National Islamic Front (NIF), by which time it was much enlarged and had infiltrated student organizations in secondary schools and universities. It had also made its presence felt in government and private business (Prunier, 2005: 82). Although this group and many other religious conservatives had previously opposed Nimeiri's policies, and perhaps because they were becoming a threat to him, Nimeiri chose to support their position that government and society should be organized according to Islamic principles. They began to assert themselves as a force to be reckoned with, and their principal concern was the unjustness of the Addis Ababa accord as it related to the north. They believed that the inclusion of secularism in governing the south was too much of a compromise, because they viewed the south – which the government should actively seek to convert – as a challenge to Islam. One significant development which gave them a foothold in the government was the 1977 appointment of al-Turabi as Attorney General. From this point onward members of the NIF and Muslim Brotherhood began to gain power within the civil service, intelligence, and institutions of government that influenced social organization such as education and welfare.

It became apparent that the military regimes that had ruled Sudan were as interested in an Islamic constitution as were the NIF, but they had always tried to apply their ideology without openly announcing the religious and philosophical views that informed their methods of governing. This may have been a tactic to achieve gradually what they hoped would be Sudan's cultural and religious landscape without the inflammatory pronouncements that the NIF racial–religious movement has often made, and which have always brought immediate confrontation. It is here that the family based sectarian political parties and the military regimes differ from the radical Islamic groups. There have been numerous indications that the Umma Party and the Democratic Unionist Party actually want to apply the Islamic laws, but fear a backlash. The working internal manifestos for these parties speak clearly of their Islamic ideologies and their vision for the future Sudan as a Muslim nation. When Nimeiri invited the NIF into his government, it quickly became apparent that the more educated and student based NIF was not going to be timid about its ideology of Islamic-based rule. The rise of the NIF was actually built on the view that previous governments were both un-Islamic and run by ill-educated persons who could not articulate the importance of shari'a. Unlike many other Islamic movements in north Africa and Asia, which rely on the poor and the disenfranchised to turn them against the regimes or alleged foreign infidels, Sudan's Islamic movement was eventually able to take power and control for so long by targeting the educated class for recruitment. Once established and confident, they began to expand their network and to recruit (at least for the militia armies) everyone else, including the largely uneducated Muslim immigrants from West Africa, especially the Hausa or the Fulani, known in Sudan as the Felata. Al-Turabi is said to have boasted, after they had successfully backed the military coup of 1989, that it had taken the Islamic movement forty years to take the helm of government and that it would take twice as long for any other political organization to replace them. Given their prominence in government and society, Sudanese fundamentalists wage their anti-Western policies from a position of power, not one of impoverishment and resentment, which characterizes the radical Islamic movements in Algeria and Egypt.

The rise of the NIF to control of the government in Khartoum appears to have begun with a pragmatic decision by Nimeiri that since he could not defeat them, he should join them. He sided with them when, in contravention of the Addis Ababa accord, he instituted shari'a, the Islamic law, in September 1983, with no exemption for non-Muslim regions.[85] This was one of his most divisive policies. Political movements were gathering momentum in the south in protest at many other policies that seemed to be attempts to thwart southern political and economic gains in the period following the end of the war. The Jonglei Canal project, the re-division of the south into three weaker provinces and the piping of oil to a refinery in the north were clear violations of the Addis Ababa accord and had already triggered considerable political turmoil. The anti-Nimeiri movement was boosted by adverse reaction to the application of Islamic law without exemptions. Moderate Muslims and the political left were also opposed to the application of shari'a, which meant that the Addis Ababa accord was falling apart: Nimeiri dealt the death blow to the accord by deciding to reform Sudanese law immediately according to shari'a. Public executions, amputation of limbs for theft, and lashing for alcohol consumption became common practices and were highly publicized in the national media. The fact that Christians also fell victim to these gruesome punishments meant that many non-Muslims, mainly from the south, had to leave Khartoum. Many of them joined the new rebellion, which had formed soon after several military units had mutinied in the south earlier in May 1983. Joining the opposition became the only viable refuge for some southerners and was also an outlet for the anger they felt over the poor treatment they were receiving at the hands of the police in Khartoum during *Kasha*. The SPLA was formed shortly afterwards and the second round of the North–South civil war commenced; a development that contributed to the eventual fall of Nimeiri. His association with the Islamic movement did not earn him much support elsewhere and Western foreign aid began to diminish, while those Islamic states that had been a source of finance began to worry about the brand of Islam being advocated in Sudan. With intensification of war in the south the economy suffered, and with it came an increased mass protest in the north. While he was visiting Washington in 1985 to renew his request for loans and development aid and military assistance for the war effort, a popular uprising broke out in Khartoum and Nimeiri was deposed when his military took the side of the protestors. He was to go into exile in Egypt where he lived for the next fifteen years until the current Islamist government allowed him to return in 2000.

The September laws, as Nimeiri's Islamic laws became known, have been the subject of much caricature throughout north Sudan. In the initial phases of shari'a, national television aired pictures of Nimeiri throwing alcohol from shops, bars, restaurants and hotels into the river Nile once the new constitution had completely banned its sale and consumption in Sudan. However, the pictures were subject to much derision and contrasted with gossip about him drinking heavily in his office, and there were many other stories about his drinking habits while serving as a young military officer in the south. One depicts him in a confrontation with a southern woman, a single mother who used to brew and sell alcohol in her house to generate income for her family in Yei town, where Nimeiri had once served as a junior officer in the Sudan armed forces. The story said he had taken alcohol on credit but failed to pay the woman back because he was transferred to the north shortly afterwards. He eventually staged the coup that made him president, and was not able to settle the debt until years later, when he was visiting Juba as president of the country and was reminded of the circumstances of extreme poverty in which female-headed households existed. Even after he had declared Islamic law, Nimeiri allegedly continued to drink at parties and other social events, using a trusted servant who would spike his soft drinks with liquor. Such anecdotes cannot be verified, neither is it important to establish their validity. They serve here to describe the political milieu in Sudan in which people had no open platform to criticize the government: such informal discussions, gossip and humor were the only medium for criticism, an act of regaining the freedom of expression that had been stolen by the dictator. Satires about African dictators are common in countries as diverse as Moi's Kenya, Eyadema's Togo, and Boukasa's Central African Republic.[86]

Their purpose is the same. They are the only way for people to vent their anger about the socio-economic conditions of the country, or what Jean-François Bayart has called 'political decompression.'[87] It shows that even regimes as repressive as that of Nimeiri can still be criticized. This depiction of Nimeiri highlighted suspicions that his Islamic policies were not a result of a genuine religious sentiment or a new-found spirituality, but politically motivated to appease the growing Islamic movement – a clear example of politicization of religion and Islamization of politics.

By the time Nimeiri was deposed, the Islamic policies had added to the other cultural issues that had driven a wedge between the north and the south and contributed nothing toward unity, creating extremism among non-Muslims. Conversion to Christianity in 1983 as a direct response to shari'a, much as it was when Abbud expelled the missionaries from the south in the early 1960s, increased to unprecedented levels. The cathedral in Wau town could no longer hold Sunday Mass inside the church after September 1983 as the numbers had increased beyond capacity: it was as if non-Muslims had to prove that they had a different faith and were committed to it. In June 2003, I interviewed Commander Lual Diing Wol, a member of SPLA High Command Council, and a man people in Sudan consider an elder, about the fate of the nation given these government efforts for cultural and racial homogenization. Voicing his concern that Sudan might not survive as a unified state for much longer, he offered the following historical reference:

> In the past, our people never used to talk about being African or Christian or non-Arab because they did not need to prove to anyone what their identity was. People professing Christianity used to go to church when they felt like it and not because they wanted to demonstrate their Christian commitments to anyone. But since 1983, it has become a question of showing the government and its Muslim zealots that we are proud of our identity and do not want anybody to change us. This insistence of northern rulers that our country must become Arab or Muslim has only created a sense of extremism to prove the opposite ... To give you one example,

before 1983, the churches in the south were not attended that much. Yes, most urban populations professed Christianity but they were not really practicing, but since the introduction of Islamic laws, not only did more people attend church more regularly, conversions to Christianity increased dramatically once the people felt that they had to protect their faith. This terribly polarized situation has now become characteristic of the North–South relations, and Sudan is perhaps going to split two ways. It may even split many ways now that similar developments are occurring throughout the country. I cannot see how all of its regions will remain together in a united country if one group feels that their identity should become the identity of the entire nation. What I am saying should not be construed as motivated by my separatist standpoint. I may be a separatist, but this is an observation from someone who has lived through all of the period during which Sudan has been grappling with the issues of unity or break up. To not share this experience as a warning to the rulers is to be dishonest to posterity.[88]

CONCLUSION

This chapter has chronicled the beginnings of the increasing possibility of the disintegration of Sudan, particularly regarding North–South relations. After the hasty exit of the British colonial authorities and the northern assumption of the apparatus of state, coupled with the southern feeling that it was short-changed in the process that brought independence, the country plunged into a chaotic civil conflict. The British had created a mess by ruling the south and the north as separate entities without setting up two separate countries. At the time of 'Sudanization,' the south felt that it had merely moved from European to Arab colonialism, and opted to fight for a better arrangement. At independence, northern politicians had made verbal promises that either development of the south would reach the level of the north or they would set up an autonomous system in which the south would exercise rights over its resources to develop itself. Neither of these happened. Instead, the south experienced an influx of Arab teachers, Muslim clergy, traders, army, police, and security agents, many of whom were instructed to turn the south into a province of the north to be Arabized and Islamicized. This was the genesis of the North–South conflict that would last seventeen years.

Since independence different governments had engaged in the politics of a struggle for power and used the 'southern problem' as a campaign slogan, which meant that governments in Khartoum changed several times, from the post-independence multiparty democracy to the extremism of the Islamist-military complex. Each one beat its chest and declared itself better able to resolve the conflict and keep the country united. They all used similar tactics in an attempt to forge a united northern front against the south and to confuse and weaken the south by proliferating the political parties within it.[89] Rather than address southern grievances, the various governments opted for a military solution. The result was a protraction of the conflict, hardening positions on both sides and potentially causing the people of the south to look at secession as the only solution. In short, an array of issues, from the snuffing-out of the question of federalism, the silencing of southern calls for a referendum and the north's aggressive campaign to change the cultures of the south all justified war in the region. This was the beginning of the rise of southern political activities, the formation of the guerilla movement and the war. The coming to power of General Abbud through his 1958 military coup and his Islamization of politics marked the beginning of the end for Sudanese unity.

2

RACE, RELIGION AND THE POLITICS OF REGIONAL NATIONALISM

The previous chapter showed how at independence the gulf between north and south immediately appeared to be growing wider. Sudan was quickly embroiled in a war over the question of national identity, the imposition of Arabic as the official language and medium of instruction in schools, and the use of Arabic in all government-controlled media. Religious fanaticism, inequitable distribution of resources and political power, and development policies objectionable to the populations of the peripheral regions exacerbated the rift between the state and the people of the peripheries. When Sudan became a member of the Arab League, for example, ignoring the importance of other groups who wanted to maintain their indigenous identity and without proper parliamentary representation on this matter, the large non-Arab populations saw this as both an exclusion and a denial of their citizenship. These developments created a wave of fear throughout south Sudan, particularly among the educated class, and signalled to other non-Arab communities within the north the government's determination to regulate the country culturally. In the south independence was regarded as a transition from European colonialism to Arab colonialism, which was perceived as an extension of foreign rule under a different name: in remote regions of Sudan Arabs were just as foreign as the British. Soon after independence, for example, a Shaigiyya from the far north became the district commissioner in the small town of Gogrial in Bahr el-Ghazal. Faustino Ngot Riny, a Dinka chief in the 1950s who passed away in 2005 at the age of ninety-one, once remarked that the Arab commissioner was more of a foreigner in his dealings with the local Dinka than his European predecessor had been.

> At least the *Khawaja* [White foreigner] was willing to learn our ways and values and respected them. He asked questions so as to better understand the situation before he made any decisions affecting the lives of the people he governed. But Arab commissioners, like this man we had named Majok Ajok, expected the people to be at his disposal, no questions asked ... Why was it that they could not bring a southerner?[90]

This difficulty was more apparent in what was seen in the south as a deliberate exclusion of southerners from the 'Sudanized' administration and from the vibrant political process that characterized the immediate post-colonial Sudan, from the civil service and from commanding positions in the army, including intelligence. The installation of Arabic teachers in the south was regarded by southerners as the start of a cultural engineering project that had been evident in numerous contexts in the past. The same views were still in place years later when the imposition of Islamic teaching was promulgated in the constitution by Ibrahim Abbud when he seized power in the 1958 military coup.

It has been observed, and for the most part I agree, that the exclusion of southerners was not solely a function of racism or cultural bias, as the inhabitants of remote regions would be quick to assert, but also a result of particular dynamics within the peripheries. For example, colonial education had not been even-handed with the regions that were distant from the centers of power: consequently there was a shortage of a strong educated class in non-Arab regions to take up seats in the new government when independence came. Of course colonial education, having favored Arab regions, may have enforced this racial imbalance within the country: therefore the racism of the post-colonial government was a result of the new bureaucratic elites replicating the mechanisms of the colonial state to reproduce their power and wealth.[91] There was also the question of disunity among southern political leaders, a reality which rendered those few who were consulted readily susceptible to exploitation in conference rooms by northern politicians.[92]

While the southern reactions to the state policies of exclusion, whether real or perceived, were based on racial, religious and cultural differences as the motivating factors behind government's exclusionary policies, the responses of the vast non-Arab populations within the traditional north were built upon race and ethnicity as the leading factors in the way they were treated by the Arab-controlled state and its local allies. This chapter will focus on the rationale behind these divisive policies in relation to the non-Arab populations whose pride in their indigenous traditions and cultures, which are mediated through language, economics and rituals, were the subject of aggressive efforts by such post-colonial policies to influence or eradicate them. These efforts have more recently manifested themselves through increased marginalization of non-Arab regions and in the highly racialized manner with which the Khartoum governments have responded to regional or ethnic insurgencies in different parts of the country.

The material presented in this chapter is not new, but rather a retelling of a well-known story in order to make a point about how religious and racial extremism by members of a single faith in a multi-faith society or the deliberate hegemonic control by one racial group in a racially diverse society can only lead to extremism in all others. Although this period in Sudan's history has been well studied, there is no agreement on the significance of these events in relation to the civil wars, their impact on the unity of the country, and whether or not they form enough evidence to suggest the possibility of the country's disintegration. My aim in revisiting this recent history is to make the case for the contention expressed in earlier pages about the fate of the nation: despite the breadth of evidence indicating the trend toward a further spiral into violence and the potential break-up of Sudan, there is still resistance on the part of scholars, practitioners and policy-makers, both internationally and within the country, to this prospect. Many of them seem convinced that as national unity is the best option for all the Sudanese, territorial unity must be maintained at any cost.[93] The yardstick by which this 'best option' is measured remains a mystery, given that the outcome of this insistence on maintaining unity in the interest of specific groups has been almost total destruction and widespread death. The cost of this adamant quest for unity, however, has been far greater for the populations of the ethnic regions that are peripheral to the government. Their right to opt out of the union should have been at least recognized, if not supported, as the break-up of countries is in keeping with the post-Cold War democratic trends seen in the former Soviet Union, former Yugoslavia, Ethiopia, and others. It is absurd for the world to allow and even encourage the dissolution of the old boundaries of these countries but insist that Africans must find a way to live with these unworkable colonial structures. The notion of a unified Sudanese nation has been challenged in the southern third of the country, the Nuba mountains, southern Blue Nile, Nubia in the far north, and the Beja in the east. Their grievances, goals, and ideological approaches, despite variations in the expression, have a great deal in common. They include objection to what they see as racial and religious domination by Arabs and political Islamists, marginalization of their territories in the distribution of the national pie, and the restriction of the political space in which they could have peacefully presented their views on how to restructure the state in order to accommodate all now that colonial frontiers have become national frontiers.

SOUTHERN REACTIONS

As mentioned in Chapter one, the second round of the North–South war began in 1983. At the time of writing, a peace agreement to end this war had been signed after a long struggle, but its implementation is still underway and its success uncertain, given the difficulties of post-war reconstruction and rehabilitation in order to persuade the people that peace has dividends. The failure of previous peace accords overshadows the current one, and the southern people have not been as quick to embrace this peace accord as they did the one signed in 1972. Many are still suspicious of Khartoum's commitment to the agreement.

The Sudanese conflicts have often been framed as setting the Muslim and Arabized north against the Christian south, where followers of various African traditional religious beliefs also live, and where the opposition SPLA was fighting for more religious, economic and political freedoms. The root causes of these conflicts are many and complex. Under British colonial rule the 'Southern Policy' had barred northern Sudanese from entering or living in the south. In 1946, a decade before Sudan became independent, this policy was reversed under pressure from a growing Sudanese nationalist movement in the north and movement of people between the two regions was allowed once again. When independence came in 1956, northerners hurried to resume all the activities that the Southern Policy had interdicted. Arabic was imposed as the only official language of administration and education, Muslim preachers flocked into the south, and northern merchants, the Jallaba, poured in to take advantage of those southern resources that had not been fully tapped in the past. Large numbers of Arabs, who were better educated under colonialism, overwhelmed the region and managed to monopolize all the institutions in the south. They soon controlled the civil service, finance and banking, education, and law enforcement agencies, including the many national and provincial security outfits.

Southern fears of Arab domination, which they had expressed to the British before independence, were now confirmed.[94] Southerners were critical of the objective of northern leaders whose drive for independence was not only to free Sudan of colonial domination, but also to establish an Arabized and Islamic culture throughout the country. This was obvious during pre-independence negotiations on self-determination of the country in the 1950s, during which southerners were frequently excluded and did not become a part of the 'Sudanized' administration. These and other measures taken against the south soon led to the development of a secessionist sentiment. It was this sentiment that inspired the first round of civil war, which began in 1955 when southerners in the army mutinied in the southern town of Torit. Armed secessionist activity grew stronger after the organization of a guerrilla army known as the Anyanya. The war between Anyanya forces and the successive governments in Khartoum went on for seventeen years (1955–1972) before it was ended through an accord signed in Addis Ababa, Ethiopia. The agreement between Nimeiri's government and Lagu's SSLA granted the south an autonomous status but had too many loopholes, and Nimeiri was quick to take advantage of these weaknesses. He contravened the pillar clauses of the agreement, including the integrity of the autonomous southern government itself, without consulting the southern leaders. For example, in the early 1980s, he redesigned the North–South boundaries, planned to build refinery in the north for exploitation of the southern oil resources, divided the south into smaller and weaker states, created self-governing states within the north, which was meant to dilute the concept of southern autonomy, and finally declared the imposition of shari'a or Islamic law all over the country.[95]

Nimeiri's disappointing policies triggered widespread anger among southerners: although they had initially been strong supporters of Nimeiri for ending the first civil war, many in the south organized into underground opposition groups. The period of relative calm brought by the Addis Ababa agreement and the serious attempts to pacify and unite the country by granting autonomous status for the south were interrupted in 1983.[96] A group of former Anyanya officers who had been absorbed in the National Army mutinied in the southern town of Bor: shortly afterwards, the SPLA was formed under the leadership of Colonel John Garang de Mabior. A fully fledged second round of war between the north and the south ensued immediately. With Ethiopian and Libyan support for the SPLA, the SPLA endured everything Khartoum threw at it and also made significant military gains against Nimeiri's government in 1984.[97]

This phase of the war revealed another face of southern aspirations when the SPLA claimed that it was not fighting for the secession of the south, but for liberation of the whole country from the tyranny of the minority clique of riverine Arabs and for the creation of a 'New Sudan,' free from any discrimination based on race, ethnicity, religion or cultural background. Although this stipulation was perceived by many southerners as a diplomatic tactic necessary to win the support or neutrality of countries that opposed the break-up of Sudan, such as Libya and Egypt, it appealed to those living in other regions of the country who felt that they too had been economically neglected by the central government. This reconfigured the age-old North–South framework of conflicts, and many non-southerners including the Nuba of central Sudan and the people of southern Blue Nile joined the SPLA in large numbers.

SPLA military gains, the burden of war on the national economy, and the political achievements within the north as the SPLA's ideology garnered some support among the northern opposition groups, led to the fall of Nimeiri in 1985 through a popular uprising. Since then a succession of governments have come to power including the Transitional Military Council led by A. Swar al-Dahab, the elected government of the Umma Party led by Sadiq al-Mahdi, and the present military regime of General Omar Hassan el Bashir backed by the fundamentalist NIF which came to power through a military coup on June 30, 1989. Although the deposed and current governments had differing ideologies as to how to govern Sudan, it is fair to say that they agreed on two things. The first is their shared Arab and Islamist stand: the second their commitment to a military solution to the conflict in the south. They all showed no indication of any intention to enter into serious peace negotiations with the SPLA until 2002 (we will examine this further in Chapter seven). These are the two most important factors that further fueled the wars long after the fall of Nimeiri. The military junta presently in power is made up of NIF members but has disingenuously sought to rename itself the National Congress Party and has pursued a policy of Arabization and Islamization since it came to power. It continues to have little respect for other racial groups and faiths. This racist outlook and religious zeal heightens their willingness to fight, and in turn further radicalizes the perpheries.[98]

The year 1991 was a turning point in the history of the SPLA for two reasons. The first was the loss of its main supply lines and military bases in southwestern Ethiopia, following the collapse of Mengistu's Dergue government in May. This provoked the mass exodus of southern Sudanese refugees from their Ethiopian hiding places into southern Sudan, where they fell prey to the bombing by the Khartoum government. They sought refuge in Kenya and Uganda where some 250,000 refugees are still living at the time of writing. The second and most debilitating was the split in the SPLA's ranks in August, which was initially thought to be based on ideological differences between the leaders but quickly led to the formation of rival factions along ethnic lines. This in turn led to militarization and polarization of the two largest ethnic groups in south Sudan, Nuer and Dinka. John Garang (Dinka) controlled the SPLA-mainstream and Riek Machar (Nuer) led the SPLA-Nasir.[99] Leadership wrangles between the two men prompted them to play the ethnic card, and each started preying on one another's civilian population. The Khartoum government fanned the flames of these conflicts between southern rebel leaders, and the southern opposition was greatly weakened causing the SPLA to lose military ground for several years until 1997 when it regained its footing once again (Jok and Hutchinson, 1999; Nyaba, 1997). Unfortunately, the SPLA's military gains were not able to halt the ethnic clashes, nor did they prevent continued raiding by the government and its militia on the southern civilian population. These raids were the cause of a major famine in the Bahr el-Ghazal region, which led to the death of 60,000 people between April and August 1998.[100]

It is now over two decades since the war resumed and, according to many studies and estimates including one conducted by the United States Refugee Committee,[101] it has caused the death of over two million southerners. The bombing and raiding of civilian villages has driven close to one million southern refugees to the neighboring countries of Uganda, Kenya, Eritrea, Congo, Egypt, and the Central African Republic and another three million southerners have fled to northern Sudan. About two million of these internally displaced persons struggle to make a living in and around

Khartoum, the remainder are scattered over Kordofan, Darfur, and other northern provinces. Internally displaced southerners in the north and foreign observers including diplomats and humanitarian aid workers complain of the lack of schools, restrictions on their use of places of worship, lack of decent living spaces, and drinking water, not to speak of the lack of employment opportunities.[102] Those living in the camps around Khartoum escaped prolonged conflicts in their native regions and braved the capital hoping for protection, only to face more horrors in which the government itself was either complicit or an outright perpetrator. People were forced to renounce their faith and embrace Islam before they could receive food aid. Their churches and schools, run by NGOs or churches, were demolished by the city under the pretext that they had violated zoning policies and they were denied permits to build new churches in the zoned parts of the city. It is an open secret in Sudan that Islamic law does not allow the building of new churches in what is supposedly an Islamic nation, but this has never been offered to the IDPs as a reason for their eviction. This is a calculated and politicized interpretation of Islam which applies Islamic laws comprehensively without the appearance of religious intolerance for fear of international condemnation and of radicalizing the non-Muslim population. The effort to accomplish goals of radical Islam while maintaining the façade of a tolerant government, usually a ploy intended to mislead the diplomatic and NGO communities in Khartoum, has not been entirely successful. Most reports about the conditions of the displaced are full of vivid testimony in which religious persecution is always more frequently cited by non-Muslims in Khartoum as the main reason behind these government practices.

In response to criticism on exercising the right to freedom of expression, Khartoum has outlawed such rights since the NIF came to power. Public protest in objection to these policies is now a treasonable offense. Between 1989 and 2000 opposition parties were banned and their leaders exiled, denying the people the only platform on which to question the government with regard to these practices. Newspapers were banned or kept on a tight leash with national security agencies reading and approving newspaper content before they hit the newsstands. A tight security system has been developed to ensure that all internal opposition is suppressed and that persecuted ethnic and religious minorities do not have a channel through which to seek justice or speak out against discrimination. Denying that it practices religious discrimination in one context and embarking upon activities that contradicted it in another, the government left no doubt in the minds of non-Muslims or moderate Muslims that it had chosen Islamic theocracy as the only way to govern. Criticism of government policies was considered an insult to Islam, and Muslims who were critical of the regime were threatened with charges of apostasy. Despite attempts to conceal it, as the rhetoric shows, Khartoum's choice of radical policies in the name of Islam was clearly self-serving and this has not been lost on its opponents. The regime has pursued a policy of forced Islamization of the country, strengthening the Islamic laws, and declaring the war in the south a holy war – Jihad. The potential for these policies to cause disunity has spurred the leading opposition parties in the north, including the religious-based sectarian parties, to join the SPLA's call for changes to the whole system of governance and the establishment of a pluralistic, secular state with equal rights for all citizens. It was the view of this opposition that a referendum would resolve whether the 'marginalized' groups want secession or a united Sudan with a federal structure. In 1995, the parties in exile joined hands with the SPLA to form a united opposition front called the National Democratic Alliance (NDA), based in Asmara, Eritrea. This group sought to overthrow the NIF government by all means, including military force. The SPLA's John Garang was chosen to command the joint NDA forces.

In their quest for power and in order to maintain it the NIF have used all and any means at their disposal including Jihad against unbelievers, denying the human rights of others in the process. Many now fear that as long as the NIF is at the helm of state affairs in Khartoum, the production and reproduction of conflict in Sudan, with an inevitable spill-over into neighboring countries, will continue unabated. Perhaps this is one of the historical experiences that have propelled the south toward the path of separation, even though the SPLA had fought for many years to persuade the Sudanese marginalized regions to work together to end the hegemony of the central region, and liberate Sudan from them instead of each wanting to break off. Years of war and the frustration that has built up due to the intransigence of the government have caused the south to revert to its old desire to secede.

However, based on interviews and conversations with a variety of Sudanese, both within the country and in the diaspora communities, there were a variety of views on the question of southern independence. Many northerners, including those who sympathize with southern grievances, have tried to make a case against southern secession even though they acknowledge the need for a democratic resolution of this issue. I have discussed with southerners many of the points made about the secessionist stand and they do not find them terribly convincing, neither to southerners or non-Sudanese observers. Northerners argue that a new state in the south would not be viable given the interests of neighbors such as Uganda and Kenya who might find it easy to annexe or influence the position of the young state. Others have suggested that the independence of the south is not a panacea for the internal problems within the south: in fact, the argument goes, independence might lead to more ethnic wars among southern groups and further disintegration, especially since the north's monopoly of power, which most southerners agree to fight collectively, will no longer be there to represent the common enemy and act as the unifying force that it has always been in the eyes of most southerners.

Another argument advanced against southern independence is the lack of structures necessary for a state, such as an educated class to run it and the vital institutions and infrastructure. At a meeting hosted by Nigeria and aimed at negotiating a settlement between the SPLA and the government in Abuja in 1992, it was reported that a member of the government's delegation wondered why the SPLA was demanding so many positions of power when the movement clearly does not have skilled people to take up these positions

(Wöndu and Lesch, 2000). A further claim against southern secession is that there has never been an opinion poll or a plebiscite in which most southern Sudanese have decided against the maintenance of a unified state with the north. It goes without saying that by advancing these claims, the northerners' intention is to make the point that unity is the best option for the whole of Sudan. However, given that a comprehensive peace agreement was signed in January 2005 between the SPLA and the government, the verdict on the status of the south is yet to come after a six-year interim period when the south will hold a referendum on unity or separation according to this agreement.

THE NUBIAN NORTH: RISING AGAINST THE MEROWE DAM

Nubia occupies the northern third of the country. This region has almost always been at the margin of the contemporary Sudanese state in terms of services as well as in the ability of the state to absorb the Nubians into the Arab identity to which Khartoum governments aspire. However, unlike the other marginalized regions, the Nubians have never resorted to an armed resistance. The inhabitants of the northernmost region of Sudan, except for the few who are absorbed into the Arab group and who detach themselves from their roots due to migration for work, have always resorted to silent resistance, keeping a low profile in Sudanese politics and maintaining their cultural character through distance from government-sponsored cultural practices. In fact, many Nubians had taken to the idea of participation in the Arabized state, and had adopted aspects of popular culture that portray Sudan as an Arab country until angered by specific events. What eventually catapulted Nubia into resistance to the state power was the manner in which the government had handled the impact of the Aswan High Dam. The dam destroyed much of ancient Nubian heritage and also led to the death of thousands, as a direct result of relocation to unfamiliar places in the country, and indirectly due to flooding. Many Nubian lives were destroyed in the wake of the dam construction as a consequence of population relocation from Wadi Halfa and the surrounding areas in the northernmost parts of the country to the arid Butana plains at Khashm el-Ghirba in central Sudan between 1959 and 1963. Of all the issues that have caused the Nubians to resent the Sudanese state, it is questions concerning physical survival that have most politicized much of the Nubian populace that remains un-Arabized: mass relocation of the entire Nubian population from its ancestral home, where a very distinct way of life had evolved, to a new alien home, enraged them. This relocation resulted in the loss of property, mainly the date palms, which had been the primary staple of the Nubian economy, as the Nubian country was devastated by the rising waters. The loss of Nubia's abundant archaeological treasures, despite the international effort to save them, was a disaster both to Nubia as a distinct cultural group and to the Sudanese nation as a whole. John Ryle, a Sudan specialist, once remarked on the difference in the way the Sudanese state and other countries memorialize their ancient cultures by preserving monuments from that past. He found it curious that the Sudanese state does not take national pride in ancient Nubian civilization or make it a national symbol in the way that Egypt and many other countries with ancient cultures have done.[103]

The Nubians would probably have come to grips with this destruction had it ended there. However, since 1999 the government of Sudan has embarked on another project similar to that at Wadi Halfa, which has stirred the Nubians into a more concerted opposition. The construction of the Merowe Dam at Hamadab is a hydrological project conceived and implemented 'by an influential group within the military government of Sudan to serve its own purposes in monopolizing the electricity sector.'[104] The new dam, which will produce 1,250 megawatts of electricity, is expected to cost $1.8 billion and is financed by China's Exim Bank and several Arab funds. It is being executed by Chinese and European companies including Alstom and Lahmeyer International. Once it is finished in 2008, the Merowe Dam will roughly double Sudan's power supply and will help irrigate land that is now barely arable. Sudan's leaders see it as a symbol of the country's future. 'Our battle against poverty starts from here,' President Omar al-Bashir said in March 2005 during a visit to the dam site, 215 miles north of Khartoum.[105] For the inhabitants of the area, modernization that comes with such a hefty price is questionable. The dam, which experts say is the largest hydropower project under development in Africa, is expected to create a sprawling 100-mile long lake that will displace 50,000 people who currently live in villages along the river. John Ryle, who had visited the project site, was to write that

> although it is much smaller than the Aswan High Dam and set to flood a lesser area, the Merowe Dam raises comparable social and political questions. It involves the forcible displacement of tens of thousands of local people as well as the inundation of an unknown number of unexplored archaeological sites.

> (Ryle, 2004)

Local and international criticism of the project remains fierce, particularly among outside environmental groups and the directly affected Nubian people. The International Rivers Network and the Corner House published a report in 2005 that complained that displaced residents were being resettled to areas with far less fertile soil and distant from water sources. 'The re-settlers were promised free services such as water, electricity and fertilizers for a two-year transition period, but are being cheated out of most of these services' (Bosshard and Hildyard 2005). The groups also said that what threatens to be a tremendous environmental effect of the project has never been properly assessed and that an appropriate plan for handling the cultural heritage of the area is lacking. The dam was first proposed in the 1940s and has been discussed and deferred by the authorities ever since. Local residents who eke out existence along the banks of the Nile near the fourth cataract and admire the beauty of the area, say they are opposed to the project. Although they see the future value in terms of industrialization for the whole country, Nubian people argue that it is being carried out at the expense of their heritage and dignity. They are aware that any benefits that might accrue from the project will probably not trickle back to them and that the little that might reach them will not compensate them for the loss of what they consider to be the fabric of their identity. The Nubians are quick to point out that had their territory been inhabited by the more favored Arab groups the government would have probably put more resources into studying the impact first, but does not care what happens to the supposedly disposable Nubians as long as the elite make their gains. In April 2006, their fears were proved to be well placed when a group of them gathered in the project affected area in order to hammer out an approach to their resistance to displacement. They were attacked with machine guns by what was reported as the dam militia and scores of civilians were killed. Affected Nubians are demanding resettlement around the dam reservoir, but the dam authority insists on resettling them far away in the desert, a location to which they have bitterly objected. The population of the affected areas suspects that the dam authority has sold their land to some rich Arab investors. A local activist group, the Leadership Office of Hamadab Affected People (LOHAP) frequently calls on the UN and Western embassies in Khartoum to find ways to protect the people affected by the Merowe Dam from such government abuses.

Because the implementation of the dam project began at a sensitive time in the history of the nation, when the government appeared bent on brutal suppression of any peaceful protests against such major works, it has stirred a major anti-government movement in Nubia and added to the threat of state disintegration. Instead of using this major cultural heritage, a civilization that reflects the multiplicity in the Sudanese heritage, as a rallying point for national identity, the Sudan government has embraced a form of political Islam and Arabist ideology that is unrepresentative of the Sudanese multitudes of cultures that ancient and contemporary heritage reveals. The destruction of ancient Nubia seems aimed at eventual denial of this heritage and the promotion of Arab culture in its place. Nubian activists I have interviewed say that the government is reported to have invited foreign archaeologists from Poland, Germany, the US, and Britain to support a speedy archaeological dig to uncover what they can before the project begins in exchange for some of the relics for museums in the home countries of these scientists. Local opponents of the project say that a government that ransoms off its own heritage before knowing what the ruins contain is one that is trying to sever its connections to the past, lest that past contradict the Arab and Islamic roots they want to promote as more autochthonous. This has caused a serious problem in Nubia; to resist more vigorously is to invite the wrath of a ruthless government, especially in light of government atrocities in Darfur which could easily be replicated on a large scale in the north. The establishment of a dam militia and the attack on the resettlement meeting clearly point to this possibility. Despite this, to allow it to go on as did the previous project which decimated so much of their way of life and so many of their people, is to risk the repeat of that destruction: this is the kind of fear and frustration that has caused many regions to be cautious about their loyalty to the Sudanese state.

THE EASTERN REGION AND THE GROWTH OF LOCAL NATIONALISM

The most prominent ethnic group that has argued strongly against the marginalization of the eastern region is the Beja, a semi-nomadic group of people comprising several sub-tribes whose livelihoods have enabled them to cover the region spanning nearly all the Sudanese-Eritrean border and the strip of land along the Red Sea. Estimates put the Beja population in the area at between 150,000 and 190,000. It is one of the most under-served and remote areas of all Sudan's conflict-affected regions. Its humanitarian needs – basic issues of physical survival, nutrition and safe water, and more complex health and educational problems – are immense, and the likelihood of foreign humanitarian aid reaching them is slender. The Beja people have been left to themselves for years. The government now blames their tragic existence on their own uprising, but their ordeal dates back many decades – long before the conflict began. Until recently, illiteracy rates were more than 95 percent, and the little that exists by way of services was offered by international agencies over the course of the ongoing conflict. Maternal mortality is also said to be unusually high, according to NGO reports.[106] Female genital mutilation is universal, and traditional childbirth practices, under such rapidly changing social and economic circumstances, kill or injure many women. For example, the Beja believe that a small baby is easier to deliver, and starve their women during pregnancy. Nutritional problems arising from the many dietary prohibitions surrounding pregnancy were traditionally offset by the availability of a variety of options, especially through market activity, but these options are currently unavailable due to conflict and reduction in the local peoples' purchasing capacity. Mineral deficiencies during pregnancy abound, and many women die during labor, simply because they do not have enough energy for the delivery. However, the main causes of death for the Beja are preventable diseases: acute respiratory infections and diarrhea.

The northeast of Sudan is a harsh environment which worsened in recent times following the droughts that have hit the Horn of Africa over the years.[107] There were no rains at all in the area between 2000 and 2004, and a shortage of water magnified the serious problems of food scarcity. Fresh drinking water is usually very hard to come by in northeast Sudan. All the settlements in the Beja region focus around dry river beds, and people rely on hand-dug wells. Most worrying is the trend that has been recurring for generations: whenever there has been a year of severe drought, for example 2004, a swarm of locusts always follows and consumes the foliage that usually sustains the goats and camels upon which the Beja depend almost entirely for survival. In early 2005 the UN Food and Agriculture Organization reported that a few immature locust swarms had formed in northeast Sudan near the Red Sea and the border of Egypt: news which caused fear among the population of the region. The locust swarms also meant that the few who grew crops in the valleys had very little if any harvest at all the following year, which repeats the cycle of famine that has characterized the region for nearly three decades. The end of this cycle is unforeseeable as a combination of natural disasters and national policies single out the Beja for deliberate marginalization due to their assumed support for the local opposition forces.

Although the Beja can be found throughout northeast Africa, tens of thousands are currently trapped in an area of eastern Sudan near the Eritrean border, held by an amalgamation of armed Sudanese opposition groups, some of which are indigenous Beja movements such as the Beja Congress and the Sudan Alliance Forces (SAF). These opposition movements started in earnest during the last few years of Nimeiri's regime in the early 1980s but increased their activities in the 1990s to fight for their share of the national pie, complaining of deliberate exclusion due to their opposition to Arabization. More opposition groups went into this area as a result of the formation of the National Democratic Alliance (NDA) in 1995. The NDA includes major political forces of Sudan such as the SPLA, the DUP under Muhammad Usman al-Merghani, and the Umma Party that has ruled Sudan on and off under the leadership of elected Prime Minister Sadiq al-Mahdi. (It was the Umma that was in power and deposed in the military coup that brought President Bashir to power in 1989.) They also include Sudan Alliance Forces and a group of officers who were purged by the Bashir government from Sudan's armed forces and immediately organized themselves into what they called the Legitimate Command under the leadership of Brigadier Abdel Aziz Khalid, one of the generals summarily dismissed by the Islamist government (Crummey *et al.*, 2006).

In the wake of the establishment of the NDA, these groups agreed that each one would contribute forces to a joint armed opposition under the command of the SPLA's John Garang, and they have since pursued the overthrow of the al-Bashir government through various means, including the use of military force. They have capitalized on the anger of Beja youth at central government's marginalization of their region to increase recrutiment. Some opposition armies brought soldiers with them from their regional strongholds, for example the Umma Party, whose small military contingent was made up of Rezeiqat from Darfur and Missiriyya from Kordofan. The SPLA deployed a brigade from its forces in the south and called it the Eastern Brigade – it was sometimes known as the New Sudan Brigade – commanded by Pagan Amuom, one of the young and more educated SPLA officers who received military training in Cuba in the late 1980s.[108] Despite this, the bulk of new recruitment into the NDA has had to concentrate on the local youth. The Beja joined in moderate numbers but were significant enough to effect a military pressure on the government. The NDA is the only vehicle through which to convey their dissatisfaction with the conduct of central government toward the northeastern region as a whole, and more specifically its neglect of the many semi-nomadic populations, of which the Beja are only one. They have since fought a bitter war in the region in which they were able to capture garrison towns which, although they were usually quickly retaken from them, were of military significance. Besides the constant threat the opposition forces have posed to the economically vital Kassala–Port Sudan and Port Sudan–Khartoum roads, the two most significant military campaigns were the NDA's short-term occupation of Kassala, the capital of the Red Sea State, and the assault on the town of Hamesh Kreib, which the NDA forces continue to hold. These two incidents were a bitter pill for the government and its response, which targeted the civilian population suspected of supporting the occupations, affected many aspects of life. Because Kassala was the biggest town in the region, its occupation was a test of the military strength of the NDA, but the occupation of Hamesh Kreib was decried because it is a religious center. The NDA leader Mohamed Osman al-Merghani, a man known for his religious commitments, distanced himself from the attack and to the surprise of all concerned, announced that he had not ordered an assault on Hamesh Kreib and regretted this transgression on a holy town.

In that same campaign, NDA forces were also able to destabilize the transportation network of roads and railway that connects the region to the capital Khartoum and other big cities such as Wad Madani. The outcome was that having fared poorly in direct military confrontation with the opposition, the government started a war on civilians in the region. In the aftermath of the attack on Kassala there was a massacre of southern Sudanese who had been living in the town for years. This is another example of persistence of racial categorization, which is perceived in Sudan on the basis of phenotypes without determining how the individuals perceive themselves. Southerners and Nuba who had been residents of the city for decades and had not expressed any political views on North–South relations were massacred simply because they were identified by arbitrary racial characteristics.[109] An even more concerted assault on the civilian population targeted the rural population of the Beja region. Combined with a persistent drought that had gone on for years, the military cordoning off of the Beja territory caused a humanitarian crisis that was hard to relieve by the international aid community. Two NGOs, both based in Eritrea – the International Rescue Committee and Oxfam – were able to access this 15,000 sq km area since 2000. Beja grazing areas were also severely restricted by a front line between rebel forces and Khartoum government soldiers, the second to be opened by southern rebels during Sudan's twenty-two year civil war. The entire front line was mined, leaving a dangerous cache of landmines and unexploded ordnance in the area. (The actual line of control was heavily manned by soldiers from the government of Sudan.) Having their grazing areas thus restricted has made it significantly harder for the Beja to seek better pasture for their animals in times of drought. Beja men have also found it hard to move freely and look for work in the nearby towns of Kassala and Port Sudan, both of which were outside the rebel-controlled area. The Beja people had traditionally maintained a pattern of seasonal migration to Kassala both for employment and for buying food-stuffs and other requirements. This has now been curtailed as Beja men are afraid of being arrested by government security forces: many of them have already been put in jail under the pretext that they are supporters of the rebels.[110] They are also afraid of being forced into the government army and deployed to fight against their own people. While there have been no calls for separation in the eastern region, despite having faced so many hardships, the inhabitants express a desire for self-determination that the current federal system has not been able to satisfy.

The NDA has been so plagued by party and ideological differences that by early 2005 it was close to being dismantled. Earlier in 2000, the Umma branch headed by Sadiq al-Mahdi ended its membership in the NDA and al-Mahdi ended his self-imposed exile and returned to Khartoum, along with the few soldiers they had brought to the eastern front with them. The SPLA signed a peace agreement with the Khartoum government in January 2005 and has – in theory – become a partner with the National Congress Party in the formation of a national government, at least for the six-year interim period stipulated in the agreement. This membership means the SPLA can no longer pursue military options to change the government in Khartoum and by extension it has ended its membership in the NDA. Muhammad Osman al-Merghani, the head of the NDA, followed suit and agreed to talk peace with the government. A peace protocol was signed in Cairo in February 2005. Sudan Alliance Forces had merged with the SPLA years earlier and were assumed to have agreed to the SPLA decision to accept the peace agreement as negotiated in Kenya. In essence then the NDA has been reduced to a nominal existence: the biggest parties received concessions from the government, the smallest parties were left without representation in the would-be government of national unity or a clear idea as to whether they should continue to fight until they get their rights or surrender to the realities of the new political developments in the country. As this situation persists, it is the Beja and other marginalized groups in the east, whose men were put forward by the NDA to fight on behalf of the sectarian parties, who have reaped nothing from these wars except more of the same kind of suffering for the civilian population in their areas. This was not a solution to the national crises that Sudan has faced since independence: it simply meant that the Beja were driven into bitter resentment of the state, which in turn meant that central government continued to hold a grudge against them, they were still excluded from political representation and from provision of services, and they have remained outside the body politic of the nation-state. In turn this cultural hegemony has translated into either a gradual absorption of the Beja and others into the national identity framed by the elites or continuation of fighting to assert their identity, which is a recipe for state disintegration, or at least a prolongation of the time it takes to achieve that elusive unity.

THE SOUTHERN BLUE NILE: RACIAL AFFILIATIONS INSTEAD OF RELIGIOUS AFFINITIES

Southern Blue Nile was integral to the seat of the medieval Sultanate of Funj at Sennar and the inhabitants, the descendants of this Sultanate, are all Muslims. Administratively the region is part of the north, but its people look to the south for ethnic or racial affiliations. Despite being endowed with natural riches the area is depressingly underdeveloped, denied services such as education and health care and under-represented in central government. The region is lush agricultural land with a climate that accommodates the growing of a variety of crops. Since the advent of mechanized agriculture in the 1990s, more Arab-owned businesses have moved in and been granted large tracts of land by the government. Local inhabitants were wary that the government had deliberately underdeveloped the region and embarked on a policy of giving their land away to outsiders, which created a serious dilemma for the peasant communities regarding their traditional land tenure system. As in most of rural Sudan, the land in southern Blue Nile is communally owned which means that people have no individual title deeds to their property. Individual families therefore can only own land through consecutive use and that piece of land can be taken by another family if the previous one ceases to use it. This in turn means that the government assumes the legal ownership of all land. Without documented ownership the people cannot put up their land as collateral to receive loans in order to develop and mechanize their agricultural productivity. This enables Arab farmers who are backed by the government and Islamic banks to claim ownership of the land because of their ability to farm more areas using a mechanized system: a loophole which has caused much resentment toward the Arabs and the government that favors them.

When the second round of the North–South war broke out in 1983, the SPLA's vision of the 'New Sudan' became attractive to the people in this region because it explained the reasons for their marginalization. Large numbers of young people, including university students like Malik Agar, joined the SPLA in the mid-1980s and were able to boost the movement's military gains in the region. The SPLA was able to capture Kurumuk, one of the biggest towns in the region, and threatened Damazin and Roseirus Dam. These military gains demonstrated both the degree to which the SPLA's message of resistance and opposition to marginalization appealed to the inhabitants of southern Blue Nile, and the ability of non-Arab populations to effectively oppose the Arab-dominated government. This is another example of race as politics: while it cannot be verified by looking at people's physical appearances, marginalization is *read* as an act of racial discrimination. This realization caused alarm in Khartoum, and a drive for Jihad recruitment which was described as a campaign to defend the holy lands against what were called the enemies of Islam and 'black racism.' Revolt of Muslims against the state was perceived as more egregious than the revolt of the non-Muslim south: Muslims are expected to be the defenders of an Islamic state, and war against apostates is holy. This discourse of accusations of reversed racism and a military solution to the crises by means of holy war has driven the people of southern Blue Nile toward demands for self-government, with the possibility of either joining the south in case of southern secession, or forming an independent union with any number of the other regions who are in revolt, probably the central region of the Nuba Mountains.[111]

THE NUBA MOUNTAINS: NUBA IDENTITY AND THE SUDANESE NATION

'The Nuba' is a term used to refer to the inhabitants of the Nuba mountains of southern Kordofan in central Sudan – they are not to be confused with Nubians of the far north. The Nuba number about 1.5 million people, making them the largest conglomeration of tribes in southern Kordofan state, and share the province with Missiriyya Zurug Arabs who gradually moved into the mountains around the beginning of nineteenth century. Like the Funj of the Blue Nile, the Nuba are African people of mixed religious beliefs. Many of them are Muslims, some Christians, and others followers of indigenous forms of worship. The Nuba are a peaceful, hard-working agricultural and herding people whose civilizations have adapted well to the ecological zones they have inhabited and kept them independent and self-reliant for thousands of years. Historians suggest that some Nuba, particularly the herding groups among them, used to inhabit the plains of northern Kordofan until large groups of Arab pastoral tribes began to move into these plains and the Nuba were increasingly confined to the region now known as the Nuba mountains (MacMichael, 1967).[112] They had actually gradually moved and settled in the mountains partly as a result of a search for a balance of resources and as protection from the encroaching slave-taking armies and other forms of aggression presented by the increasing number of the Arabs taking over the plains. Slave raids of the Turkiyya era also contributed to this push as the Nuba moved further away to the comparative safety of the hills.[113]

However, the notion of one Nuba people remains vague. The Nuba themselves have no clear idea of what made these multitudes of subgroups who speak different languages recognize a sense of historical Nuba oneness.[114] There was no reason to forge a collective Nuba identity before they were made aware of the rising threat posed by the Arabs, especially the government-backed Missiriyya herders, to their cultural heritage and their resources. The need to emphasize 'Nubaness' was a result of the collapse of the precarious balance they had once maintained with the Arabs when the Arab and non-Arab divide became real to the Nuba. Until this point the Nuba, who speak more than fifty languages, tended to identify themselves by their specific tribal groups – Tegali, Miri, Lafofa, etc. – rather than as Nuba.[115] The use of the term Nuba is a politicized identity formation (Bauman, 1987) which emerged due to their need for a unified front against the force of the invaders. The calamities and political pressures they have had to face have imposed a sense of a shared destiny upon them, which has been conducive to a growing feeling of a common Nuba identity. A more concerted political awareness about these threats and the necessity to defend their rights within the state arose in the 1980s when Yousif Kwa Makki, Abdel Aziz A. al-Helu and many more educated Nuba led their people to the SPLA in large numbers. They were not necessarily born out of a desire to join the south (none of the Nuba leaders has ever spoken of forming a polity with the south) but simply because the SPLA's idea of reconfiguring Sudanese political structures was something all the marginalized regions found appealing. The marginalized and the liberal-minded within the north had begun to consider the SPLA concept of 'New Sudan' as a plausible alternative to the kind of Sudan the Arab elite had been trying to forge. It is safe to say that it was the weight of the historical experiences of the slave raids during the Turkiyya, the increasing Arab encroachment on Nuba land since independence, the post-independence exclusion from the development process, and state violence, that have led the people of the mountains to become more Nuba than they had originally thought of themselves. There have also been numerous cases worldwide where people were given a name that was created by outsiders and have come to accept themselves with the passage of time. The best-known instance is that of the native populations of the Americas whom Europeans insisted on calling Indians until the term stuck. In the politically correct modern US, the 'Indians' are the only ones who now prefer this term: everyone else seems to believe that the correct term is 'Native Americans.' Nuer and Dinka are further examples of such names, as are many other nationalities throughout the African continent whose present names were invented and imposed upon them, mainly by European colonizers or Arab slavers. In other words, the Nuba identity, which is now the basis for collective resistance to the state, is subjectively defined in relation to the Arabs and objectively determined by common destiny, spatial proximity, and a belief in cultural similarities. Again, Nubaness has almost become a race in itself when the people juxtapose themselves against the Arab race. It is this objective determination that has prompted them to create a collective front of resistance against cultural ethnocide and physical annihilation, and to stem the policies that have increasingly marginalized them (African Rights, 1991, 1992).

The Khartoum government's reaction to the news of Nuba people joining the southern rebellion was severe military reprisals.[116] Indiscriminate bombing of civilians was carried out, and in February 2000 at the town of Kaouda a class being held under a tree was bombed, killing eighteen students and their teacher and wounding scores of other children. An amateur video recording captured the atrocity, which was aired on the BBC to the horror of viewers worldwide. When confronted by a journalist about the military significance of such an attack, a Sudan embassy public relations official in Nairobi said that the bomb 'has landed where it was supposed to.'[117]

Over the course of the war, the government also used food as a weapon of war and the Nuba mountains were cordoned off to international humanitarian aid agencies, bringing the entire population to the brink of starvation year after year, especially throughout the 1990s. Several years of severe drought had made the region less self-reliant, but the government sent mixed signals in response to the drought: some officials denied that a crisis existed while others appealed for outside help to deal with it. There was credible evidence that even when the world community responded by providing funds to deal with the crises in the Nuba mountains, these resources were either diverted to other areas or given only to the internally displaced Nuba as a way to lure them away from the region and herd them into relief camps. Reports prepared and distributed by rebel authorities to the international community have suggested that this internal displacement of the Nuba was a deliberate policy to force the Nuba out of their homes and set up camps that were constantly watched by security agents: Khartoum was quick to dismiss these claims as war propaganda. More transparent was the policy of relocating the Nuba into what were called 'peace camps.' This policy served two purposes. First, it gave the government the opportunity to redistribute the land and Nuba property was given to Missiriyya Arab farmers, both because they were Arabs and as payment for supporting the Islamist regime. Second, it placed the Nuba under constant watch and denied the opposition army its support base among the Nuba by removing these potential supporters, a tactic that was commonly practiced in the war against the south for decades.

War and society in the Nuba mountains

From the mid-1980s to 2002, as described in Chapter two, the government of Sudan conducted a war against the Nuba people of central Sudan. The weapons of war were twofold. One was direct attacks on civilians and their sources of livelihood – land, livestock, water and property. The other was enforced political conditionality on access to essential goods and services including international humanitarian aid. Before the war, the Nuba mountains held a rich and diverse mixture of cultures. The people were surplus food producers and exporters of grain and cattle; through the major towns and market centers they secured what they did not make – basic goods like clothing, salt, and soap. During the war, they were forced to live and cultivate on only the most marginal lands in and along the mountains, as they continued to be attacked by government forces. As a result their crop production was dramatically reduced, most of their cattle were lost and they were barely able to cover their own food needs. Under these conditions, they were forced to defend not only their basic means of survival but also their way of life.

Since the beginning of the war, the government has killed and abducted several thousand civilians. They have razed villages to the ground, looted and destroyed properties, displaced the majority of people from their homes and seized their most productive farmland. The people captured in these attacks were put into so-called 'peace' villages and other government-held areas. In some cases they were able to access food and some other essential goods and services, but at a heavy price. In exchange for these services, when the government allowed them access they were forced to accept the political, cultural and religious identity imposed by the Islamist government. However, despite the attempt to annihilate them, by the time the Nuba Mountains Humanitarian Agreement was reached by the US President's special envoy for Sudan, Senator John Danforth, as one of the four confidence-building measures agreed with Khartoum, there were approximately 400,000 people still remaining in SPLA-controlled territories. They had been cut off from the rest of Sudan and the world at large and this region became Sudan's most difficult area to access. Government destruction of cross-border markets, the sanctions on trade to the SPLA Nuba and the exploitative prices of any goods that crossed from the north all prevented the majority of people from having even basic personal and household items. At the same time, little or no meaningful support could come from outside, as the Khartoum government blocked the international community from providing any humanitarian assistance to people living in SPLA-controlled areas of the mountains.

The silence of the world community only emboldened the government. Throughout 2000, Khartoum significantly increased its military targeting of civilians, their farms and villages. Beginning in March of that year, it launched an offensive against the people of Buram and Western Kadugli County. In May 2001 the government of Sudan attacked southern Heiban County, killing a large number of people (the exact count has not been verified) and abducting many, taking some to peace villages and others to garrison towns where many of the women became sex slaves for the army. Houses, farms, food stores, livestock, and other properties were systematically destroyed and looted and over 51,500 people were displaced, many of them several times.

Many people were rendered so desperate that the only way they could avoid the government attacks was to consider a pre-emptive move to the government side and thus attempt to access the food, medicine and education found there. However, due to aggressive Islamization and Arabization programs in the peace villages, they chose to remain in their homes and defend their way of life, despite the risks involved. Many reports from this region at that time indicated that majority of the people did not want to move to the government side, as they saw the overwhelming evidence that their fundamental rights of self-expression, justice and liberty would be denied. Their continued struggle to survive in a war zone was not because they believed in a long-term military solution, but because they saw no alternative if they wished to preserve their cultural identity and their right to raise their children in an environment shaped by democracy and equitable peace.

Between 1998 and 2001, escalating government attacks on civilian targets and drought-induced crop failures across the region placed the civilian population in a life-threatening situation in the SPLA-controlled areas of the Nuba mountains. Some of these civilians were killed or abducted whenever they ventured outside the peace camps that the government had set up as a way to contain them. During the raids, displaced survivors of these attacks would lose everything while the host populations were themselves facing severe food shortage as a result of war and drought. For six months in 2001 there were extensive assessments of the area by humanitarian agencies which confirmed the severity of the crisis. Because humanitarian access was often denied, immediate intervention was not possible and that resulted in widespread loss of life, especially in June and July 2001.

This tragic consequence could have been averted in the short-term if access had been granted to aid agencies. According to a report compiled by the Nuba administration and humanitarian partners, at one stage the government denied delivery of an available 2,500 metric tons of food aid plus additional medical and non-food items. People were still able to survive despite the poor response as the communities resorted to the barest minimum ration. The Nuba relied on the extraordinary resilience that has facilitated their survival over the years, but it was not sufficient to reverse the chronically deteriorating situation caused by the war and additional support for even the most basic livelihood recovery was needed throughout 2002.

The situation was further compounded by years of extremely poor rains. Across the region the harvests had been low every year since these crises began to escalate in 1998. For example, post-harvest assessments carried out by Nuba Relief in 2000 concluded that approximately 33,000 people had harvested no crops to take them into the following year, and the people reported that this had been characteristic of the two previous years. Their opportunities for finding surplus food locally were negligible as local reserves were also exhausted. Accessible areas from which wild foods were traditionally gathered had become increasingly limited as government military activities continue to restrict civilian movement. The droughts had also reduced the amounts of wild foods available. In total, over 84,500 people in the counties mentioned earlier were brought to the brink of death because of a host of consequences of the war and poor rains in 2000. With no food in their stores they were struggling to survive, and as they entered the hunger gap, i.e. June and July, they were finding less and less to help them. Acute malnutrition was unavoidable and rampant throughout this period, especially for the young, old and weak. Those who lost their homes faced additional challenges. At the onset of every rainy season, they must make their shelter as best they can – with no blankets, plastic sheets or protection from malaria. They must also find cooking materials and water containers and they desperately needed access to even the most basic of health facilities as their condition worsened.

At the height of the humanitarian crises between 1998 and 2001, the risks involved in gaining the limited access that concerned agencies had managed in previous years became too great to allow flights into SPLA areas to continue. The government of Sudan had bombed and shelled relief planes on several occasions and attacked the main airstrip from the ground. Despite dialogue between the UN and the government, the ongoing round of discussions was making no progress in establishing negotiated access. It became clear that the government was deliberately trying to delay humanitarian access to those Nuba civilians who chose to live in SPLA areas, and that such delays enabled the government to continue its use of hunger as a weapon of war.

This reluctance to secure safe access only resulted in immediate loss of life and strengthened Khartoum's undeniable aim to destroy the opportunity for Nuba people to exercise their rights to attain an equitable, just and democratic peace. Given the experience of humanitarian agencies over the years since the establishment of Operation Lifeline Sudan (OLS) in 1990 and the urgency of the situation in 2001, an appeal to the government in Khartoum was no longer a realistic option. The people of the Nuba mountains, the civil society groups in the south and a number of relief agencies called on the international community, specific world governments and the UN, invoking an agreement which the UN, the government, and the SPLA had signed on the rights of war-affected civilians in Sudan, to take immediate action to secure unrestricted and safe air access to the SPLA-controlled Nuba mountains for at least five months (June–October 2001). They also called for the enforcement of this agreement to ensure safe civilian access to relief distributions. The SPLA-controlled Nuba mountains remained excluded from the initial tripartite agreement which was the foundation of OLS. The Khartoum government blocked the UN from working in SPLA areas, effectively preventing their efforts to provide emergency humanitarian aid. Despite the commitment the government gave to the UN to establish a negotiated access, the UN has failed to provide a solution and the issue has effectively remained buried in a series of discussions that show no sign of bearing fruit. Even when agreements were reached, they were usually without clear mandates and mechanisms to enforce them.

This sort of agreement was difficult if not impossible to enforce, as the tripartite agreement between the Government of Sudan, the SPLA and the humanitarian agencies (the UN and NGOs) that brought the OLS into existence had been reached at the field level and not at the diplomatic level, involving the Secretary General of the UN, for example. The agreement was therefore not capable of ensuring continuous uninterrupted humanitarian access to areas such as Nuba. It had no mandate to stop any aggression against civilians so that even at times of relief food distribution, whenever it was allowed, the government was still able to bomb, shell, and destroy property. In the case of the Nuba mountains specifically, the government would take advantage of peoples' exodus to relief centers and seize the Nuba farmland. This was all the more disturbing because the international community had little commitment to pursuing every possible option to enforce the agreements the parties to the war had signed. The international system and the influential countries behind it had a role in allowing the tragic consequences of the crisis in Nuba to unfold. Pleas made by a few organizations on behalf of the people of the Nuba mountains, urging the world community to take action urgently to save innocent lives, were not heeded quickly enough, and sometimes policymakers in Western capitals had no clear solutions even when they knew they needed to do something.

Despite the unwillingness of the international community to secure negotiated access to the SPLA-controlled areas of the Nuba mountains, some humanitarian aid was delivered, albeit at considerable risk to those involved (both Nuba and expatriates). Although the response has never been enough, it has made a difference in the lives of the Nuba people, but because of the escalating aggression of the government, it was sometimes impossible to continue aid efforts. In May 2000, for example, the government attacked the main airstrip near Kauda and made explicit threats to shoot down planes flying into SPLA-controlled areas without clearance from Khartoum. On several occasions, they bombed and shelled relief planes while on the ground. Flying into Nuba was so dangerous as to be untenable, making it impossible to address even the most life-threatening needs.

It was not until the United Nations Commissioner for Human Rights (UNHCR) had appointed a Special Rapporteur for Sudan that world leaders and the higher echelons of the UN began to press the government of Sudan to allow the provision of aid to the Nuba mountains. Humanitarian aid distribution, when it was possible, also became the trap the government needed to congregate the population only to attack them while captive and awaiting aid provision. The Special Rapporteur, after a mission to the region, learned that on many occasions civilians were deliberately targeted as they gathered to receive food aid. So while access to humanitarian aid was often severely hampered by a combination of government war tactics in the Nuba mountains, poor roads and railways, making it hard to get food from surplus to deficit areas across Africa's biggest country, it was the government's deliberate denial of food to the region that most effected an unprecedented suffering in the Nuba mountains. It is safe to say that as genuine as the initial grievances that had propelled Nuba people into joining the rebellion were, it was the way the government had reacted – by indiscriminate attack on civilians, blocking of humanitarian aid, distribution of Nuba land to the Arabs, and the mistreatment of IDPs – that sent even more of them into opposition and increased the demands for self-government, if not total independence. In sum, the more prolonged and frustrating these violent conflicts became the more likely that the initial feelings of discrimination and demands for services were transformed by the passage of time into nationalist demands to break away from the polity.

CONCLUSION

This chapter has sought to establish the connections between the different racial/ethnic and region-based reactions to the central government's policies towards them and to the state as a monopoly of a few elites. The south, the Nubian north, the northeast, southern Blue Nile, and the Nuba mountains have all expressed concern at racially based marginalization over the years, but successive Khartoum governments have resorted to military force and political suppression as the best instruments to engage with the peripheries. The reactions from the regions have been either a passive resistance by creating a distance from the state, as was the case with Nuba, or protracted conflicts such as those that arose in other regions. The result has been the demise of state legitimacy and authority in the eyes of these populations that are remote from the centers of power. The wider the gap between the remote regions and the state apparatus, the less loyalty the peripheral regions give to the state: citizens of the peripheries become more committed to ethnic or regional citizenship than to pride in the nation. The longer this situation continues and the more militarized the relationship between Khartoum and the regions, the more likely it is that the regions will seek autonomy. The south has already reached this stage, where secession has now become a question of when rather than if it will actually materialize. A similar process is currently happening in Darfur as the next chapter will show. Given the fact that the crisis in Darfur is still ongoing at the time of writing, and the scale of genocide that it has reached, it is important to devote a separate chapter to it.

3

ARABISM, ISLAMISM AND THE RESOURCE WARS IN DARFUR

The previous chapter showed how the clashes between the Arab-run state and the peripheries are rooted in marginalization in the economic development process and exclusion from power structures. They are also related to the rise of militant Islam as a tool for political machination. These clashes also reveal the racist set-up of the state and the militarized responses to the local people's demands for their right share of power, wealth and religious space. I hope I we have also shown that if the southern experience is anything to go by, the longer these clashes drag on, the more it becomes apparent that Sudan will not be able to maintain its unified existence. This chapter examines the root causes of the brutal conflict currently taking place between the western region of Darfur and the Islamist government in Khartoum. By studying the war in Darfur, we may be able to show the connections between the different regions of Sudan in relation to causes of conflict and the ways in which people living in war zones come to grips with the upheavals of war.

In 2004, Darfur was described by the UN and by prominent diplomats from North America, Western Europe and some African states as the world's worst humanitarian crisis. The government's war tactics to suppress the opposition have made about 2.5 million people – more than a third of Darfur's total population – almost entirely reliant on aid to survive. Approximately two million were displaced from their homes, of whom 200,000 have sought refuge in the neighboring country of Chad.[118] This is a mind-boggling statistic not only because of the staggering numbers of people involved but because the conflict between Darfur and the Khartoum government and its attendant disasters are happening within the political entity called 'the north' in the Sudanese traditional political discourse.[119] The Darfur conflict surprised many observers given that the confrontations most characteristic of the tragedy that is Sudan have always been the North–South disputes. The religious sentiments that have always characterized the North–South conflicts are absent in this case, as the parties are all Sunni Muslims. The previous alliances have shifted as Darfur was always the strongest ally of the Khartoum government in the 'northern' war against the 'south.' Few had expected that Khartoum would unleash force against Darfur at this crucial juncture in the country's history, when the government is facing multiple war fronts. When the crisis erupted in early 2003, both outside observers and the people of Darfur themselves were confused as to why the region that has always functioned as the support base of some of the most influential political parties and elite politicians should become the target of horrendous state-sponsored violence and destruction. Researchers and humanitarian aid workers who have watched Darfur closely over the last two decades were not surprised at all, however, as they had witnessed a gradual unraveling of the factors that had kept this region harmonious *vis-à-vis* the state since the annexation of the Darfur Sultanate. The roots of these puzzling developments could be traced to several points in the racial/ethnic, environmental and commercial history of the region. The conflict that started in full throttle in February 2003 and continues at the time of writing can only be understood through the prism of this history. Once we have outlined this historical background, however, there is still no agreement among all concerned as to why such developments, spanning nearly three decades, should culminate in such a brutal confrontation at this particular juncture.

Many historians have demonstrated that the coming of independence in Sudan, as in many other sub-Saharan colonial territories, was a product of negotiations between an educated elite and the colonial authorities (Johnson, 2003; Collins, 1983). Such negotiations, and the agreement regarding the post-colonial set up, involved few if any representatives of the various communities that would come to form the post-colonial state. The populations of the peripheries, especially Darfur and the regions discussed in the previous chapter, had only nominal representation in the constitutional processes that brought about independence and the eventual transfer of power to the Sudanese people. This meant that all the agreements that decided their status were reached without consideration of what the inhabitants of remote regions might think about the structure of the new polity. This may have been easier and more acceptable in smaller and less ethnically diverse African communities, as the local people would see in the new government representatives that they would recognize and easily relate to, but in a large and diverse country such as Sudan it was difficult to accomplish. The result was that some regions, uncertain of what independence meant for their own status and survival, were understandably suspicious of the new rulers. This was more the case in the south, the Nuba mountains, parts of Darfur, the southern Blue Nile, and the east, as we saw earlier.

It was really in the last two decades that the skepticism of the peripheries about the Sudanese state's ability to be fair has become generalized to all these regions, as what used to look like a North–South religious and racial confrontation incrementally became a center versus periphery issue, based on new racial ideas and a new interpretation of the role of religion in the politics of state building. Since the founding of the Sudanese state when various ethnic regions had somewhat accepted exclusion, every region has now expressed, in one manner or another, its unease with the exclusionary policies of the Arab-controlled state. It was during this period from 1980 to the present that alliances have shifted in ways that would have been impossible immediately after independence and throughout the first round of the civil war. In this earlier stage, many of the peripheral regions like Darfur and the northeast were mobilized by the state to fight the south on the basis that the conflict was purely North–South, with Islam operating as the unifying factor between all the northern groups who would otherwise be as disparate as north and south. Since the early 1980s, the question of a minority Arab clique that claims ownership of the whole state and exploits the non-Arab majority by pitting them against one another has become a widespread discourse in these regions. This shift may be related to the arrival of the SPLA on the political scene in 1983, but local dynamics specific to each region are also responsible. Other reasons abound in the period since the second round of civil war began. They include the dismissal by Khartoum of all the protests and grievances of Darfur as criminal acts, and their leaders as greedy politicians driven by political frustration into armed thievery, and the assertion that Darfur's frustrations were not genuine economic and political grievances. Darfurians also began to hate the attitude of the main political parties who often took their support for granted on the basis that they were co-religionists. In fact, political parties such as the Mahdi's family party, the Umma and al-Turabi's NIF historically have both counted on the strong support of the West: the Rezeigat branch of the Baggara Arab in Darfur and the Missiriya branch in Kordofan are the historical allies of the Umma Party, and the non-Arab populations of Darfur such as the Masalit, the Zaghawa, the Tunjur and others are the supporters of the NIF. During his two terms as Prime Minister Sadiq al-Mahdi has used the Baggara as a tool to increase support for his party and to fight the south, while the NIF's al-Turabi has often used the other groups both to engage the Arabs and to forge an Islamic network in the region as part of his grand design for an Africa-wide Islamic program. After many years of this political exploitation, these groups were no longer prepared to accept being used in this manner. In exchange for their support, they wanted concrete benefits such as social services and life-saving responses to the recurrent droughts and their deadly consequences. Parties who wanted their support would have to deliver the services to Darfur and Kordofan.

Some governments – for example Sadiq al-Mahdi's elected government of 1986 and the current NIF regime – have attempted to resolve the crises in Darfur, especially the droughts – land scarcity nexus, by using this Arab-African divide. Al-Mahdi's proposed solution was to displace some non-Arab populations in Kordofan, especially in the Nuba mountains, and distribute their territories to the Baggara. Between 1987 and 1989, al-Mahdi's government adopted similar policies and caused race-driven clashes over grazing and water rights between nomad Arabs and the Fur farmers.

> The conflict began at a very limited level among some camel herding Arab tribes in northern Darfur and some sectors of the Fur in the northern part of Jebel Mara but it quickly degenerated as a result of the meddling of the political elements in Darfur's towns and 'Darfur intellectuals' in Khartoum. Propaganda, particularly in the Khartoum media, intensified and stoked the fighting until it drew all the sectors of the Fur on one side and all the Arab tribes on the other.[120]

As shown below, the current NIF regime has attempted similar policies within Darfur, which is the cause of the ongoing crises in that region.

The war in Darfur, which was declared genocide in 2004 by the US and a number of human rights agencies, covers much of Sudan's westernmost region. Although presenting it as a war between Arabs and Africans in the way the news media have done is somewhat simplistic and does not do justice to what is a complex politics of difference, it is undeniable that race matters a great deal in Sudan's conflicts. The subtle tensions among the various ethnic groups have been exploited by corrupt powers that have little interest in the people. Yet despite the tensions, Arabs and Africans have long coexisted and intermarried, creating the racial composite we see in Darfur today. The blurring of physical identity between Arabs and Africans has challenged outsiders who usually determine race through a limited definition in terms of skin color. With over 500 ethnic groups in what is a mixture of ancient civilizations, Sudan is too genetically rich to narrow people down into a basic Western racial paradigm. In Sudan, 'Arab' refers less to the appearance to which we usually affix stereotypical Arab physical identity, and more to a state of mind, as well as politicization of race. There are many Arabized populations within Sudan who may or may not look Arab as we understand that race in the Arab Middle East but are completely Arab in their behavior, cultural and religious loyalties. Although observable racial traits play a role in Darfur, if the non-Arab population submitted to complete Arabization they would have a better chance of being accepted as Arab within Darfur than any Sudanese would have in, say, Egypt.

Darfur's conflict is not religion-based in the same way as the North–South conflict: in Darfur the executed and the executioners are all Muslims. Part of the problem is that the victims are not *Arabized* Muslims, because many indigenous inhabitants of Darfur maintain their core cultural ties with their respective ethnic groups. Despite years of Darfurian support of northern policy against the south, many non-Arabs realized that Islam's racial tolerance was not always observed by the Arabs. As a result, feelings of betrayal have been expressed by many Afro-Darfurians.

Darfur has three ethnic zones. The northern includes Arab and non-Arab, mainly Zaghawa, camel nomads. The central zone is inhabited largely by non-Arab sedentary farmers such as the Fur, Masalit and others, cultivating millet. In the south there are Arabic-speaking cattle nomads, the Rezeigat branch of Baggara. All are Muslim, and despite perceptions among the groups in the region that each held title to specific territories, no part of Darfur was ever ethnically homogeneous.[121] For example, there have been cases where a successful Fur farmer had acquired a certain number of cattle, he would be absorbed into Baggara, and in a few generations, his descendants would self-identify as Arab, even tracing their genealogy to the prophet Muhammad, something many Arabized Sudanese do in order to authenticate their Arab-ness and Islamic purity.

PEOPLE, HISTORY AND THE LAND IN DARFUR

Dar Fur, Arabic for 'Land of the Fur,' is made up of some ethnic groups whose native tongue is Arabic and self-identify as Arabs, and others who are non-Arab, who belong to an array of ethnicities and call themselves by their specific group names: Fur, Zaghawa, Masalit, Tunjur etc. The Arabs generally tend to be nomadic herders of camels and goats, while the Africans are settled farmers. Due to the mixing of people explained above and despite this talk of Arabs and Africans, it is rarely possible to tell on the basis of skin color which group an individual Darfurian belongs to. All have lived there for centuries, intermarried and all are Muslims. Of course identity is more about self-identification than simply being labeled by others, and I will demonstrate in the chapters that follow why the Arab-Africa divide reflects actual historical and sociological realities of Sudan in some instances but why it may be misleading in others.

Historically, Darfur was a Sultanate founded around 1650 by Suleiman Solong. Like many of Darfur's key political leaders of the time, Solong was of a mixed ancestry, the son of an Arab father and a Fur mother. Darfur was established and dominated by the Fur people, ruled by a title-holding elite recruited from all the major ethnic groups of the region. Under the sultan, the settled peoples, basically non-Arab, were able to control or keep out the nomads: the Sultanate's ultimate sanction was heavy cavalry. The Sultanate was destroyed in 1874. Although today's conflict is much bloodier, such wars are not new and are at times reminiscent of the nineteenth century. The Sultanate was restored in 1898 by Ali Dinar, a descendant of Solong, and true to the nature of ethnic rivalries that Darfur has been witnessing in contemporary times, Sultan Ali Dinar spent most of his reign trying to keep the nomads out of his territory. It was not until 1916 that the British annexed the region and Ali Dinar was killed.[122] In order to rule this vast desert region the British had to continue this policy of governing through the old ruling elite, and many of today's educated Darfurians such as Ahmed Dreig, the former governor of Darfur during Nimeiri's reign, are descended from that elite.

Like the rest of Sudan and characteristically of British indirect rule, Darfur was governed by a handful of British officials along with a core of these elite Darfurians, who, by coercion or enticement, had become partners with the empire. This set-up was maintained more or less peacefully from 1916 until independence in 1956. During the entire colonial period the people of Darfur lived on the margins of the state, and their only involvement with the government was either through seasonal migrant labor – especially the young men who would travel to find work in the cotton schemes in the Jazirah region between the Blue and White Niles – or limited access to social services such as health care.[123] There are indications that colonial rule was regarded as neutral in dealing with the different ethnicities, but when independence came, there was anxiety that the new government, which was Arab-controlled, might be biased against non-Arabs. The result was that some Darfurians, both Arab and non-Arab, began to enter the national political arena and assert their own identity. As the effort by each group to assert itself gradually became so bitter, the national government took sides: the current crises are a result of the government's desire to maintain the racial divide as a governing asset. In other words, to pit them against one another in the event that they are both hostile to the government, or arm one against the other if either confronts the government with violence.

The established farmers of Darfur were mainly from African tribes, while the encroaching nomads were primarily Arabs. Given that Arabs were steadily coming to dominate all branches of the Sudanese government, there could be little doubt as to how any Arab-African squabble would ultimately be decided. The result was surely the opposite of what Khartoum intended: the tribes of Darfur, Arab and African alike, increasingly took matters into their own hands, availing themselves of their young warriors to defend their own communities and to conduct reprisal raids on their foes. What is more, with civil unrest becoming common across the Sahel, the entire region was now awash in modern weaponry, allowing the raiders to trade up from their old rifles, swords and spears to Kalashnikovs. The consequences were predictable: in one clash between Arab tribes and the Fur in January 1983, at least 3,000 were killed. Initially, the Darfur tribes tried to cope with these tensions as they always had, through inter-communal negotiation. If violence like this broke out, the chiefs would attempt to reconcile their people by returning stolen cattle and paying blood compensation. If a nomad's camels trampled a farmer's field or, conversely, some of his herd was stolen, the elders of both tribes would convene and thrash out a settlement: typically, a payment of cash or animals to the victim. By the mid-1980s, however, this age-old system was being dismantled by the national government in Khartoum, which sought to exert greater control over Sudan's remote and near-autonomous tribes. Instead of the age-old tribal mediation familiar to them, almost any dispute now meant going before an official and maneuvering through the state bureaucracy.

As is often the case with disasters in Africa, that which is occurring in Darfur seemed to burst into the global consciousness without warning. Until early 2003, probably few people around the world had ever heard of the remote region in western Sudan. Then, virtually overnight, it became a topic of urgent human rights campaigns, was discussed in the US Congress and the UN and became a frequent news item for the world's television stations and newspapers. It was even mentioned in the American presidential election debate between President George W. Bush and the Democratic candidate, Senator John Kerry. Within Sudan as it is in the whole region, the alarm had been sounded long before. By the summer of 2003, Darfur refugees slipping across the border into neighboring Chad were telling of a scorched-earth Sudanese army counterinsurgency campaign. In its war against rebel groups, the army had teamed up with Arab tribesmen: rather than looking for rebels these militias simply laid waste: shooting down whoever crossed their path, torching homes, and looting. These raiders were given a popular name derived from an old western Sudanese epithet for bandits: Janjaweed, or 'devils on horseback.'

The ongoing conflict, although pitching the region against the state, is carried out along this Afro-Arab demarcation. The political leaders of non-Arab groups have in recent times adopted the Arab-African divide as a way to bring the world's attention to their marginalization because this characterization was perceived to have worked in highlighting and internationalizing the southern grievances. The crisis in Darfur is now understood as Arabs against Africans, but it may be more related to recent developments than to a long-standing racial or ethnic hatred: it has more to do with the manner in which post-colonial states relate to the people and how the people see themselves fitting into the haphazard polity that was the state. For a better understanding of the competition between local groups, it is important to trace the recent crisis to its origins in the colonial era. When the British conquered Darfur in 1916, defeating the army of Sultan Ali Dinar, like many colonial administrations throughout Africa, the British rule in Sudan was based on 'native administration,' which meant the appointment of chiefs or kings to govern over and collect taxes from their own ethnic groups. To govern Darfur, an area the size of France, the territories were demarcated and awarded to each of the thirty plus groups living in Darfur, who have since taken this boundary demarcation so seriously that every group would be ready to go to war to protect that territory from any encroachment other than established peaceful cooperation. Darfur is dissected according to these ethnic groups, which means, at least superficially, that some areas are inhabited exclusively by one or other of the region's ethnic groups. This has been true since the colonial era but this notion of exclusive ownership of a territory by a bounded ethnic group can be slightly misleading. Due to the long history of internal migration, mixing and intermarriage discussed earlier, ethnic boundaries exist more in name than in reality. People have acquired different ethnic identities over the years. The post-colonial Sudanese state has found it equally convenient to maintain the system whereby the chief not only runs the day to day affairs of the ethnic group but also gives land titles to the people. The government gave the chiefs the authority to do this but did not really regard it as a system of land ownership in the real sense of the word. Darfurians however believed in this arrangement and were happy with it as long as enough land remained (farmers of any ethnicity could settle and farm any area that is nominally owned by another). This was to change with the droughts of the 1980s when the nomadic herders lost much of their grazing land, causing them to encroach further and further into farming areas while good farming land became disastrously scarce. In the past the norm had been one of cooperation: nomadic groups relied on an understanding that gave them customary rights to migrate and pasture their animals in areas dominated by farmers and this had worked for decades. But the 1980s drought, desertification and the expansion of farms were threatening these rights. The result was that a number of local conflicts erupted in Darfur in the wake of the drought and famine of 1984–1985.[124] On the whole, the pastoral groups were lined up against the farmers in what had become a bitter struggle for diminishing resources, along a dividing line that increasingly adopted racial language. The government could not intervene effectively, so herders armed themselves to protect their herds and force their way into pastures. The farmers armed themselves in response. The Chadian wars of the 1980s, in which Libya was heavily involved, made it easy for the people of Darfur to acquire arms.[125] As this study will demonstrate, this succession of local conflicts became the springboard for larger conflicts that have now led to a serious humanitarian tragedy and threaten the territorial integrity of Sudan.

Darfur has been gripped by drought for close to thirty years, and this has brought disturbing changes in the lives of both herding nomadic tribes who tend to self-identify as Arabs and the settled agricultural communities whose members belong to non-Arab groups such as Masalit, Fur, and Zaghawa (Tobin, 1985). Recurrent droughts mean the Saharan winds have been blowing sand onto fertile hillsides, and when it rains the water cuts gullies through the rich alluvial soil along the valleys. This makes the land available for herders and farmers very scarce, and meant that villagers who had always played host to cattle nomads were now barring their migrations, and stopping them from using pastures and wells. Many of the nomads, whose livelihood and social relations are built around ownership of large herds of camel, have been losing their camels and goats and are becoming desperately poor; a reality which has forced more and more of them into settling down and attempting to farm. The farming villagers from the Fur, the largest ethnic group in the region, had given them only dry, sandy soil, keeping the more fertile areas next to the valleys for themselves. Having realized the importance of legal land titles, the farming groups of Darfur, especially the Tunjur of north Darfur and the Masalit of west Darfur, were careful to register the most valuable farmland. This has caused resentment among the former nomads, now farmers, as they scratch at the arid uplands in an attempt to grow a few heads of millet. But not all nomads are resigned to an attempt at farming. Most still cling to their way of life, and it is these who are trying to take their herds for grazing wherever they can find pasture, including the farm areas of the settled villagers. This is the crux of the competition: a fight over scarce resources, coinciding with an extremely turbulent political juncture in the whole nation, which gives the government a tool for suppressing any dissent by setting these groups against one another as a way to reduce national security threats posed by either faction.

Both the farmers and the herders began to use racial slurs which were meant to degrade their opponents and to claim entitlements on the basis that the opposite group is inferior and undeserving. The Sudanese government in Khartoum has often taken sides in this competition and supported the herders, a situation that increasingly proved disastrous to the region as a whole, as violence displaced people, spread insecurity, and diminished service provision.* Throughout the 1980s and 1990s, the whole of Darfur has been increasingly marginalized and Darfurians began to debate their conditions, the causes of turmoil, and possible solutions. Racial hierarchies were often cited by an increasing number of political leaders as part of the process that seems to relegate them to second-class citizenship. It is these social and political circumstances that transformed this debate into activism and political opposition against Khartoum. The war broke out in early 2003 when two opposition groups demanding greater political representation of Darfur in Khartoum, the Sudan Liberation Army (SLA) and the Justice Equality Movement (JEM) saw an opportunity in

---

* Herding nomads also seek out the government to request state assistance in exchange for political support.

developments over the previous few years regarding North–South relations. The war in Darfur sets Sudanese government armed forces and militias allied to it against opposition armies fighting to end what they have called marginalization and discrimination of the region's inhabitants by the state and the ruling Arab elites. Darfur insurgents claimed that they were marginalized not only in terms of power and wealth, but increasingly from the North–South peace negotiations that were underway in Kenya under the auspices of the Inter-Governmental Agency for Development (IGAD), the results of which might yet again reconfigure the political structures without including Darfurians in the future. The government of Sudan, under the pretext of counterinsurgency, i.e. a drive to thwart the rebellion, recruited militia forces known as the Janjaweed and deployed them in an indiscriminate campaign against the non-Arab civilian population, who were accused of acting as the support-base for the rebel movements. The Arab attackers appear to have taken the Arab-African divide seriously and their attacks were reportedly preceded by pronouncements designed to agitate the militias into the mindset that they must fight this war if they wished to survive in Darfur. In describing their enemies the members of these militias used derogatory terms like 'slave' so as to avoid any feelings of remorse toward their victims.

Despite mounting evidence of state-sponsored destruction in Darfur and criticism from around the world, the Sudanese regime not only denied any connection with the Janjaweed, but also continued to suggest there was no crisis at all. As the number of refugees and burned villages soared, Khartoum effectively sealed off Darfur from the outside world. By early 2004, vast tracts of the region had been depopulated, the refugee population in Chad had mushroomed to 120,000 and as many as 1,200,000 people were internally displaced inside Darfur. Scattered over vast dry lands, they became the concern of the humanitarian aid community. There, they were subject to continuing attacks by the Janjaweed, rapidly running out of food and drinking water.

The spring of 2004 marked the tenth anniversary of the Rwandan genocide, and many of the world's politicians, military

experts, human rights campaigners, and research institutions organized commemorative events to mark this tragedy, while a similar
catastrophe was in the making in Darfur. In fact it had been going on
for many years in Sudan, given that the tactics the government used
in Darfur were some of the old tricks long in use in the war against the
south. The anniversary of the Rwandan genocide coincided with
these particularly vicious campaigns of human destruction in the
western region of Sudan. John Ryle describes the conflict:

> The catastrophe in western Sudan is the result of a long-term
> divide-and-rule policy pursued unscrupulously by successive
> Sudanese governments. Like previous mass killings in other parts
> of the country, it reveals the decay of the state, the routine
> impunity accorded to the perpetrators of violence – and the incon-
> stancy of the western powers.[126]

In late 2004, after many missions by foreign service officials and
human rights investigators to Darfur and to Chad to interview
refugees and IDPs, the government of the US made the determination that the Darfur situation was genocide. In fact Collin Powell,
then US Secretary of State, had earlier declared that the crisis in
Darfur was the worst humanitarian tragedy in the world at that
time (he swiftly qualified this declaration with the assertion that a
determination of genocide did not necessarily obligate the US to
get involved directly in any effort to stop the killing). Instead, the
US called for the involvement of other countries with some US military, technical and logistical support. The UN sent in a fact-
finding mission in January 2005 and the team found that there had
been many gruesome atrocities carried out by government-
sponsored Arab militias, but that the situation did not amount to
genocide, especially that the element of the intent to commit genocide, a major part of the genocide convention, could not be proved.[127]
By the middle of 2005, the conflict had affected over 2.5 million
people and was continuing to do so, but the Janjaweed attacks had
resulted in the displacement of two million people, some of whom
have been forced to flee to neighboring Chad. This had caused an
appalling humanitarian situation, and as the attacks continue,

international aid agencies have had serious difficulties in their effort to deliver relief to the victims. The result was that more people died of starvation, thirst, and disease than from the weapons of the government and its allied militias. Judging by their effort to deny access to humanitarian assistance, it seems that the perpetrators view death by starvation as serving the same purpose. The NGO Physicians for Human Rights also carried out investigations into the genocide allegations since June 2004, and declared that what they saw in all three regions of Darfur, north, west and south presented evidence of genocide by attrition, i.e. compared to that in Rwanda, this was a slow but effective program of death and destruction. They documented an organized attempt to affect group annihilation. In particular, the findings of their livelihood study were found applicable to Article 6c of the Rome Statute for the International Criminal Court which defines genocide as 'acts committed with intent to destroy, in whole or in part, a national, ethnical, racial or religious group, as such deliberately inflicting on the group conditions of life calculated to bring about its physical destruction in whole or in part.' To this effect, they concluded that there was:

> full range of loss of livelihoods, including loss of community, economic structures, livestock, food production, wells and irrigation, farming capacity, and household structures. When this detail is applied to the estimated 700–2,000 villages destroyed in Darfur, the scale and cost of livelihood destruction is enormous. From the air and land, the [Physicians for Human Rights] team also photographically documented the utter devastation of dozens of villages in the southern border with Chad.[128]

It was surprising that the Darfur conflict, which erupted early in 2003, was covered so quickly by the international media with an urgency that was never generated by the destruction effected in the south for many years before. The media often likened the Darfur crisis to the Rwandan experience with the same qualification that this was Rwanda in slow motion, as the numbers of deaths were not as large as in Rwanda. For those of us who have watched the situation in south Sudan closely over the last twenty years, what was taking place in Darfur was an extension of what had been happening in south Sudan since the start of the second round of the war between Khartoum and the opposition SPLA. The tactics the government employed in Darfur had been tested, refined and proved extremely effective after two decades of similar activities in the south. Darfur was also a repeat of south Sudan at high speed. As will become clear in what follows, this was one of the many Sudanese conflicts that most baffled the world community, because the parties had not traditionally been known to hold such extreme enmity toward one another. While there were some historical disagreements that may have helped in predicting this eventual development, these were mainly between some embittered groups in Darfur and the government in Khartoum. That it would set Arabs against Africans within Darfur itself was unexpected, and this requires further explanation which this study will attempt to present in a more nuanced picture.

In hindsight, however, when this conflict finally broke out between Darfur armed opposition groups and the government of Sudan, many observers said it was a culmination of long-standing grievances felt by the people of Darfur for years. Precisely when and how such resentment started is a subject of debate, but it began to manifest itself more acutely during the last ten years of Nimeiri's government. In the late 1970s there had been frequent incidents of armed assaults on trucks, buses, and trains traveling between Darfur and the capital Khartoum and other big northern towns. Trade goods being transported within the western region or en route to other regions were also frequently attacked. The government media reported these attacks as armed robberies, while the Sudanese populace, as evident in the everyday popular discourse in northern Sudan, spoke of these events as manifestations of an organized political action against the government for neglecting Darfur. Indeed, for many years there was a plethora of angry voices speaking of how Darfur, a region which makes up one-third of the country, had been sidelined in terms of wealth-sharing, provision of basic social services, and political representation at the center. In reaction to what it had described as armed crime, the government often cracked down on specific ethnic groups that were thought to be behind these incidents, but because there was no evidence linking these groups to the crimes they were charged with, many were detained for long periods of time without trial (Harir, 1992). This angered their immediate families and the entire ethnic groups they belonged to, and this resentment would later become a tool for organized opposition as disgruntled youths joined the rebel armies when they were eventually formed. Some of these youths had joined the south-based SPLA when it was formed in the early 1980s when its then inspirational leader, John Garang de Mabior, had begun to talk about the concept of marginalization of the peripheries by the elite in Khartoum, and that the conflict in Sudan was no longer between north and south as it had traditionally been framed, but rather one between the politically and economically entrenched northern minority Arab elite and the exploited and neglected African majority in peripheries. One young man from Darfur called Daoud Yahya Bolad, a one-time Muslim radical during his days as a student at the University of Khartoum, shifted his political orientation and joined the SPLA in response to the way Darfur had been marginalized. The SPLA trained him and after he had risen to the rank of commander he was sent to his home region to mobilize the youth to join the SPLA on the basis of the newly redefined conflict. Bolad was not able to recruit a significant number of people in Darfur as the small contingent that went with him had to operate in an environment hostile to the SPLA. His mission was thwarted and he was reportedly captured and interrogated by the governor of Darfur, Colonel al-Tayeb Ibrahim. He may have perished from the encounter: certainly he has never been heard from again. There is no record of the interrogation, but in 1995 I was able to interview Alesio Makuc Makuac, an SPLA officer who was a member of Bolad's team. Alesio and a handful of other fighters had escaped and walked for months through the Central African Republic back to south Sudan after their force was scattered. He thought that Bolad had either been in possession of written evidence that the interrogators may have seized and used to track down the members of the Darfur pro-SPLA clandestine network, or he had to divulge the details of their names during the interrogation under torture. Despite the failure of this attempt, it had stirred debate within Darfur about the nature of Sudan's conflicts. In 2003 when the SLA and JEM were formed, the two opposition armies had no shortage of able-bodied men to swell their ranks.

The National Islamic Front and Darfur

When the Islamists toppled Sadiq al-Mahdi's government in 1989, the Sudanese people in the north were less jubilant than on previous occasions when incompetent governments had been overthrown. The October Revolution that toppled Abbud in 1964 and the popular uprising that deposed Nimeiri in 1985 were still considered significant evidence of the ability of the Sudanese people to bring down dictatorships after all other measures had been frustrated over many years. The NIF coup, however, was regarded differently because al-Madhi's government had not been in power long enough to be judged correctly. It was also decried because the head of the DUP, Mohammed Osman al-Mirghani, who had been party to a coalition government with al-Mahdi, had met with SPLA leader John Garang in Koka Dam, Ethiopia in May 1989 and agreed with him to initiate peace talks, news that was received with great jubilation when al-Mirghani returned to Khartoum. Eric Reeves correctly observed that 'It was precisely to stop this peace agreement that the NIF timed its military coup for June 30, 1989.'[129] In other words, the NIF coup had spoiled what could have been the beginning of the end for a civil war which was becoming increasingly destructive and hated as much by the northern populace for its economic consequences as it was by the south for its bloodiness. Sadiq al-Mahdi had won elections in 1986, a year after Nimeiri was deposed in a popular uprising in which the military had taken the side of the protestors and refrained from cracking down on them as had happened on many similar occasions in the past.[130] This popular skepticism was as much about history as it was about what the people feared the future held for the country. Nimeiri's violent and oppressive days were still fresh in the minds of the majority, and a return to military rule after such a brief period was not something the Sudanese were ready for. The reason for this somber mood became apparent shortly after the military junta took power: the head of state was Omar al-Bashir, a devout and ruthless soldier who ruled in uneasy alliance with Hassan al-Turabi, the charismatic leader of the country's Islamist party.

Since al-Bashir came to power, the Islamist and Arab-centric regime has increased its militarization of ethnicity and racialization of the conflict. This has caused the rapid advance of the ideological and racist dimensions of the conflict, with the sides defining themselves as 'Arab' or 'Zurq' (Black). Many of the racist attitudes traditionally directed toward southern slaves have been redirected to the sedentary non-Arab communities within the north. The racist dimension comes to the fore in reports of rape and mass killings, all reportedly supported by the Khartoum government, which is determined to retain control over the area. Consequently, the Janjaweed have a fully developed racist ideology, a warrior culture, weapons and plenty of horses and camels (a camel is still the easiest way to get around Darfur). With the Islamists in power, the Darfur regional government tried to compensate for the rarity with which it caught criminals by the savagery of the punishments it meted out – execution and public display of the corpses for armed robbers, amputation of limbs for thieves, and extended periods of detention for suspected enemies of the state.

In 1994 the government redrew administrative boundaries, dividing the region into northern, southern, and western Darfur states, thus splitting the Fur and their centrally located fertile land among the three states. It then brought back the old native administration council and allocated territories to chiefs. With no funds to provide services, a suddenly renewed authority to distribute land (now becoming scarce) and self-armed vigilantes all around, this was a charter for local-level ethnic cleansing. Immediately after this administrative reform, there was another round of killings in the far west of Darfur, the area known as Dar Masalit, named after the dominant group. In addition to racial, ethnic and cultural issues in Darfur, much of the ongoing conflict also has its origins in land rights and the shortcomings of local administration, but central government is implicated in Darfur's plight, with neglect and manipulation playing equal parts. Despite reports by its own officials that the situation was threatening to become an ethnic conflict between the Arabs and the non-Arab tribes, the ruling National Congress Party remained focused on military victory against the rebels and 'armed robbers,' as Khartoum continued to describe the insurgency. For example, President al-Bashir, in a televised speech in December 2003, placed the responsibility for the insurgency on the Zaghawa, and the government has been trying since then to isolate this tribe from the Fur, the Massalit, and other groups that were part of the revolt. The government attempted to mobilize some tribal leaders under the National Congress Party, preaching peaceful coexistence to them while at the same time planning for a military victory that would remove the need to negotiate for a political settlement.

Geography is against Darfur. The large town of el Geneina, at the westernmost edge of Darfur, close to the border with Chad, is distant from the centers of power and so under-served that it may as well be a territory outside the bounds of Sudan. This part of Darfur, Dar Masalit particularly, was only absorbed into Sudan in 1922, by a treaty between the sultan and the British. 'Quite recently, the sultan's grandson, holding court in a decrepit palace, used to joke that he still had the right to secede from Sudan, and he pointedly hung maps of Dar Masalit and Africa on his wall, but not of Sudan.'[131] This sort of sentiment is rampant in the remote areas of Sudan, where services are hard to access and complaints are suppressed by force. The use of brute force without anyone ever brought to account for it is also a function of geography: the state abuses peoples' rights in remote regions where it is difficult to get news to the outside world and reporters and human rights activists are barred by both the terrain and the state.

Underdevelopment, some have argued, is at the crux of all the crises in Darfur, and one of the reasons it gets framed in ethnic, racial or religious terms is the unevenness of such undervelopment as some regions are deliberately neglected.[132] Despite being part of the north from the perspective of the traditional North–South divide, Darfur suffers nearly the same level of poverty and lack of infrastructure as in the south. For example, the train from Khartoum terminates at Nyala in southern Darfur: the journey takes anywhere between three to five days, depending on a number of factors along the way, and it is at least another day's drive to el Geneina, the capital of west Darfur, if the road is not cut by rainwater coming down from the massif of Jebel Marra. Khartoum has ignored Darfur and its people have received less education, healthcare, development assistance and fewer government posts than any other region in the northern two-thirds of the country. Even the southerners, because of the fights for their rights and the different arrangements of autonomy, may have had better deals in some respects. Within Darfur the non-Arabs have been even more marginalized, and attempts by the leaders of these groups to make common cause in the face of Khartoum's indifference also explain the conflicts.

Hassan al-Turabi, the Islamist movement and the war in Darfur

The triggers of this latest phase in Sudan's conflicts are to be found in the politics of power-sharing within the Islamist regime. They may also be traced to the changing geopolitics of war against terrorism declared by the US in the wake of the September 11 attacks on New York and Washington in 2001. The signing of a peace protocol between the Khartoum government and the southern-based SPLA in 2002 may be relevant as well. The conflict is also about the government taking advantage of an ongoing competition between the semi-nomadic herding Arab groups and the sedentary agricultural African communities of the region, whose relationships have become increasingly strained by the diminishing natural resources due to recurrent droughts that have plagued the region for decades. The next section will address these factors in more detail.

With regard to the struggle over power, many Sudanese seem to believe that Omar al-Bashir was made president at the time of the

1989 military coup by the NIF leaders to be a figurehead while the real power lay in the hands of powerful Islamists such as Hassan al-Turabi, Ali Osman Taha, Mustafa Osman Ismail, Nafie Ali Nafie and many others. (Two important and influential members of this group, Shams al-Deen Ibrahim and Muhammad al-Amin Khalifa, perished in the south in uncertain circumstances while directing the war.) The officers who took power arrested al-Turabi and he was detained briefly. On his release he went straight from jail to a position of power in the new government: proof for many Sudanese that he had been behind the putsch all along and had sought to cover up this fact. Al-Turabi has been a man of many contradictions throughout his political career. Prior to the coup, he had denounced change of power by military means: to be seen supporting the military takeover was to be caught in a lie, and he therefore disguised himself as another victim of the coup. He became a dominant force in Sudanese politics from about 1990 until 1999. Al-Turabi became the speaker of the national assembly, a position he used to push for a variety of self-aggrandizing legislations, brutally prosecuting the war against the south and making Sudan a base for extremists from all over the Islamic world. Most notable in this regard was his making Sudan a base for Osama bin Laden and other 'terrorists.' During this period the Islamists changed the name of their ruling organization from the National Islamic Front to the National Congress Party; a response to increasing criticism from around the world for their Islamic militancy. The change in the name was intended to move the party away from its image of Islamic extremism so as to push the Islamist agenda while exhibiting tolerance. In a puzzling turn of events that took place in 1999, al-Turabi had a falling-out with his former allies in the military, most of whom were his own protégés. This made the differences between President al-Bashir and al-Turabi that had existed since the coup ever more apparent. Al-Turabi had ambitions for an Islamic revolution throughout Africa and the Middle East, while al-Bashir held to the traditional view of Sudan as the possession of Arabized elite. It was a protracted struggle over ideology, foreign policy, the constitution, and ultimately power itself. The Islamist coalition was divided down the middle and al-Bashir won. He dismissed al-Turabi from the post of Speaker of the National Assembly, a move that gave al-Bashir the cover he needed to approach the US.[133] Most of the administration, and all of the security elite in control of the military and various secret security agencies, stayed with him, and al-Turabi broke away from the party to set up a splinter group called the Popular Congress Party. Some formerly prominent figures in the Islamist movement such as Ali al-Hajj Osman went with him. The students and the regional Islamist party cells also went into opposition alongside al-Turabi.

This new Islamist group immediately started jockeying for ways to return to power, none of which has yet proved successful, and they seem to have lost this battle for now. One of their more surprising moves was the contacts they made with the SPLA, in particular the arrangement of a meeting that took place in Germany in 2000 between the SPLA and Popular Congress Party representatives, after which they issued a joint communiqué condemning the government and declaring a plan of action to change the government, including the use of military force. Many Sudanese expressed unease and disappointment over these developments, which were seen as acts of political promiscuity of a desperate kind. Southerners were puzzled as to how the SPLA could bring itself to agree on anything with al-Turabi, one of the northern politicians most despised in the south; and the followers of al-Turabi who supported his move against al-Bashir were angered that their party had sold its soul to the infidels of the south. Because of this agreement al-Turabi was accused of the crime of a plot to overthrow the government by illegal means, a treasonable charge in Sudan's constitution, and was imprisoned. He was later released from jail and placed under house arrest for nearly a year, but was back in jail in 2003 and remained at Khober prison in Khartoum for the next three years.[134] The other leading figures of the new party fled the country, and many of them remain in exile. Al-Turabi decided to fight from jail. Many Sudanese believe that he was directing part of the insurrection in Darfur. The leader of the opposition JEM, Khalil Ibrahim, a man from a leading Zaghawa family, was a close associate of Hassan al-Turabi before 2000 and has been particularly hardline, resisting pressure to negotiate with Khartoum.

Geography, history and the Janjaweed militias

A further issue at the core of Darfur's misfortune is that it borders Chad and Libya. In the 1980s, Colonel Gaddafi dreamed of an 'Arab belt' across the Sahel region of West Africa. The key element of his plan was to gain control of Chad, starting with the Aouzou strip in the north of the country. He mounted a succession of military adventures in Chad, and from 1987 to 1989, Chadian factions backed by Libya used Darfur as a rear base, provisioning themselves freely from the crops and cattle of local villagers. Many of the guns in Darfur came from those factions. Alex de Waal neatly summarized the situation:

> Gaddafi's formula for war was expansive: he collected discontented Sahelian Arabs and Tuaregs, armed them, and formed them into an Islamic Legion that served as the spearhead of his offensives. Among the legionnaires were Arabs from western Sudan, many of them followers of the Mahdist Ansar sect, who had been forced into exile in 1970 by President Nimeiri. The Libyans were defeated by a nimble Chadian force at Ouadi Doum in 1988, and Gaddafi abandoned his venture all together. He began dismantling the Islamic Legion, but its members, armed, trained and – most significant of all – possessed of a virulent Arab supremacism, did not vanish. The legacy of the Islamic Legion lives on in Darfur: Janjaweed leaders are among those said to have been trained in Libya.[135]

It was in the mid-1980s, when Nimeiri was overthrown, that the Ansar exiles began to return. In 1987, returnees from Libya took the lead in forming a political bloc known as the Arab Gathering. They announced their presence with a letter to Prime Minister al-Mahdi in which a number of Darfur leaders of Arab descent complained of under-representation at the local, regional and national level although 'the Arab race created civilization in this region ... in the areas of governance, religion, and language.'[136] The Gathering could be described as a political coalition that aimed to protect the interests of a disadvantaged group in the region. They demanded a 50 percent share of political posts and other services at the local, regional and national levels, claiming that their demographic weight, contribution to the development of the region through their wealth, and role as bearers of civilization granted them such a share. However it also became a vehicle for a new racist ideology: the language of the letter was supremacist, presenting Arabs as more civilized, productive, and inclined to reason, as opposed to the ignorant, uncultured, and ill-natured farmers. These racist epithets date back decades if not centuries, but were now taking on an increased political significance in Darfur. Their address to the Prime Minister warned that if the Arab race continued to be neglected and the situation got out of hand the consequences could be grave. The Gathering seems to have latched on to the dominant ideology of the Sudanese state, the very different Arabism that has threatened to break up Sudan. The war in Darfur at the end of the 1980s was more than a conflict over the distribution of power and resources: it was the first step in constructing a new Arab ideology in Sudan.

This is partly what seems to have given the Darfur rebel leaders the idea of using the Arab-African divide unsparingly, having realized that the SPLA had gained a high international standing by characterizing the southern plight in the simplified terms that had proved so effective in winning foreign sympathy for the south. The southerners were of course the victims of an Arab regime, but the Darfur rebel movement's decision to portray the problems of Darfur as that of Arab versus African simply pandered to the established notion of Arab-African rivalries in Sudan. The 'African' label played well to international audiences on the issue of the south in the 1990s, but the situation in western Sudan is more subtle. One complicating factor is the prevalence of radical Islam and its appeal to many Darfurians – the result of the success of a political experiment by the regime in Khartoum, masterminded by

Hassan al-Turabi. As indicated earlier, political Islam in Sudan was dominated by an Arabized elite originating in the Nile Valley, with strong links to the Egyptian Muslim Brotherhood. Theirs was a conservative movement, identified with Arabization. Most of Sudan's ruling elite have attempted a form of Islamic government at some point, but al-Turabi broadened the agenda and constituency of the Islamist movement. For example, he encouraged women's education and other rights he claims Islam grants to women (being student-based, the Islamist movement in Sudan is today very popular among young women in schools and on university campuses). Unlike the Arab Gathering, al-Turabi also embraced all African Muslims, at least in rhetoric, as authentic, therefore focusing on religion as unifying factor. In ensuring that citizenship was extended to all devout Muslims, al-Turabi revolutionized the status of the non-Arabs of western Sudan, including the Felata of West Africa who had either settled in Sudan during their journeys back from pilgrimage to Mecca, or had come to work on the agricultural schemes of al-Jazirah.

As a result the split in the ruling Islamist movement in 2000 had an equally destabilizing impact on Darfur. When al-Turabi formed his Popular Congress following the infamous power struggle with al-Bashir's NIF or National Congress Party as it was now called, he reached out to the religious leaders of the Fur, Masalit, and other non-Arab groups with an eye to renewing his power base among them. It is thought the widely circulated pamphlet, 'The Black Book' was an appeal by al-Turabi's Popular Congress to Sudanese African constituencies, arguing that the ruling Islamist faction was Arab-centric and trying to block people from Darfur and other peripheral regions from senior posts while giving preference in appointments to those from the privileged northern region. This was an attempt on the part of Popular Congress to gain support of the non-Arab Darfurians on the basis that a common faith – Islam – rather than race was the route to Darfurian national emancipation. The Bashir–Turabi face-off reverberated in Darfur. Many Darfurians who had come into the Islamist movement under al-Turabi's leadership now left government and decided to organize on their own. This maneuvering backfired on al-Turabi and al-Bashir as both the region and the whole of northern Sudan is becoming polarized along racial rather than religious lines. The rapprochement between the Islamists and the secular radicals of Darfur is evidence of this polarization, as seen in this otherwise unlikely alliance between the Darfur secularists who founded the Sudan Liberation Army (SLA) and the Islamist-leaning who formed the JEM. The Popular Congress is unapologetic about its political backing of the rebels, but says that it does not approve of their use of force. Those who had been watching Darfur over the years were less surprised when rebellion broke out than many in journalism and policy circles in the West. The Sudanese government had a hand in the confusion in Darfur and faked its surprise at the eruption of the war. It had indirectly fanned the conflict by engaging in internal initiatives to reconcile the ethnic groups, meeting separately with tribal leaders of one group after the other, but telling each group something different. These peace gestures in the early months were as half-hearted as its military preparations, and their double-dealing continued to fuel the conflict. In April 2003, the rebels attacked el Fasher airport, destroyed half a dozen military aircraft and kidnapped an air force general. Unlike the SPLA's earlier attempts to gain a foothold in Darfur which had failed miserably due to the hostility of the whole environment to southern rebels – a hostility built upon race and religion – the rebels in Darfur had mobility, good intelligence and popular support.

When it looked as if the two-decades long North–South conflict was going to end in a peace deal, which at the time was being worked out in Kenya under the auspices of the IGAD, the Darfur opposition armies, SLA and JEM, may have realized that the time was ripe to strike. The North–South peace agreement was widely criticized for privileging the SPLA and the government of Sudan and directing little attention to the other aggrieved regions and political forces: the opposition leaders in Darfur may have come to the conclusion that a military action would guarantee them at least a seat at the negotiating table. So the timing of the Darfur attacks on the government was not entirely coincidental. It was also clear that the Darfur opposition movements were receiving help, perhaps not directly, from the SPLA as a way to present the government with multiple war fronts and forcing it to be serious about negotiating a peaceful settlement. The more war fronts the less likely that the government would pursue the military option in the same way it had done over the years when the war with the south was the only military engagement.

While it is uncertain how the Darfur conflict will eventually be resolved to the satisfaction of all, it appears that the people of Darfur, at least judging by what their political leaders have declared, are not fighting for secession. At this stage the Darfur conflict does not appear to represent an instance of the possible disintegration of the Sudanese state, at least not in the same way that the southern conflict does. What makes the Darfur crisis a challenge to the unity of Sudan is the intransigence of the Khartoum government with regard to the search for a peaceful settlement of the conflict. Many attempts have been made to establish a ceasefire and peace deals, all coordinated and sponsored initially by Chad and Nigeria (and later by Libya) and partly financed by the African Union and the European Union, but they met with little success and were violated by both sides to the conflict as quickly as they were signed. Given the brutality that has characterized the Darfur conflict since 2003, the longer it goes on the more it polarizes the situation, and as the people of Darfur become increasingly frustrated, a break away will be considered as a viable option, at least by some of the larger groups such as the Fur, Masalit, and the Zaghawa. A situation similar to that which led the south to desire secession is already in the making in Darfur.

The Darfur conflicts have been as much about resource distribution along ethnic lines as they are a contestation of history, with each side wanting their history told to reflect who they are and to which territories they have always held title. In the 1980s, the contest was magnified to the state of crisis that exists today after prolonged droughts accelerated the desertification of northern and central Darfur and led to pressure on water and grazing resources as the camel nomads were forced to move southwards. Conflicts over wells that had once been settled with spears or mediation became far more intractable in an area awash with automatic guns. The situation disintegrated with the decision of the prime minister, Sadiq al-Mahdi, in the mid-1980s, to give arms to the Arabic-speaking cattle nomads of southern Darfur, the Baggara, ostensibly to defend themselves against the SPLA. With the war against the SPLA degenerating into the targeting of Dinka civilians for slave raids, the program fell short of its ultimate goal of defeating the insurgents. Neither did it guarantee the Baggara an easy access to the southern grazing plains of the Kiir River, one of the reasons they had agreed to sign up for the militia force in the first place. When they failed to make a significant headway in the south, the Baggara turned the guns on their northern neighbors, the Fur, Masalit, and others. As we saw earlier, the SPLA's decision to send Bolad and his contingent to southern Darfur in an attempt to open a front in that region exacerbated the situation. It was at this point that the Arab tribal militias, known at that time as the Murahileen, began to get out of control. Just as the Murahileen had been sent down south to suppress opposition, so now the Janjaweed were being used for the same purpose within Darfur two decades after the militias had proven effective tools of suppression.

Genocide and the world community

Destruction of assets so as to render people desperate, dependent on outside handouts, and starving to death, has been one of the measures to effect genocide in Darfur. Many human rights researchers have been to Darfur over the course of the last years and amassed a wealth of detailed information about how the victims of Sudan's genocidal campaigns live. According to accounts given by some individuals who had never left their villages, nearly all the pre-war livestock was lost: 40 percent were killed as a direct result of the attack and 20 percent stolen or eaten by attacking Janjaweed forces. Of the remaining animals, 30 percent died as a result of lack of food and water either during the long trek to Chad or from neglect. Food production for family consumption and for upkeep of their livestock was completely wiped out as homes were attacked, looted and/or destroyed, crops were burned and fruit trees were cut down. Because of continuing intimidation and regular return attacks against Africans, villagers are unable to return home. Michael Van Rooyen, a humanitarian aid expert at the Harvard School of Public Health, commented, 'An essential part of survival is community structure. People can't and won't return unless their entire village returns. It is vital that the international community and the government of Sudan take concrete steps to rebuild these people's lives.'[137]

Without access to their land there is no home, and no farm, and without the farm there is no way to eat or feed livestock. Without livestock, African villagers have reduced access to water and no more economy to speak of. The continuation of attacks and intimidation has forced the population into the harsh desert to live off wild grains and berries. It is only the presence of humanitarian aid organizations that has prevented the starvation and annihilation of the targeted population. A return to their homes, saving lives and preventing further attacks, will only happen if the international system; i.e. the UN Security Council, the European Union, the African Union, and concerned individual countries act promptly to deploy a military force with a mandate to protect the civilians.* Such a force, along with the Sudanese government, would also be given powers to disarm and disband the Janjaweed militias. Above all, to ensure the return of normality to Darfur, there must be a mechanism for restitution so that the people of Darfur can restore their livelihoods. It is hard to see how they can get back on their feet without a system that will ensure the return of seized lands, compensation for stolen livestock or damaged crops and houses.

Based on these findings and many others, most human rights groups working on Sudan and the US Congress have called for targeted sanctions to be imposed on the government of Sudan and others responsible for the destruction of Darfur. Calls to hold

---

* (The Arab League and the Organization of Islamic Countries have both been suspiciously silent on the Darfur crisis.)

perpetrators accountable by referring the crimes they committed in Darfur to the International Criminal Court (ICC) have also been made. With a concerted voice from a number of European countries, the Security Council passed a resolution in March 2005 to refer these cases to the ICC. This resolution was still awaiting implementation at the time of writing, and is unlikely to make headway.

The international community, including the European Union, China, India, and Pakistan all stress the importance of keeping away from what they view as an internal affair. Yet surely they must be aware that their interests in excavating oil include destroying those communities that stand in the way of that oil development. The Arab League, on the other hand, has been unashamedly passive while watching Sudanese Arabs dishonor Arab identity with misguided agendas of Arabization and Islamization. The US is equally implicated because it knows that its power and resources could bring an end to the genocide yet it does not have the will to intervene. The Sudanese leaders themselves, starting with the heirs of the colonial structures who have chosen to wage war for longer than the country has been independent, stand accused of political promiscuity that has led them to switching alliances and using ethnic differences for their own political gains.* If anyone is to broker a successful peace deal in Darfur, they must be conscious of the absurdity of attempting to talk peace in the midst of genocide.

The destruction carried out by the Janjaweed is aimed at all non-Arabs, and its effects are disproportionate to the military threat of the rebellion. The mass rape and branding of victims speaks of the deliberate destruction of a community and appears to aim at achieving a long-standing solution to the problem of racial diversity. It has been seen before in similar situations in the country. The genocidal campaign in Darfur bears the same ideological appearance as the slave raiding in northern Bahr el-Ghazal from the mid-1980s to 2001, the 1992 Jihad against the Nuba, and the

---

* This has left many people in Sudan with a pessimistic view of the world; that the evil doers in Sudan and elsewhere will continue doing evil, and the potential do-gooders will continue to do nothing.

more recent oil-related destruction in Upper Nile. Ideology is being used here to attract the fighters and imbue them with routine cruelty toward non-Arabs. What is really at the bottom of these campaigns, and common between all of them, is that they were determined efforts to secure natural resources.

The nomads of Darfur, due to their unstable lifestyle, have in recent years found themselves fighting to carve out niches in territories that were not originally their own, and therefore displacing the people who lived there before them. Normally the people of Darfur would probably resolve these problems using the traditional approaches of mediation, reconciliation, and compensation of property. Unfortunately, because the system has been reconfigured by the successive governments, with Khartoum backing the Arabs, coupled with years of ignoring the overall need of this remote region, rebels within Darfur organized to contest disputes.

One reason for Khartoum's neglect of the region may have been that in the wake of the September 11 attacks the Bashir regime was energetically trying to clean up its international image: a task whose size left little time for new distractions. With the oil industry getting under way in eastern Sudan, Khartoum was eager to end American economic sanctions, which kept foreign investors away and blocked access to international markets. Having already ended its romance with the most notorious Islamic radicals, Khartoum has set about mending relations with many of its neighbors, quietly cutting off its support to a variety of guerrilla and dissident groups throughout the region. Certainly its most significant overture was agreeing to a strong American role in mediating negotiations to end the southern civil war, a move that would have been unthinkable just a short time earlier.

Nevertheless, Khartoum claims that through the humanitarian operations, the SLA and JEM are being armed with US backing. This allegation scarcely seems plausible, as attempts to end 'the world's largest humanitarian crisis' cannot be done through training and arming rebel groups such as the SLA and JEM, especially when the latter is controlled by Hassan al-Turabi. After all, al-Turabi was once among the most powerful men behind

Khartoum's military regime and the mastermind of the Islamist regime that invited Osama bin Laden to set up training camps for Hammas and other terrorist groups in eastern Sudan. Since his fall-out with al-Bashir, al-Turabi has used Darfur as a recruiting field with an eye to reclaiming power in Khartoum. Having been the Speaker of Parliament, the spiritual leader of the NIF, which aimed to apply shari'a law, and a clandestine supporter of JEM, it is unlikely that the US could use al-Turabi as a way to rein in Khartoum. If the US decided to intervene using military strength by backing al-Turabi, as the government of Sudan alleges, they would be funding another rebel who would almost certainly turn on them as did the Mujahidin whom the US funded during the Soviet invasion of Afghanistan in the 1980s.

In response to the rebels in Darfur, Khartoum admits to mobilizing counterinsurgency measures, but has denied any relationship to the Janjaweed militias. Janjaweed convoys travel on horseback and cover their faces, both to protect themselves against the dust of the desert and to conceal their identities from their victims who may survive to identify them later. A journalist has likened their appearance to the images of the Ku Klux Klan (KKK) in the United States. Much like the KKK the Janjaweed have no political power and are exploited by their government in Sudan, which plays on their bigotry to equip these otherwise poor Arabs with expensive weapons.[138] This is the power that allows the Janjaweed the authority to prevent the entry of food, water and medicine into IDP and refugee camps in Darfur. Like most corrupt governments, the NIF government has denied ties with this renegade group, suggesting that the violence is random: but random violence does not involve a scorched earth policy that drives specific groups from their land so that they are open to systematic rape, slavery and murder. As the indigenous Darfur African customs, social structure, and means of livelihood are ground into extinction, the notion of random violence has no currency in Sudan. These acts of violence are genocide.

The idea that Darfur's crisis is not really the government's fault is not borne out by the facts. In response to a rebellion by two local armed groups, Sudan's government attacked civilians with helicopter gunships and armed a local militia to raze villages. Rather than solicit international help to deal with the humanitarian crisis, Sudan's government actually blocked aid groups from entering Darfur for a long time: aid was only allowed in after considerable diplomatic pressure and the deaths of many thousands of people, and even then was subject to severe restrictions.[139] Its policy toward displaced people was to deprive them of food, health and protection. These are the actions of a government intending to kill people, not one which has lost control of outlawed militias. Horrifying reports tell how government troops and their militia allies have engaged in a systematic policy of raping civilians. Médecins sans Frontières (MSF) documented and reported these offenses in May 2005 and its staff were targeted for harassment, including the detention of its country director.

The harassment of aid workers poses an immediate risk to Darfur's two million or so displaced people, who have been unable to plant food and so remain dependent on humanitarian assistance for the near term. But it also poses a challenge for outsiders. Western diplomacy toward Sudan has oscillated between the pressure that is brought to bear on the government and the engagement that implicitly endorses the government's claim that Darfur's suffering reflects anarchy and poverty. On occasion the US has persuaded its allies to threaten to bring UN sanctions against Sudan: but some nations have treated the government as a partner that is working to control the violence. At a Sudan donor conference in Oslo in March 2005 they pledged large amounts of aid to support the tentative North–South peace deal, imagining that this will help solve the Darfur crisis. These countries sometimes condemn the Sudanese government for its atrocities in Darfur and have at other times acted as though Khartoum, the perpetrator, could be expected to provide the solution to this crisis.

President Bush has called the Darfur killings genocide on several occasions, a description that implies some moral obligation on the part of the US to act to stop the killing. His administration qualifies that determination by asserting that there is little they can do about it: in their view the best solution requires cooperation with other countries. But such cooperation has been made difficult, if not impossible, by European escapism, US lack of commitment, and Asian greed for Sudanese oil. Given that the Bush administration is paralyzed by more burning issues, not least of which is the indifference of possible allies, it was unlikely from the first instance that the US would intervene on behalf of the victims of genocide. China already looks at Sudan from the perspective of its oil interest; Russia wishes to sell arms to Sudan. The Arab and Islamic Leagues appear unmoved by the killing of Darfur's Muslim people, perhaps because of race, again justifying the suspicion of many Darfurians that when it comes to the Arab countries Islam, the religion they share with most Arabs, will not help them. While the US may believe that the government of Sudan is the problem and not the solution, it is unlikely that the other countries mentioned above, which have more clout in Khartoum, will ever look at the government of Sudan in the same way the US government does.

The genocide declaration of the US government is still being debated in the international community. The UN says that war crimes have been committed but not genocide: the only country that has classified it as genocide is unwilling to take steps toward stopping it, even though the genocide convention obliges them to do so. Compared to south Sudan, Darfur has not lost as many civilians, but the US government under President Clinton refused to determine the south Sudanese situation as genocide, allegedly because of the claims that such a determination would have forced them to take actions which they were not prepared to take. Ironically, genocide is not declared where many people have died because of the fear that it could force world governments into undesirable action: when it is declared where fewer people have died, no action is taken in accordance with the obligations of the genocide convention, which most of the world's countries have signed. Current debate over Darfur suggests that the world is waiting for it to catch up to south Sudan in terms of numbers and the scale of destruction before any action is taken. The death and destruction in Darfur are fulfilling the reasoning behind genocide, which is to destroy cultures and re-induct the survivors into the image of the conqueror through language, education, and customs. Perhaps the world does not take genocide seriously. Many Western countries who championed the passing of the genocide convention had themselves engaged in horrendous acts, and the convention came to pass as self-criticism.[140] Genocide conducted by distant governments upon distant citizens does not seem to generate the levels of concern that caused the West to establish the genocide convention after World War II. It seems that the superpower of the world is slower to act because its allies in the Arab world are unwilling to intervene because the oppressed African Sudanese are not like Palestinians or Iraqis. African countries, on the other hand, are too poor to engage the government of Sudan, which may soon replace Nigeria as the country with the largest oil reserves on the continent. Yet this is an issue that should not be about any other considerations: it should be about stopping genocide, and African governments surely are just as capable of stopping it as any other if there was a political will.

Outside intervention makes the government of Sudan nervous because it fears further estrangement between Darfur and Khartoum. While conscious of the fact that the peace-keeping forces and military interventions will come and go, the Sudanese will still have to contend with one another, but rather than acting quickly to avoid foreign intervention, Khartoum regards reconciliation with the Darfur rebels as surrender. The people of Sudan will need to solve their national problems in the end, but the destruction of humanity is no longer an internal difficulty but a universal one. Every nation that continues to do nothing to stop the genocide is just as responsible for it as the government of Sudan, especially in the light of the 2004 UN Security Council resolution that made a pledge to protect the most basic of all human rights; the right to life.

WHAT ABOUT PEACE WITH JUSTICE?

What is clear from the above is that the Darfur crisis is not about one people assaulting another in a frenzy of long-buried ethnic hatred, as African wars are sometimes depicted. It is a mob of armed thugs and a corrupt government that are taking advantage of each other. The militias are cashing in on the opportunity to loot at will while securing political objectives set by their handlers, and the politicians in Khartoum are fighting over power using what are otherwise reconcilable ethnic differences to fight one another. Additionally, the government wishes to quash an uprising that could not only threaten the government's hold on this region but also unravel its efforts to reach a lasting peace with the rebellious south and perhaps start new revolts in the restive east and north. The nature and scope of this disaster is not the responsibility of the current regime alone, but the outcome of a decades-long strategy of divide and rule that successive governments – all drawn from the fractious elite that reside in and around Khartoum – have used to put down challenges, mostly out of the international spotlight.

Horrific as it is, the focus on violence in Darfur has masked the politics behind the crisis. Many parties have got what they desired from this situation. The Sudanese government has used its Janjaweed proxies to defeat the two rebel groups, the SLA and JEM. For their part the militias have booty pillaged from their victims, and have now established expanded access to grazing land for their herds. It now seems that the Khartoum government has achieved control over the rebels. If it can also bring the Janjaweed under control the Bush administration will consider this a diplomatic success, more so if the peace brought to the south is extended to Darfur: then sanctions could be lifted and Sudan's extensive oil reserves opened up to American oil companies.[141]

As for the millions of terrified and impoverished Darfurians who have lost everything and are currently relying on international aid, ending the fighting is sufficient gain for them and they are unlikely to gain little else – neither compensation for their destroyed property or prosecution of the perpetrators of genocide. The other marginalized groups in the Nuba mountains, the Blue Nile, and the northeastern Beja are not likely to gain much either. It is highly desirable that the killing should stop, but the possibility of ending this ordeal in a just peace is nowhere on the horizon. The government of Sudan, with the assistance of its allied militias, has committed such horrendous acts that officials will probably admit only the most minor of them, and the international community will probably pressure the victims to accept a compromise that does not restore justice to them. For example, Sudan's first vice-president and one of the regime's toughest hardliners, Ali Uthman Taha, urged a reconciliation conference for the tribes of north Darfur in March 2005 to promote unity and dialogue and affirmed the government's determination to embrace dialogue and negotiations as a way to solve the country's conflicts. Historically such government-sponsored mediations without international observation have been the best way for the government to get away with such violent acts. It has enabled the government to erect a façade of reconciliation to mislead the international community while it pursued war in other parts of the country. In the dialogue regarding the case of the Baggara versus Dinka, the promised compensation never materialized, leaving some parties even more embittered against both the state and their tribal foes. This duplicity is why and how Sudan's wars have never achieved any lasting resolution.

Some members of the international community are aware of the callous nature of the NIF government. While urging the government of Sudan to seek reconciliation, the UN Security Council adopted two consecutive resolutions in May 2005 aimed at pressuring Khartoum and seeking real internationally mediated solutions to the crisis. One of these resolutions was on an arms embargo and asset freeze, and a travel ban on those who were deemed responsible for the atrocities in Darfur. The other called for the trial of those implicated in the region's crimes by the ICC. Earlier in January 2005, the UN International Commission of Inquiry had reported reprehensible abuses and recommended referral of the Darfur crimes to the ICC. This was followed in March by UN Security Council Resolution 1593, which accepted the recommendation and referred the situation in Darfur to the ICC to probe further with a view to an eventual prosecution of the perpetrators. It is hoped that the investigation will lead to the prosecution of all those who ordered, condoned or carried out crimes such as killings, rapes and mass displacement – including senior figures in the government, armed forces and armed militia. There is no shortage of evidence that the ICC could use. Most of the human rights agencies that have been working in Darfur since the crisis began have documented specific abuses such as unlawful killings or extrajudicial executions by government forces and Janjaweed militia, which were armed and funded by the Sudanese authorities. These agencies have also estimated the number of people who were forcibly displaced from their villages and have lost all their property. Thousands of women have been raped and rapes are reportedly continuing.

The government and their allied militia forces have also harassed the humanitarian aid agencies and even attacked aid convoys, denying the displaced persons access to food, medicines and other basic necessities, and exposing more people to preventable deaths. The government, while denying its role in the atrocities, has failed or refused to disarm the Janjaweed militias or bring those accused of crimes to justice. The national justice system was already crumbling in the face of the bias that it held against non-Arab groups and it is absurd to expect the Sudanese government to support the work of the ICC in bringing to justice, at trials that meet international standards of fairness, those accused of committing war crimes. The decision by the ICC prosecutor to open the investigation was applauded by human rights groups and many Sudanese people, and the announcement brought hope for justice and accountability for the victims of killings, massive forced displacement and rape in Darfur. If this is to be meaningful for the people of Darfur, there has to be a commitment on the part of the Sudanese government to fully support the ICC investigation by protecting victims and witnesses and arresting and surrendering persons subject to ICC arrest warrants, none of which the government seem willing to do, and no international mechanism is capable of forcing it to do so.

However, the move to refer Sudan's human rights abuses to the ICC was condemned in the strongest terms by Sudanese National Assembly. The Sudanese authorities asserted that it would interfere with the African Union peace initiative being undertaken by Mu'ammar al-Gaddafi, the Libyan leader. Amnesty International issued a statement indicating that traditional reconciliation methods should complement, as opposed to replace, justice for victims. The statement said that 'Justice should not be seen as an obstacle to peace, but as part of the essential foundation for building a durable peace through individual – not group – responsibility.'

The government of Sudan also suggested that the two resolutions ignored international law because they bypassed regional organizations and were an attempt to undermine the Sudanese judiciary, which they said was capable of trying those accused of war crimes. President Omar al-Bashir described the resolutions as 'negative signals and unfair pressures from the Security Council.' He declared that several measures had been successfully implemented to 'contain the Darfur crisis.' Other officials echoed the president's words about the government's determination to continue the efforts for the realization of a comprehensive peace in the country. Once again there was a glaring gap between the rhetoric of peace and the actions of the government on the ground in Darfur, where reports of sexual violence around IDP camps were still being received while the government was making these pronouncements. This situation continued well into late 2006, prompting the UN Security Council to pass yet another resolution (1705) to sent UN peace keeping troops to Darfur, to which the Sudanese government has bitterly objected.

CONCLUSION

This chapter has described the complex historical background to the Darfur rising: scarcity of resources, the politics of Islamic militancy, and the history of race relations between Africans and Arabs within Darfur. Above all, the wars of Darfur were fanned by the NIF government in its effort to reconfigure political demographics and resource allocation to these demographics. The NIF also perpetrated and intensified genocide in order to fight the opposition armies of the SLA and JEM by proxy. The chapter has introduced the various sides to this devastating conflict, which has caused such unprecedented human suffering in the region and has threatened national unity. Darfur has become the face of the Sudanese crisis of national identity. It began as a periphery versus center politics that has characterized all post-colonial societies, but degenerated into a long drawn-out war in which Sudanese racial ideas combined with Islamic militancy to create a recipe for disintegration. That genocide has taken place in Sudan is unsurprising given the North–South long history of warring relationships: that it should have happened in Darfur, the region that had been the staunchest ally of various Khartoum governments in their wars against the south, was puzzling. I have also chronicled the difficulties faced by the international community in Darfur both in terms of stopping the killing and destruction and in pressuring the parties to talk peace. While the parties have agreed to sit at a negotiating table, none of the peace initiatives – the efforts of Chad, Libyan attempts and now the ongoing talks in Abuja, Nigeria – have resulted in a narrowing of differences. Equally distressing are the reports of continuing violence against civilians within Darfur, in IDP camps and in refugee settlements in Chad, and that the government's own security agents are put in charge of the camp's security, where they perpetrate rapes and other types of violence while the world community continues to debate whether genocide has taken place despite the mounting evidence.

4

ISLAMIC MILITANCY, MEMORY OF
THE CONFLICT AND STATE ILLEGITIMACY

There is little doubt that the North–South wars have left significant wounds that will take years to heal, if they do at all. That they have racially and religiously polarized the country is evident and the possibility of this leading to the secession of the south is no longer a distant prospect. As I mentioned in the Introduction, when General Lazaro Sumbeiywo, the Kenyan chief mediator in the IGAD-sponsored Sudanese peace talks, landed in Malualkon in northern Bahr el-Ghazal to solicit local Sudanese views regarding the ongoing peace process, his meeting with the local community revealed a variety of issues that indicate the near impossibility of reconciliation. He arrived having held meetings with government officials as well as other various sectors of the Sudanese population in the north and held a meeting with the population of the town in which all civil society groups were represented. The county admin-istration, youth leaders, an SPLA commander, traditional chiefs, the spiritual leaders, and a women's representative all spoke one after the other, and all focused on one theme. They all wanted the visiting general to carry a message to the peace negotiations that the people of south Sudan have had enough of this war and the many broken promises of peace, and that the only solution was to sever their relationships with the north. In addition to Chief Makuec, who spoke about the racial boundaries that set northerners and southerners apart, the rest of the representatives spoke on matters relating to how the racial violence has affected the specific sector of the population they represent. But the man who related his speech to the issue of peace at hand was an elderly spiritual leader,[142] a spear master, as anthropologists of religion call the Nilotic priests,[143] who stood up to loud applause and spoke about separation, but for slightly different reasons from the racial issues raised by the others. He emphasized the history of violence between the Arabs and the Dinka and its lasting scars, religious differences between the Dinka and Muslims of the north, and that 'if God had intended us to be one people, the almighty would have been wise enough to tell the Muslims that their faith is a matter between them and their gods ... that he did not identify a single human group to impose its worship system upon the rest.' Historically religious difference has been very much politicized in Sudan, and the old man asked General Sumbeiywo to tell the rest of the mediators about the importance of separating north and south for the good of both. He continued:

> It is too late for unity. That we are different people is evident in the way they have killed our people without remorse for many years ... if you were staying here for more than a few hours, we would have gone to nearby villages to bring to you women, men and children whose limbs were cut off during the raids for slaves, and many others who were maimed in many different ways by [shrapnel] from aerial cluster bombs. How do you expect us to just forget about these things and become brothers and sisters once again with people who do such things? The wounds of their atrocities are everywhere on peoples' bodies and in our hearts and are far too painful to massage away with speeches of forgiveness ... we have done that many times before and we are not repeating it again. It is my opinion, and I speak for my people sitting here and all over the land, to simply cut this country up, the Arabs take their part and we take ours.[144]

His speech strongly attests not only to the fragility of North–South relations and to the pervasiveness of racial perceptions that are used in order to characterize the lines that separate certain groups from one another as part of the natural scheme of things. It talks about the depth of the wounds that this war will leave behind: if a lasting peace is to be found and trust restored, it is necessary to address these in any peace process so as to give the Dinka, Nuer, and Shilluk populations that share borders with the Arabs a sense that security will return to their homelands and that accountability for these crimes will be established and justice restored. However, there is reason to doubt that such programs will come to pass, given that a commitment to a human rights culture has not been laid down during the peace processes as a foundation upon which such actions could be built.

Sudan is a nation of 175 major ethnic and linguistic groups, plus another 325 smaller groups, and these belong to various religious traditions, making it one of the most ethnically and linguistically diverse countries in Africa. Currently, it is estimated that 30 percent of the south's 8 million people profess Christianity, 5 percent are Muslim and 65 percent followers of various systems of worship indigenous to the region. The north is over 90 percent Muslim, but 2 million of the displaced southerners reside in Khartoum and are mostly Christian.[145] Few countries are so culturally diverse and would oppose a notion of cultural pluralism in social programs such as access to education. This chapter deals with the forces that have hampered a multicultural existence in Sudan. Despite the insistence of many academics of Sudan that religion plays a limited role in Sudan's conflicts, this chapter will show how religion, especially Islamic ideas, have come to form one of the most important causes of discord and violence. The purpose of this chapter is to elucidate what the impact of this debate on the unity of the country has been, especially after 1989 when the current military Islamic extremist regime took power. There is no question that the rise of political Islam threatens the unity of Sudan. Gérard Prunier noted:

> The southern rebels refuse to accept the notion that law in the Sudan should be based on the *shari'a*, the traditional fountain of legal creation in Muslim countries. And the Government in Khartoum keeps repeating – rightly so – that it has never applied *shari'a* to the southern provinces and has no intention of doing so. But in fact this is a very sophistic line of argumentation because

shari'a mentions, *inter alia*, the impossibility for true believers to be ruled by *kuffar* (unbelievers, whether Christians, Animists or anything else), a provision which statutarily prevents a non-Muslim from ever reaching high office. Furthermore, there are now over three million non-Muslims in the north, who must either submit to culturally alien religious laws or move back to the southern part of the country. Thus one sees that the apparently innocuous argument of self-determination – 'people have a right to choose their own laws, so *shari'a* is all right in the north while secular law will apply in the south' – in fact negates the very concept of citizenship, which presupposes equality in the eyes of the law and the right to live anywhere within the national territory regardless of religion, ethnic origin or sex. So one can see that the rejection of *shari'a* is not religious *per se*, non-Muslim southerners have no objection to Islam as a religion and to freedom of worship. And the increasingly diffident western and eastern parts of the country are themselves Muslim.[146]

What the non-Muslims of Sudan have objected to has been their relegation to a lower type of citizenry that is inherent in the idea of an Islamic state. Since 1983, when President Ja'afer Nimeiri promulgated Islamic law as the basis of the legal system in the country, this act was seen by non-Muslims or moderate Muslims as the final straw of the many misguided policies of successive Khartoum governments. The opponents of Nimeiri could no longer contain their anger at something which intrinsically gave them the status of second-class citizenship, and to assert their right of citizenship meant going to war as there was no peaceful debate. This was essentially the beginning of the end for Nimeiri's regime. It became a turning point in the history of the opposition to Nimeiri not only by non-Muslims of the south, but also by a large number of northern Muslims who viewed Nimeiri's new-found Islamic piety as a mere political game. Some found it an offense to Islam that a man like Nimeiri implemented Islamic law. It added to a host of other grievances and together sparked the second round of the North–South civil war in 1983. Religion is widely known to address conscience, and it is not easy to understand why people engage in such brutal violence and various forms of killing that are inspired by religious beliefs, to which they are committed in the name of God. This is more so in the case of politicized Islam. The only aspect of it that is accessible to all and that could be subjected to analysis, is the observable consequences of policies prompted by religion such as those of Nimeiri. As the Muslim Canadian writer Irshad Manji says, the problem with Islam is that unlike Christianity and Judaism, it is not subject to criticism and interpretation by members of the faith. 'Most Muslims treat the Koran as a document to imitate rather than interpret, suffocating our capacity to think for ourselves,' (Manji, 2004: 30). It is beyond the scope of this book to assess why the application of Islamic laws was necessary at this sensitive point in the history of this multi-faith country, but we will consider why some Muslims insist on the application of Islamic laws as the only way for Sudan to pass as a truly Muslim nation, and why others are opposed to the brand of Islam that has emerged in Sudan over the last several decades. The consequences of the application of shari'a for the nation's future are clearly important here.

The proponents of an Islamic state argue that it is incumbent upon Muslims to invoke the teachings of their holy book as the guide to public as well as private life, that a true Islamic country must derive its laws from the Koran, and that there is no separation between state and religion. The opponents suggest that those who are applying Islamic law in Sudan, whether it is Nimeiri in the 1980s or the current government of the NIF, are not genuinely interested in advancing the cause of Islam or improving the lives of Muslims but rather in advancing their political agenda, strengthening the hegemony of a political party, controlling businesses, and silencing opponents in an attempt to imply that the regime and its supporters are more Muslim than the rest. It is this politicized Islam that has most threatened the unity of the Sudanese nation, not only by alienating non-Muslims and driving them toward separation, but also by branding any Muslim opposed to Islamic laws as a bad Muslim: some are even accused of apostasy. Opposition to the application of Islamic laws – and many other policies of the NIF government, for that matter – is quickly twisted by its supporters to suggest that opponents are anti-Islam. The activities of prominent NIF leaders and their followers are most frequently mentioned as evidence of this manipulation of religion for political and economic ends. Those most strongly associated with this radical form of Islam are accused of engaging in dealings that are entirely contrary to the way true Muslims must conduct themselves. For example, the families of prominent and well-connected people such as Hassan al-Turabi[147] have been gradually taking control of major corporations: banks, telecommunication companies, transportation companies, agricultural schemes, and many more. This is taken as evidence of self-enrichment at the expense of the poor, something that runs contrary to the Islamic teachings they profess to follow.

Despite the existence of a large liberal intelligentsia in northern Sudan, which is largely opposed to the application of Islamic law or the rise of a theocratic state, one is hard-pressed to find them speaking unequivocally against shari'a. On the contrary, at least in recent years following the relative success of the peace talks between the government and the SPLA, they have found themselves blaming the SPLA for agreeing to the application of shari'a in the north and the exemption of the south. The SPLA and the southern population have found themselves facing a dilemma: on the one hand, to continue to fight against shari'a even after the government has agreed to confine it to the Muslim north would appear contradictory to southern demands for religious freedom.[148] On the other hand, to say that they are non-Muslim and therefore without the right to prevent Muslims from applying their own laws to themselves, was to withdraw from the commitment of fighting for a secular state, a fight which many Muslims in the marginalized areas have joined.

There have been incidents in northern Sudan's recent past where it would have been opportune to speak out against shari'a, but it has not happened. One shocking event that was expected to give rise to criticism was the execution of Mahmud Muhammad Taha, founder and leader of the Republican Brothers[149] and himself a renowned scholar of Islamic theology, who was sentenced to death on charges of apostasy in 1985 by President Nimeiri for his criticism of the application of shari'a laws (the so-called September laws). Many of the informants for this project say that if the northern Sudanese had truly been opposed to Islamic laws they would have taken advantage of this incident to make their views known, perhaps by means of mass protest. Instead, Taha and four of his followers were executed while 3,000 spectators watched the execution and chanted 'Death to enemy of God.' There were protests against Nimeiri's government which eventually led to his overthrow, but not particularly against shari'a, nor for the execution of Taha. Again, when the current military government took power in 1989 in a coup d'etat staged by the NIF, the speedy implementation of the September laws led to the execution of twenty-eight senior officers of the Sudan Armed Forces, and of businessmen on charges of corruption, money-laundering, and illegal currency trading. All the executions were carried out in the name of shari'a, but it did not escape the Sudanese people that all the practices for which these executions were meted out gradually became the norm which the NIF followers used to conduct business. In response to these events, very little anti-shari'a sentiment is visible in the north, at least not in a way that represented a critical mass. This unclear northern stance regarding the application of Islamic law suggests three things. The first is that none of the Sudanese Muslims, especially the politicians or members of the sectarian political parties led by the Umma and the DUP, want to come out openly against shari'a and risk losing the popular support base they have established by appearing to be anti-Islam. The second is that the few northern Sudanese who may be opposed to shari'a expect the south to fight for them against the shari'a because southerners would be perceived as demanding secularism as their political and religious right, while northern Muslims might appear as religious traitors. In other words, northerners may feel that a non-Muslim can best fight the application of Islamic law without worrying about appearing to oppose his or her own faith, or of being labeled anti-Islamic. Some may even fear the risk of being accused of apostasy and executed like Taha. If the south succeeded in opposing the application of Islamic law, the secret northern opponents would rejoice. The third is that there have been many indications in Sudan's recent history suggesting that the majority of northerners may be more inclined toward an Islamic state than they admit.

Many Muslims interviewed for this book suggested that the socioeconomic conditions in Sudan are not suitable for the application of Islamic law: in essence such law can only be applied in a state similar to Medina, where the prophet Muhammad lived and first recommended the use of these laws; a state where the authorities have first to establish a welfare system to care for the poor. A place like Sudan, where people might steal because of their impoverished circumstances, would not qualify as an Islamic state. According to these respondents, the goal of Islamic law should not be and is not meant to be the punishment of wrongdoing, but rather the reform of society so that there is no need for individuals to go out and commit crimes which force the application of Islamic law. They also say that a multi-religious country such as Sudan must be cautious about privileging certain faiths over others if the country wishes to remain united and maintain a sense of belonging for all its citizens, where they can exercise loyalty to their country. Instead, the Islamist government has made a crucial choice in insisting on developing a theocratic state over the unity of the nation. This decision has led to a religious polarization of the nation between non-Muslims and moderate Muslims on the one hand and the radical Islamists on the other: this in turn has provoked extremism on both sides and led to deadly confrontations. Unfortunately, the victims are usually not the combatants: the civilian populations largely pay the cost of these wars, both literally, in terms of material provisions for the war effort, and in a physical sense. National resources are sidetracked into a religious war that many people do not support, young children who are conscripted by force pay with their blood for a cause they do not understand; and social relations between Africans and Arabs, Muslims and non-Muslims are necessarily strained beyond reconciliation.

Since the start of the current outbreak of the North–South war, a product of the frustration felt by non-Muslims, Khartoum's attacks on villagers everywhere in the south have been documented as viciously aimed at civilians and are executed either directly by the regular army, through aerial bombardment, or by use of militias recruited from the northern tribal groups hostile to southerners and from a few southern groups allied with the north. These tactics have reduced the people in the south to a precarious level of subsistence, without food, clean drinking water, electricity or modern agricultural implements, and the outright denial of their rights to services, including those war-displaced southerners living in towns under the government's own control. This level of deprivation was deliberate and was made possible by well-coordinated attacks on civilian targets, during which property was looted and the people forced to flee their homes. During these raids what was of no use to the raiders was destroyed. For example, water hand-pumps are blown up and cultivated fields set on fire, and civilians have been driven into extreme poverty by these mechanisms over the years. Large southern populations have braved the gauntlet of the military onslaught through what was supposedly an 'enemy' territory to seek refuge in Darfur, Kordofan and as far north as Khartoum. They have sought refuge in SPLA-controlled areas as well as moving south and east to the neighboring countries of Ethiopia, Kenya, Uganda, and Congo. Families that have fled to government-controlled towns have continued to live under constant and deliberate harassment. Once under government control, for example, the cultural aspect of the war was promoted through conversion to Islam, banning their native languages and constantly trying to infuse them with Arab culture. Such activities, which were aimed at undermining the cultural identity of the non-Arab regions such as the south and Nuba mountains, were particularly pursued in government-controlled garrison towns in the south, away from the eyes of foreign journalists or human rights agencies. Journalists or human rights investigators were denied travel permits to Juba, Wau, Malakal and other smaller towns. Even when given, travel is under such strict and constant monitoring of government security agents as to make their work impossible. Certain parts of the towns where the most grave violations take place are usually off limits to foreign observers.[150] Military actions in the rural south were meant to force people into government areas, where they would be rendered vulnerable and less likely to cling to their ideals in the face of such a calamity. This forced regroupment of population has also been a military and political tool and was deliberately exercised to bring them under the close watch of the Islamist government, thus eliminating the possibility of lending their support to the opposition and rendering them so vulnerable as to accept religious conversion. Throughout the 1990s the government set up what it called peace camps in the Nuba mountains and herded most of the civilian population under its control into these camps.

WOMEN, FAMILY, AND STATE VIOLENCE

In addition to the government's security forces destroying harvests and looting livestock, creating massive forcible displacements of populations, government security forces and government-allied troops carried out a pattern of extrajudicial and indiscriminate killings and rape of women and girls throughout 1986 to 2001. Children and women were also carried off to northern towns to function as domestic servants and concubines for the army, and any captured able-bodied men were executed by shooting or by nailing them to the trees with iron spikes. The endeavor to regroup non-Arab populations from the dissenting regions into government-controlled towns was particularly directed at women and children. This was because the young were thought to be impressionable and easily absorbed by force, persuasion or trickery. The logic of forcing the women into government garrison towns was threefold. They became concubines, sex servants or 'wives' whose potential children are raised Arab and Muslim, therefore injecting Arab blood and culture into the southern population. Women were also feared by the army as the 'secret organizers' without whom southern opposition forces would lack the support services necessary for their military success. Finally, women in many

Sudanese communities are regarded as the caregivers: when the men joined the opposition forces they could count on their womenfolk to sustain the society in the men's absence. Many fighters in the south have suggested that they would probably not have joined the revolution if they did not have what they believed were 'strong women to look after things, a woman who would take up both her role and the husband's role.' The government's action suggests that their approach was to destabilize this basic foundation in order to weaken the resistance army. It was often reported by women returning from government-controlled towns or from the north that these were the issues they had always heard the army officers or security agents discussing. These questions were usually raised during interrogation conducted by security agents with women recently abducted during the raids or displaced from the war zones.

After the raiding and burning of villages in the south and the Nuba mountains that have been witnessed in the years of war and which are still going on in Darfur, what followed was ominous. Raping and enslavement of women and children, kidnapping and forcible conversion of children to Islam are common. Human Rights Watch (2001) confirmed these charges in its report on human rights in Sudan. The report described Sudan's government as 'a gross human rights abuser.' Many other international bodies have also protested the situation in Sudan. For example, Christian Aid and International Christian Concern describe in their reports issued in 2001 how in many cases the northern military forces follow a scorched-earth policy.[151] Areas were sealed off by road and air, and government forces were often sent in to 'depopulate' those regions designated hostile. People and livestock were taken or killed and buildings destroyed. Survivors were then forcibly relocated to peace camps, where the young were taken away from their adult guardians and sent to other camps for indoctrination by Islamic fundamentalists.

As gruesome as the killings have been and depopulating as the war has been in the south, it was the experience of those who have survived to tell that is most terrifying. They cannot yet qualify as survivors until the carnage is over, an end that is not currently foreseeable, and many of these 'survivors' may themselves become victims, particularly as such atrocities are being carried out in other regions of the country, as described earlier. In all of these confrontations, whether attacks by government-recruited militias on civilians, the scorched-earth tactics of the regular army, or government-sponsored south-on-south wars, it is their impact on women, children, and the family in general that is testimony to a two-pronged military action. It threatens physical elimination and attempts to reconfigure the cultural identity of a sector of people in order to achieve national unity at the expense of some sectors of the nation's population. Such destruction is unspeakable, but without prospects of the situation letting up, the future of the south as a cultural, political and social entity is even more challenging. It threatens to create a situation where south Sudan has to choose between continuing the fight, in which case the better-equipped northern army might cause total annihilation, or surrender to a position of second-class citizenship and servitude. The peace deal reached in January 2005 holds the promise of a middle ground between these two extremes, but the agreement is only as good as its implementation, and the NIF government is dragging its feet about executing the peace agreement.

Of the situation as it was between the 1990s and 2001, Roger Winter, executive director of the United States Committee for Refugees in Washington, said, 'I would argue that there is a genocide going on.'[152] As much of Sudan's war is religious and non-Muslims are treated as second-class citizens throughout the country, numerous human rights organizations have publicized the Sudan government's lack of respect for individual freedoms and religious liberty. The US-based Freedom House's Center for Religious Freedom condemned the government as 'the only one in the world today engaged in chattel slavery, as documented by the United Nations Special Rapporteur on Sudan and the US State Department.' Freedom House also accused the military forces of repeatedly bombing and burning hospitals, refugee camps, churches and other civilian targets and, by manipulating foreign food aid, the government brought 2.6 million south Sudanese to the brink of starvation in 1998. About 100,000 people died of hunger between February and September of that year alone, most of them women and children. This is because times of severe food deficit are often more detrimental to children, whose resistance to starvation is weaker than that of adults. In south Sudan, it was equally deleterious to women due to limited access to the few resources that existed because such access is influenced by local political and military power, neither of which women have. It is also because in the wartime Sudanese context, women are the ones who have to juggle the preferred and traditional livelihood options of rural people – consisting of a mixture of horticulture and pastoralism bolstered by wild foods, seasonal fishing and trading. These options have become increasingly untenable as more and more families become both destitute and displaced. Combined with the fact that people's survival techniques had become more individualistic and/or household-oriented, their abilities to sustain the community-wide institutions and practices that formerly restrained abusive behavior or emphasized sharing within rural communities had declined dramatically. Extreme food deficit was also more virulent to women because households made destitute in this manner often fled to foreign aid centers, where their congregation made them easy targets for the military activities of the Sudan government. The government disrupted relief activities simply because they gave southern communities a sense of independence from the government and a degree of world recognition for the distinct southern identity.

The situation was particularly grave between 1991 and 2001, when aerial bombing of civilian facilities in Equatoria and Upper Nile regions was a daily cause of agony, when the slave raiding in Bahr el-Ghazal saw a marked increase in traffic, and the government had become convinced of the viability of the military solution to the conflict. Select groups of agencies, however, struggled on to bring these tragedies to the attention of the world community. In this vein, the United States Holocaust Museum began the campaign and insisted that responsibility is not merely to remember the past, but to respond to the genocidal realities of the present. In 1999, for the first time in its history, the Committee on Conscience of the Holocaust Museum issued a genocide warning for a country outside Europe. Citing the terrible human destruction in Sudan, the Committee on Conscience declared that 'organized violence is under way that threatens to become genocide.' Khartoum's conduct of the war on the peoples of south Sudan and the various African peoples of the Nuba mountains provided ample justification for such characterization. In addition to the consistent denial of humanitarian food aid as a means of destroying what it regards as the opposition support base, Khartoum had encouraged its allied militias to raid civilian villages, followed by enslavement of women and children of the targeted areas. The regime had also engaged in widespread and vicious persecution animated by racism and religious intolerance, and had disrupted and destabilized the displaced communities of those southerners who had fled the war zones to other parts of Sudan, especially to Darfur, Kordofan and the capital Khartoum.

INTERNALLY DISPLACED PERSONS AND THE STATE

In the north, outside the conflict zone, where hundreds of thousands of women and children had sought refuge, the demolition of IDPs' spontaneous settlements without compensation and the relocation of the populations involved, often with little or no advance warning, continue to be a major source of disruption. Here the displaced, most of them female-headed households, are at the mercy of the army and security agents. Because the activities that put them in this situation were part of a concerted government effort to render people helpless, they had nowhere to file complaints. Once they are dependent on the government's meager assistance with handouts, the policy of cultural Jihad can proceed unhindered.[153] For example, humanitarian assistance, where available, was distributed in coordination with Islamic relief organizations that required conversion to Islam in exchange for relief goods. Most displaced people objected to such blackmail. Those who accepted such conditional aid did so at the cost of their pride, apparent humiliation and loss of face: those who have objected to this practice have tried their own survival techniques which are exercised under harsh conditions of harassment. The Islamist government, for instance, abhors the fact that most female-headed households rely on low-level income-generating activities such as brewing alcohol to make ends meet instead of the 'food-for-faith' policy that is adopted by Islamic aid agencies. To counter this displaced persons' effort to ensure their economic independence, and because brewing alcohol is illegal according to the Islamic constitution, large numbers of women were sent to jail without due course of the law. Where such legal procedures existed, the women did not have legal defense and the sentencing was often summarily carried out. Those who protested this kind of treatment were labeled fifth columnists and supporters of the opposition: they were either jailed or relocated to desert settlements in the peripheries of Khartoum where there were no services whatsoever and mortality rates were appalling. The harassment of the displaced suggests that even those civilians who had sought refuge in government centers continued to suffer from lack of protection and constant mobility as the government periodically bulldozed housing sites and relocated the IDPs to new sites without consulting them beforehand. Any popular resistance to these removals was ruthlessly suppressed by government security forces. Following demolition, the residents of these shanty towns are either left to fend for themselves or loaded into trucks at gunpoint and moved to a fluctuating series of camps far from the economic heartlands of the capital. Mortality rates at these new settlements are reportedly even more abysmal, especially those of young children, pregnant women, and the elderly. The United States Ambassador to Khartoum, Donald Patterson, explained that this treatment of the IDPs by a government that was supposed to protect them was one of the many reasons why the US government began to single out Sudan as a major human rights abuser. Patterson enumerated the 'factors putting Sudan in such a bad light,' including the military takeover in 1989 and the government's repressive steps to neutralize its opponents (or suspected opponents), in which large numbers of people were detained and denied legal rights. The authorities in Washington were also unhappy about Khartoum's tight control of the political process, denying basic civil rights such as freedom of speech and assembly and fair elections. There was also the question of thousands of southern IDPs living in Khartoum who were 'forcibly moved to the fringes of the city, to areas that lacked the most basic amenities, like potable water' (Patterson, 1999: 136).

A BATTLE OVER IDENTITY

Within the south, some of the important tools of war that have characterized the conflict have included massive killings of civilians, bombing of refugee camps, forced population transfers, separation of families, sexual abuse of women, and herding of population into controlled areas. All of these are employed as low cost counterinsurgency measures, supposedly to guard against rebel attacks, but in reality they are meant to prevent the southern civilian population from giving any support to southern resistance armies. Southern civilian populations are randomly accused of abetting the SPLA and other southern opposition forces, which gives the government a license to use all means of terror to preempt any decisions they might make to support SPLA. These assaults are, for the most part, because the majority of northern Sudanese politicians, especially those that seized power in the 1989 coup d'etat, want Sudan to become an Arab and orthodox Islamic nation.[154]

More subtle and gradual ways of achieving such an identity have been tried since the Mahdiyya,[155] but to no avail. They have succeeded in projecting the Islamic-Arab image outside the country so that Sudan is now known to the world as an Arab country, but have failed within Sudan: most Sudanese do not regard themselves as Arabs, and the only alternative for the government has been the use of more heavy-handed military options to cow them. The religious and racial homogenization policy has failed internally in terms of peoples' self-identification and increased the resistance to the state policy of reconfiguring national identity. This is especially the case in the south, the Nuba mountains and in the Ingessina hills, where people are self-identified as black, African, or simply call themselves by their specific ethnic identification: Dinka, Nuer, Nuba, Acholi, etc. Southern protest at the imposition of Arab identity on the Sudanese people has also spread over the years of the war to the west, east and the far north, where people would rather call themselves either Sudanese or Fur (west), Hadandawa (east), or Nubian (north), etc. (Deng, 1995).

Due to the failure or slowness of the more gradual and peaceful assimilation and due to its drive to reconfigure the multicultural society of Sudan, the government has clearly committed itself to a military solution to Sudan's problems. Currently, despite the country-wide spread of resistance to the notion of Arabism, the south takes the brunt of Khartoum's wrath as it is being blamed for having triggered what the government has called an anti-Arab movement throughout Sudan, and the government has vowed to fight it at any cost.[156] Since 1983 when the war resumed, Khartoum has shown no signs of lessening its brutal conduct of the war on the civilian population despite the international pressure to conform to the laws of war and respect for the rights of non-combatants, and clearly regards the military options chosen as most effective. However, military force does not always achieve its military and political objectives if it is not brutal against those least involved – civilians. For example, when Sudan's war resumed in 1983, it was not long before events unfolded to the disadvantage of government forces. Throughout 1986 and 1987 the regular army suffered a series of defeats at the hands of the growing SPLA, and the government resorted to an unprecedented dismantling of codes of warfare ethics that condemn civilian atrocities and destruction of property.

By early 1988 the SPLA had become a major threat to the government's survival. When Sadiq al-Mahdi's government realized that it might very well lose the war militarily, it resorted to recruitment of militias from various ethnic backgrounds. Many were themselves southern, such as the remnants of the Anyanya II guerrillas in Upper Nile or the Mundari or Toposa ethnic groups in Equatoria whose leaders had disagreed with the SPLA's approach to the liberation struggle. After being roughly treated by the advancing SPLA forces, these groups chose to join the government's camp, and the government immediately trumped up accusations that the SPLA was a Dinka occupation force. The Dinka predominate in the SPLA and Dinka civilians have all characteristically been stigmatized as supporters of the SPLA, so the entire Dinka nation was now regarded by Khartoum as a legitimate military foe. The government started recruiting the militias from Arab groups against the Dinka and the SPLA, alleging that the Arabs needed to protect themselves. The consequences for the civilians were devastating both on the Dinka side and among the groups from whom the militias were recruited. Again, it was more disastrous for women and children, as young men are usually quick to either escape or join the opposition armies to defend themselves. Since then the situation has become a cyclical tragedy. Militias attack Dinka villages, young men are provoked into taking up arms for defense, and the government responds with increased anger, larger armies, more powerful weapons, and therefore total destruction of civilian lives under the pretext that the whole Dinka nation has rebelled against the state.

Another factor central to the genocidal ambitions of the NIF regime since 1998 was oil development in the Nuer areas of south Sudan. This development can only proceed if the regime first creates a sanitized security corridor for the oil companies operating in the various concession areas. This development was a disincentive for Khartoum to talk peace or to follow the laws of war. An assessment commissioned by the government of Canada in 1999 concluded that the security situation had worsened with the beginning of oil exploration, including asset destruction and mass population displacement. This massive displacement of the local population followed the deployment of additional weaponry and forces specifically drafted to protect the oilfields. The tactics of destroying harvests, looting livestock and occupying the area were designed to prevent the return of the displaced population and is all carried out in the name of providing security for foreign oil companies. Amnesty International bluntly chronicled these events in its 2000 report, *Sudan: The Human Price of Oil*. I will return to these events in the next chapter.

POPULATION DISPLACEMENT AND THE THREAT TO UNITY

One of the most strenuous aspects of the war for the rural civilian population was the internal displacement made possible by various military activities of the government. As we saw earlier, when families were displaced, their most common response was to move to humanitarian relief stations. It is therefore important to examine the causes of displacement to assess how people decided where to move once they had come under a military attack, how they reached such a decision and why. Because each factor in civilian displacement has been an effective weapon of genocide, it is also important to explore how the government used each of these weapons to effect a solution to the conflict and to the crises of culture and identity that Sudan was facing as a nation.

The causes for internal displacements were multiple and complex, as were the driving forces behind them. A typology might, among others, include categories such as mass evictions. Displacement may simply be a collateral effect of indiscriminate warfare, but it was direct military action with the clear intent to displace civilians which became the major cause of displacement in south Sudan and the Nuba mountains. As the examples of slave raids in northern Bahr-el-Ghazal and oil-related evictions indicate, the practice was used by all government troops and allied militias, including the deployment of militias engaged in factional warfare within the south. During the many years spent conducting this research I constantly met and interviewed people who said that systematic attempts were underway to evict the indigenous population from the oil-rich western Upper Nile region. There was also the forced regrouping in peace villages undertaken by government forces in the Nuba mountains: once the Nuba were evicted or relocated, Arab peasants were settled on the agricultural land owned by the Nuba. Credible sources also suggest that Toposa and Dedinga of Eastern Equatoria were forcibly held in Torit to be used as a human shield against SPLA attacks. Their circumstances in the town were reportedly horrendous. Military commanders in government garrison towns within the south seemed to assume that the presence of civilians in the towns prevented the SPLA from attacking them out of fear of high civilian casualties. The displaced may have opted to move to these garrison towns to flee military confrontations in the rural areas, only to find themselves trapped in the towns under harsh conditions and without the option to move again as displaced persons would normally do.[157]

MILITARY ACTIONS AND DISPLACEMENT

The causes of the displacement in the conflict in Sudan are typical of the increasing trend to violence that has been directed less between armed groups, and more by armed groups against civilians. The primary cause of the internal displacement in Sudan has been direct armed attack, or threat of armed attack on civilian populations, rather than innocent populations finding themselves in the crossfire of military against military operations. In an environment where civilians are the target of armed attacks, displacement would be significantly reduced if combatants respected the essential elements of international human rights and humanitarian law. This distinction does not exist in the tactics that the Sudan government has adopted in training soldiers or in how the war is conducted. Given that most non-Arabs in all of the conflict zones are suspected of being natural supporters of the opposition forces, civilians are often indiscriminately accused of lending support to all local non-state armies simply by virtue of their residence in a given locale. Such generalized military actions are more about the racial or religious lines that are perceived as dividers between government supporters and opponents than winning war against an armed opponent.

One way deliberate displacement of civilians is made possible is the creation of tribal militias to aid the army. There is an old northern Sudanese adage: 'Kill a slave by using another slave'. Once the government found that some south Sudanese were hostile to the SPLA, it did not waste any time before building anti-Dinka militias to fight the war by proxy. To persuade Arab Sudanese to join militias, the old Sudanese ideas of racial cleavage between the north and the south were deployed. Southerners were characterized as *abid* (slaves) and *kufaar* (infidels) in order to justify fighting the south to the would-be militias. Racial and religious ideas work well in Sudan as a means to entice people into war. Various militia forces are formed on the basis that Arabs and Muslims have to defend their identity and maintain the good name and the territorial integrity of the country. Arab militias are to execute the policy of ethnocide, the southern militias are intended to weaken opposition armies within the south. Southern popular discourse attributes the observation 'If we cannot persuade the southerners to see the importance of becoming Arabs and Muslims, they will just have to leave the country,' to numerous northern politicians.

South Sudanese explain the atrocities meted out against them over the years in terms of this alleged northern reasoning. Many acts of horror have been committed against southerners by armed or security agents since 1955, when the first round of North–South conflict began, and especially during the course of the current war. Whether or not such acts were actually a part of a grand design is no longer the issue: it is deplorable that they continue to take place. Still the worst excesses were to be committed by those militias that were built by using Sudanese cultural divides. Militia forces such as the Fertit 'Army of Peace' based in Wau, or the Baggara Murahileen from Kordofan and Darfur became the norm in government's conduct of war, and these ethnic-based forces were meant to break the back of the Dinka groups in Bahr el-Ghazal. The violence has been gruesome and hundreds of thousands of civilians have died by the guns and spears of the militias, and also of starvation after the militia raids had destroyed property or caused massive population displacement.

During a mission to Sudan, the UN Special Rapporteur for Human Rights received well-documented information, often from first-hand sources, pointing to the perpetration by the army of massive and systematic violations of human rights and international humanitarian law, the principal targets of which were innocent civilians. In the war zones affected by direct fighting, the Sudanese Army, the Popular Defence Force, and all of their allied militias, have repeatedly targeted civilian populations. During the early phases of the war (1984–1988) such activities were intended to deny the opposing side supplies or civilian support: hence the rural subsistence economy and its assets were the primary target for attack. In addition, relief inputs have also become targets. Since 1994 especially, food drops, primary healthcare facilities and relief agency compounds have invited attacks. For example, on February 20, 2002 an aerial attack on a food aid distribution center in western Upper Nile instantly killed forty-seven people and injured hundreds of women who were receiving relief. A UN World Food Program staff member who was in charge of food distribution described the attack: 'The gunship maintained its position right over the WFP compound and started shooting sideways aiming at the huts across the compound. Missiles/rockets were used to blow up hut after hut with large numbers of people inside, followed by machine guns aimed at those running for cover.' Those who were in the huts were either children, sick people, or elderly, the more vulnerable, who were waiting for their mothers or sisters to return with food from WFP distribution.

All these activities have produced widespread displacement, as specific populations have been denied the opportunity or means to feed themselves, and as groups of people have fled areas of conflict seeking refuge elsewhere. Both parties to the conflict have also organized forcible relocations of populations at different times during the war. In the north, outside the conflict zone, the demolition of displaced settlements and the relocation of the populations involved continue to be a major source of disruption.

Whatever the broader political and military objectives of the warring parties, the civil war has been fought on the ground as a resource war. Battles between organized armed groups, with the intention of seizing or holding territory, were only one aspect of the fighting, but the most devastating confrontations have taken place in areas where the government wants to extract resources. Civilians have been systematically targeted in asset-stripping raids since the outset. The government's intention has been not only to seize whatever resources the opposition possesses, but to deny these resources to the opposition side. Civilian populations themselves have often been treated as resources to be controlled. The pattern of this resource war was also expanded throughout the 1990s to include relief supplies, with various government armies and militias adapting their strategies either to secure relief items, or to interdict the delivery of such items to the areas under the control of their opponents. To control relief resources, Khartoum seemed convinced that controlling access to displaced persons will redirect the flow of aid from the international community to locations under its own control and has been very clever in this respect. The distribution of aid resources, especially in Bahr-el-Ghazal and Upper Nile, is a factor in government attempts to control the displaced persons' political action, as well as in the government strategy of depopulating the rural areas where the SPLA receives support. Such 'aid-farming,' – the use of aid by the strong to exploit the subordinate – became commonplace in the government's conduct of war. In government areas there is a complex system of relief committees and structures which present lists of needs to aid agencies in the areas of nutrition, health, education, water and sanitation training. When it was provided, the aid did not reach its intended beneficiaries and was instead diverted among soldiers and other government officials who earned their living in its design and distribution.

The net effect of these activities has been increased and continuous massive population movement. In some cases, individual families as well as large groups of people have moved into more secure areas near their original homes. In other cases, there have been movements of large groups of people out of the war zone alto-gether. For example, the Dinka of Abyei and northern Bahr el-Ghazal have moved to sites in the Transitional Zone,[158] or to Khartoum, while other populations have moved out of Equatoria and across the border to become refugees in Kenya, Uganda, Congo, and the Central African Republic. Such movement out of the south was to the military advantage of the government and it seems that it was regarded as such in Khartoum, and promoted as an effective military tactic.

Naturally, the government's response to allegations of forced evictions has triggered some debate as to whether or not civilians were actually retrieved by force in a systematic manner. Khartoum flatly denied any wrongdoing, and said that people moved on their own account to government areas fleeing 'rebel' abuses and short-age of food in opposition-controlled areas. But even if civilians were 'only' entrapped because the lack of supplies and the danger of being caught between battlelines forced them to regroup, there was clearly a military strategy behind the process. For example, the disruption of subsistence farming, and the cutting off of civilians from emergency supplies, denying them access to international aid, left many women and children with one option: to move to government-controlled areas where they were at the mercy of the army and security agents. The result of this was either to hang on and live through the abuse at the hands of security forces or to embark on dramatic migration, often over great distances, as in Bahr-el-Ghazal in 1988 and 1998, usually back and forth between government-controlled areas and opposition-held territories, despite the dangers involved. Consider the following statement from a displaced man from the Tuic section of Dinka who had tried to live in a government-controlled town of Wau, but found it unbearable and had to move to the SPLA-controlled town of Tambura in western Equatoria:

My cattle were looted twice, both times by the Baggara ... I had nothing left, I could no longer look after my family, and so I slipped away and headed to Wau. I did not even tell my children that I was leaving because I was so ashamed. While in Wau, along with tens of thousands of others, one would receive an occasional meal from this or that organization. But the abuse that accompanied the food, the insults, interrogation by the security agents and all the rest of it were too much to endure. So we may have been filthy poor and black, but did that mean we were no longer human beings [*koc*]? When you think about those things at night, and you see images of abuse meted out against women, they all pierce at your very being more than the hunger, the cold weather at night, and more than the fear of being killed on your way out of the town ... I could not last in that place, I could not go on helplessly watching Arab soldiers take young girls away at night and return them in the morning stripped of their humanity [*deek*], so I left.

AERIAL BOMBARDMENT

As we saw earlier, aerial bombing in various war zones was not merely a military activity against military opponents. It has been a deliberate assault on innocent civilians in the south and Nuba mountains as well as on the international humanitarian relief efforts attempting to aid this terribly stricken population. It was intended to displace civilians and to clear oil development areas. Numerous aid agencies, responding in particular to aerial bombing, have sent complaints to Khartoum, all of which have proved ineffectual in halting or even slowing the regime's campaign of aerial terror. Indeed, since Darfur plunged into conflict, civilian bombings have increased. Until July 2002 reports from the ground in south Sudan and our interviews of the residents indicated that the bombs being used in these terror attacks were getting bigger, more powerful, and made with case-hardened metal (which makes the shrapnel from detonation more deadly). This is Khartoum's oil revenues at work. The high altitude Russian Antonov bombers were being flown for Khartoum by Russian pilots and mark the time when aid organizations reported increased accuracy in the bombing runs. Even with improved accuracy, these attacks were still useless for true military purposes; they were wholly ineffective in attacking opposition forces or materials but more deadly and terrifying to civilians. And it is civilian terror that is the true goal of the attacks. Khartoum wishes to destroy civil society and civilian morale in the dissenting regions as a means of weakening the entire opposition. For the authorities in Khartoum, such destruction is the easiest – if cruelest and most brutal – way of gaining further military control of the regions. With a devastated Darfur, as was the case in the south, Khartoum reasons, there will be nothing left to support military opposition.

SLAVE RAIDING AS WAR TACTIC

Despite refusing to apply the term 'slavery' and referring instead to 'abduction,' a 1998 UN report estimated that 800 women and 1,500 children were abducted in that year, and were transferred to the areas of the Arab Baggara. The abduction was carried out by the Murahileen militia which captured these women and children as war booty. This UN report, although a sign of overdue international recognition of what had been a serious problem, was a mere scratch on the surface of a much more elaborate government plan of genocide, ethnic mixing, or cultural reconfiguration that targeted the south. The government denied involvement or complicity in slavery but it took no action to halt these practices. An earlier study demonstrated that there were really three different phenomena in the slavery/abduction issue. First, there was armed and organized raiding in which the role of the government is not clear, and is likely complex. Field research has unearthed credible information that the government sometimes provided arms, on other occasions the groups of Murahileen went off on their own. Northern tribal groups have been known to organize raids with 'representatives' from other Arab groups; returning with children, women and cattle taken in these raids, all of them frequently holding common celebrations (Jok, 2001; Collins, 1992).

Then there was the state-owned military supply train escorted by the Popular Defense Forces (PDF) which carries government supplies and travels slowly from the north down through the contested territory of Aweil and Wau in Bahr el-Ghazal. It is evident that there is formal recruitment by the government of militia to guard the train from possible SPLA attack. These Murahileen (or Mujahideen, holy warriors) then go out from the train and attack villages suspected of supporting the SPLA on the way from Babanusa to Wau and back. According to eye-witness accounts that we have received over the years, the Murahileen ride on horseback along both sides of the railroad tracks, fanning out within a radius of up to 50 km, and systematically raid villages, torch houses, steal cattle, kill men. Their booty consists not just of goods, but also of women and children. Often, abducted women and children are taken up to the north and remain in the possession of the captors or other persons.

Finally, we have documented over the years the joint punitive raids carried out by the government and the Murahileen, who, under the Popular Defense Act, enjoyed status as state-sponsored militias, the PDF. The raids by the militia continue to be a major source of violation of human rights, as the militias are not subject to any legal measures for their destructive activities. Our interviews and many NGO reports contain lengthy and detailed testimonies of women and children abducted and kept in these circumstances, who regained freedom only by escaping or through ransom. The captors are often referred to as PDF, Murahileen militia, or sometimes even as government soldiers. Doubtless, regular troops also take part in or facilitate the raids. According to certain accounts the perpetrators were wearing uniforms; whereas Murahileen and other militias usually wear plain clothes. Although an auxiliary force, the PDF are directly under the control of the Sudanese authorities, sometimes conducting raids jointly with the regular Sudanese troops. Moreover, the militias are armed by the Sudanese authorities and receive ammunition from the Sudanese Army. Raid preparations follow established patterns, leaving little doubt as to the Murahileen's intentions of capturing women and children for enslavement.

The testimonies of abducted women and children contain descriptions of the ill-treatment and forced work to which they are subjected, usually involving cooking, cultivation, tending animals in the desert, collecting firewood, fetching water from the wells, washing clothes and other domestic chores. Domestic servants report being made to sleep in the kitchen, cattle tenders sleeping in the same space as the cattle, and various other forms of abuse such as being addressed with demeaning terms like *Abd*, 'slave.' Women and girls' testimonies cite rape, forced 'marriage' and other sexual abuses amounting, in certain cases, to sexual slavery. Many of those who were freed were either pregnant or gave birth to children fathered by their captors. In some cases, women were freed and instructed to return to the south but leaving the children behind with the Arab men who fathered them. Consider the following remarks by a Dinka woman who had been enslaved for years:

> The man in whose house I had worked for a few months following my abduction was nice at first, but when he decided one day to force himself onto me he would not stop any more and there was nothing I could do as he told me that he would tell his other friends to rape me if I did not comply with his demands. He demanded that I become his wife, but he had no courage to tell his real wife and did not want his neighbors to know about it. His wife still found out and she became furious but aimed her anger at me instead. She would not stop yelling all kinds of insults at me and threatened to kill me, at which point the husband decided to let me go because it was going to bring disgrace to him. At this time I was already two months pregnant. I moved to a displaced persons camp in el-Daein where I met up with other Dinka people from my home area. I remained there for nearly five years ... Although my child is an Arab child, I consider him my compensation. I am blessed that my child was not taken away like all the other women who were forced to have children with Arab men and were forced again to leave the children behind.

CONCLUSION

This chapter examined the language with which the war is described in the south. It described the testimonies of men, women and children about their own experiences with the various instruments that the Khartoum government has employed in its war against the SPLA. There were aerial bombings of civilian villages, the indiscriminate targeting of whole populations that were stigmatized as anti-government, oil-related massacres, slave raiding as a counterinsurgency tactic, the miserable life in IDP camps in government-held towns in the north and south, the fanning by the government of inter-factional wars within the south as a way to weaken the southern opposition block, and rape and sexual slavery as tools for humiliation of not just the women but their communities as well. The language used to describe the memory of the conflict emphasized the racial divides that pervade the Sudanese society, the religious ideas that view non-Muslim women as trophies for Muslim soldiers who want to assert their masculinity, and the North–South national divides in which the north is depicted as a colonial power over the south and in which southerners speak of their struggle as a nationalist opposition to colonial-style domination by the north. Throughout the war, there were voices within the south that saw these dichotomies of North–South, Muslim/non-Muslim, and Arab-African as realities of the situation in Sudan, but as things that could be righted with correct national policies that emphasize equal citizenship and opportunities. As for the majority of southerners, there is no mistaking their desire to be independent of the north as the only solution to the crisis of the state.

5

A DEADLY COMBINATION
Militant Islam and Oil Production

From 1998 to the present, Sudan has dominated news headlines for various reasons, most of which have been bad news. First among these issues has been the rise of militant Islam and Sudan's support of international terrorism, the role of oil production in government atrocities that have reached genocidal levels in western upper Nile, the wars between the government and regional rebel movements, and the consequential humanitarian disasters as the more recent case of Darfur has shown. These are all interrelated issues and have spurred human rights groups to step up their scrutiny of Sudan's human rights record. They have also led to the formation of constituencies around the world that are concerned about the use of oil revenues for the benefit of some and the destruction of other sections of the Sudanese population. Most prominent among these constituencies were the European Coalition on Oil in Sudan (ECOS), an alliance of Canadian Evangelical churches, the American Anti-Slavery Group, and a host of other small groups which have constantly staged protests against the oil companies involved in Sudan. Demonstrations, for example, were made in front of Talisman Energy Inc.'s offices every year during Talisman's annual shareholders meeting in Calgary, Alberta in Canada, where Talisman is headquartered. Others were held at Sudan's Mission to the UN in New York. There also were human rights research groups and think tanks in Europe, South Africa and the US that were equally outraged by the human rights abuses associated with oil production in Sudan. Among them were Human Rights Watch, Amnesty International, the International Crisis Group, Justice Africa, and the Institute for Security Studies, all of whom wrote extensive exposés of the role of oil production in human destruction.

What was it about oil activities in Sudan that angered so many people? Disturbing reports of human rights abuses, including the destruction of villages to make way for oil explorations, the use of oil revenues by the government of Sudan to fight the war with impunity, the development of various ways to fight these wars, including the use of militant Islamic discourse to attract large numbers of radical recruits into militias and the PDF, and the intransigence of the government regarding peace negotiations. These groups campaigned for the governments of the countries of origin of foreign oil companies to rein in these corporations who should either suspend oil production until such time when peace and security had been achieved, or guarantee that their infrastructure did not facilitate the government's war effort. Refusing to deal with the human rights abuses brought on by their presence, the oil companies became the target of criticism by these coalitions, who began to demand that people in North America and Europe divest and disinvest from these oil companies. American activist groups demanded that the US government impose sanctions on these companies and de-list them from the American stock market. They became as disappointed as they were outraged when a Chinese oil company, a holder of a 40 percent stake in the Sudanese oil business, was listed on the New Stock Exchange with an Initial Public Offering (IPO) of US $5 billion, and underwritten by the market giant, Goldman Sachs. Although the IPO was eventually reduced to US $2 billion because of the campaigns against the company, it was listed nonetheless. For the first time in the US since apartheid South Africa, these demands started a debate about the use of financial markets to achieve political goals. The US Congress drafted a resolution for debate on this question, but the outcome was unsatisfactory for the Sudan constituency. Congress resolved not to 'mix business with politics,' but that it would press ahead to force the government of Sudan to have regard for human rights and to agree to good faith peace negotiations. Congress also vowed to pressure the mother countries of the oil companies to rein in these organizations so that they would cease abetting human rights violations enacted by the government of Sudan in the name of securing the safety of oil workers and their property. (US oil corporations were not active in Sudan because of the long-standing US-sponsored UN sanctions that were imposed on Sudan in 1995 due to human rights violations and Sudan's sponsorship of international terrorism.[159])

Sudan's oil industry is a network of state and business that focuses on promoting the north. It is localized in the capital, Khartoum, and is not a national economy that connects all parts of the country, a development James Ferguson aptly described as the ability of the state to legitimate itself by controlling resources simply because it controls the capital city (Ferguson, 2006).[160] Having lost vast territory of the country to opposition forces, the Sudanese state is free of the obligation to care for its citizens. The result has been a deal between Khartoum and foreign oil firms to finance the state in order to remove the insurgency along with the indigenous population thought to aid the insurgents. Control over the capital has given the state international recognition to sign contracts and sell resources for its own benefit to the exclusion of the bulk of the population. By utilizing the economic predations of the resource-extracting foreign companies owned by other nation states, the Sudanese state has escaped taking responsibility for the people beyond its control, concentrating the nation's resources in the hands of its narrow support base in the capital city and other northern towns.

This chapter will chronicle the aggressive insistence of the government in pushing ahead with oil production amid protests. It will also address the ruthless measures the al-Bashir government took against the civilians in the oil region of western Upper Nile in the wake of oil production. Some of these measures involved the use of high altitude bombers, helicopter gunships, and calls for

Jihad to entice the radical Muslim youth into the PDF for the alleged protection of national resources and to displace the inhabitants of the oil areas to clear the region of any threats that the local population may pose to oil facilities and foreign oil workers.

OIL DEVELOPMENT AND THE CONDUCT OF WAR

Sudan's war, like all of Africa's resource wars, has been by no means a purely local affair. After oil exploration and production had been halted by the war for so many years, and foreign oil companies, especially US-based Chevron, pulled out when the war escalated, Sudan resumed the development of southern oil resources and started exporting them in 1998. Soon after the oil began to flow government forces and allied militias were able to obtain weapons from China, Iran, Russia, former Soviet republics and Bulgaria in exchange for loans to be paid by future oil exports. This oil development was made possible by the Greater Nile Petroleum Operating Company (GNOC), a consortium of Talisman Energy Inc., China National Petroleum Corporation, and Malaysian Petronas. The human rights abuses associated with oil production led to these companies and their countries of origin being subject to considerable criticism for their complicity if not outright abetting of government atrocities. Talisman was forced to sell its 25 percent stake in the GNOC to an Indian company and left the operation in 2002, but by the time they left, Talisman had helped the consortium to generate and turn over to the government approximately US $500 million a year. Following in the footsteps of Nimeiri's designs for the exploitation of southern oil resources, al-Bashir's government decided to pipe the oil to a refinery in Port Sudan, passing through a number of other refinery facilities within the northern territory along the way. To expand oil exploration and to build the pipeline from western Upper Nile to Port Sudan, the Sudanese regime, taking advantage of its new-found wealth and military equipment, immediately began to wage war against the civilian population inhabiting the oil region with a view to eliminating any threats these people might pose to the pipeline. This oil-related destruction was decried locally and internationally for its genocidal nature. It has since occasioned a 'genocide warning' from human rights groups and civil society organizations, including the United States Holocaust Memorial Museum and humanitarian agencies working in the affected regions of western Upper Nile and eastern Bahr el-Ghazal.

Oil revenues are probably larger and expected to grow bigger than any other resource the country has ever seen. It is expected that more oil will be found along the Nile all the way south to Juba, and for a country of an impoverished majority of population oil is being looked on as a blessing, but independent and foreign government-sponsored reports on the role of oil in destruction and genocide have all proved unequivocally that oil revenues have brought more evil than good to Sudan.[161] Before the ceasefire agreements were signed between the SPLA and the government of Sudan in July 2002, military helicopter gunships and Antonov bombers had reportedly used oil company airstrips on their way to bombing raids in south Sudan. These facts were documented by Christian Aid in a report published in May 2001 and detailed how foreign oil companies were subsidizing the war machine of the Sudanese regime. In October 2001, another independent investigative team commissioned by Canadian NGOs published a report in which the government of Sudan and its part partners were indicted for serious human rights violations in the oil region (Ryle and Gagnon, 2003). The report

> documents a range of abuses connected with forced displacement of the inhabitants of the area. Defecting soldiers from the government of Sudan's military base at Heglig testified that they had been ordered to force the inhabitants out of the area. The soldiers said they had been instructed to kill civilians and any persons believed not to be loyal to the government. This, they stated, was for the purpose of securing the oil fields for development.[162]

The report concluded that nowhere else in the world is corporate complicity in human suffering and destruction as direct and as consequential as in Sudan today.

Judging by their revamped military activities, it is clear that Khartoum has used oil proceeds to acquire a great deal of additional military hardware. In its November 2000 report, the International Monetary Fund revealed that Khartoum's military expenditures had doubled since oil revenues began to come on line. Helicopter gunships in particular were deployed with considerable effectiveness in fighting, especially in targeting civilians for displacement, a military tactic the government had been using since the war began. Destruction of civilian lives and livelihoods and displacement was often portrayed by the state as collateral damage, an inevitable consequence of such a war, but there has been abundance of evidence that such destruction was a deliberate action with military goals in mind. For example, helicopters are vulnerable to ground-fire, and were hard to use in a conventional combat against the opposition armies; and despite the flat, open terrain of southern Sudan – ideal for air-to-ground combat – the government has yet to demonstrate the significance of its arsenal in terms of military success against its armed opponents. In fact, they deliberately avoided using these helicopters in direct engagement with the SPLA. All that they were able to achieve with these deadly air force assets was civilian destruction, which local people have argued was intended for military ends. 'If they chase away the civilian population, then the rebel forces would have to go with the population as well,' explained one local resident who had observed the pattern since the war began. Civilian displacement, however, could easily have been effected by infantry and militias, but the terrifying image and the speed of the helicopters prove more effective in gaining ground in the shortest amount of time possible. When deployed in actual military engagement with the opposition forces, for example when they were deployed in the east, it was not clear how the government assessed the cost–benefit of their deployment of the new weapons, as they were often shot down. But they have clearly succeeded in more than one way. The new weapons were most effective in destroying civilian life and terrorizing the people, which in itself had military consequences to the advantage of the government. They also boosted the morale of the government forces, and probably functioned as a scare tactic against the rebel armies.

Since the government started receiving petrodollars, the army has been equipped with around 350 battle tanks and 25 light tanks, as well as various reconnaissance vehicles, troop carriers and self-propelled artillery. The air force, with around 3,000 personnel, has 44 combat planes and 28 attack helicopters, although it is unknown how many of these are airworthy. Military equipment comes from a wide variety of suppliers, and is generally in poor condition. Oil revenues promise to improve the situation and emphasis has initially been placed upon boosting stocks of battlefield armor, long-range artillery and attack helicopters, mainly from Russia.

Khartoum was reported in 2002 to have taken delivery of the last of ten MiG-29SE fighter aircraft and two MiG-29UB trainers. Although the government claimed that these were to defend against external threats, Human Rights Watch and Amnesty International have identified MiG aircraft as being involved in attacks on civilians when the Darfur crisis began in 2003, as well as the ubiquitous Antonovs, known for their terror in the south for many years. The US, by means of its terrorism-related sanctions on Sudan, has interdicted any delivery of weapons to the Islamist government, not just due to accusations of atrocities against its own citizens, but also because of sponsorship of international terrorists. Officials at the US State Department have threatened the source countries that deliveries of military hardware to countries that sponsor international terrorism will be punished with sanctions, in line with US law. Despite this the Russian Foreign Ministry has taken every opportunity to justify its country's arms trade with Sudan, saying that the business did not breach any of its existing international commitments. The Sudanese regime was reported to have expressed satisfaction with Russia for filling the arms order without delay, and said the aircraft were bought to prevent Sudan from being 'an easy target' for other nations. An official in the Sudanese embassy in Moscow declared, 'We need these jets to safeguard our economic interests.' It is noteworthy that the Sudan government exaggerates the existence of external threats as a pretext to arm itself against its internal opponents. Sudan's potential external threats appear based on the fact that it had always had a low-key stand-off with its neighbors, usually just Egypt and Ethiopia, but in recent years with Uganda and Eritrea, both of which have openly supported Sudanese opposition forces, but none of these stand-offs have ever escalated so much as to warrant the purchase of such a large arsenal. It was clear that internal threats were more pressing than external ones, and these could not be fought with such heavy weaponry without destroying civilian life.

A policy paper issued by the Center for Strategic and International Studies in Washington, DC in March 2001 also highlighted the connection between oil development and human displacement. Participants on the team that authored the document included government officials, regional experts including representatives of relief and development groups, academic authorities, former senior policy-makers, experts on religious rights, human rights advocates, and officials of the UN.[163] Though controversial in many respects, the document spoke authoritatively in assessing the realities of oil development in south Sudan, an issue which it highlighted repeatedly. The CSIS report declared forcefully: 'Sudan's exploitation of oil assets has created forced mass displacements and other gross human rights abuses. If war persists, future exploitation of other promising energy fields in populated areas of the south will almost certainly involve more forced displacement and abuses.'[164] In reaching this conclusion, the CSIS report had, of course, echoed the extensive and detailed findings on this topic that had previously come from Amnesty International, the UN's Special Rapporteurs (Leonardo Franco and Gâspâr Bíro), Human Rights Watch, the Harker Report commissioned by the Canadian Foreign Ministry to verify activists' claims about the damaging role of oil production for human security, and numerous other credible sources.[165]

The Sudanese regime, like that of many countries whose regimes have lost their legitimacy in the eyes of their citizens due to their failure to provide basic services, enjoys a monopoly of legitimate use of force, and has therefore never been forcefully confronted by the international community as a whole. Competing national interests between countries interested in Sudan have barred a concerted effort to force the regime to cease destroying lives in order to get oil and to share oil proceeds equitably with producing regions. Lack of forceful pressure has caused the government to act with impunity toward the civilian population who were suspected of being a security threat to oil production. Having received huge petrodollars from oil concessions in south Sudan, Khartoum has the economic power to buy protection in the form of commercial contracts, many with European countries that refuse to criticize the regime's worst offenses against its own citizens.

To put a human face to some of these reports, we conducted interviews in the summer of 2001 with Nuer families who had witnessed the attacks and had fled from western Upper Nile into Dinka villages in eastern Bahr el-Ghazal. The picture that emerged was a grim one. The displaced Nuer reported that government troops on the ground drove people out of their homes by committing gross human rights violations; male villagers were killed in mass executions; women and children were sometimes thrown into burning huts. We met a few Nuer who were from villages north and south of Bentiu such as Guk and Rik, who said that soldiers slit the throats of children and killed male prisoners after tortuous interrogations. Some of them had nails hammered into their foreheads. The displaced told us that there had been a massacre in a village called Panyejier in July 2001, where people had been shot at, houses burned, and people crushed by tanks.

> And that was when we had to flee in disarray ... with some of us ending up here alone without knowledge about one's family and not knowing what to do next [said one man]. I constantly think of going back to look for my family, but where do I begin since our village is no longer there.

A direct link between the nature of the war and guarantees for security for oil exploration by foreign oil companies has been obvious since the intensification of warfare at the beginning of 1999.[166] The interviews have revealed a pattern of gross human rights violations in the areas in which foreign oil companies had rights for exploitation, both those who were actively operating with staff and those that had withdrawn, leaving assets and retaining their rights to oil production. Over the years following the initial flow of the oil, numerous reports of massive forcible displacements of populations have appeared, testimonies about government security forces and government-allied troops raiding the villages, carrying out aerial bombardments and strafing villages from helicopter gunships. There is also plenty of documentary evidence indicating a pattern of extrajudicial and indiscriminate killings, with torture and rape committed against unarmed civilians who were not taking active part in the hostilities. More armed conflict in some districts of western Upper Nile that followed the coming of oil into the pipeline has displaced almost 75 percent of the population from the villages in the immediate vicinity of oil operations, or close to the pipeline. An astonishing 95 percent of the population of these villages has, for the same reason, also reported cattle losses – the main source of trade and livelihood in the region. Moreover, during our trips in eastern Bahr el-Ghazal and interviews with displaced Nuer, we found that those districts most affected by oil-related displacement have never received UN or other general food rations and that despite the presence of a large number of aid agencies ready to help, there had been virtually no NGO presence since June 1998. This was because the humanitarian work carried out by Operation Lifeline Sudan (OLS) was commandeered by the government and its delivery of aid was dictated by Khartoum. Western Upper Nile, due to the military activity that targets civilians, was declared a no-go zone for aid agencies, including the UN.

The Khartoum regime execute the war in a savage fashion and the government received all of Sudan's portion of revenues from the southern resources. Unencumbered by any mechanism for equitable distribution, neither the local communities nor south Sudan at large received any benefits by way of services as had been promised. Oil companies such as Talisman reported having built schools and health centers for the local population, but reports from the displaced persons and human rights groups indicate that where such facilities were actually built, they were serving the Arab communities that had come to resettle in areas where the Nuer had been displaced. In Bentiu for example, the southerners who have taken refuge there live in camps on the outskirts of town, far from the facilities the companies claimed to have established for them: only the new population of northerners who occupied the center of town were taking advantage of these services.

The effect of oil production on the local communities has been negative in the extreme: it has emboldened Khartoum militarily; indeed, apart from the arms purchases discussed above, by 2000 the regime had begun to boast openly of its military ambitions as more oil revenues were projected to flow in; it was beginning to manufacture weapons, including the capacity to assemble tanks in its factory at Shendy, north of Khartoum. As a result, the revenues became a powerful disincentive for Khartoum's junta to negotiate a just peace to end the civil war. Instead, the government came to believe that it could achieve a military 'final solution' to the war, in the face of a silent and seemingly complicit world community, partly because of business interests and partly due to the geopolitics of the war on terrorism. It had become a perfect war for Khartoum: it was confined to distant peripheries and therefore far removed from the view of the northern population, reducing the risk of being a negative point against the government. Revenues from southern resources were being used against the southern population, and the government was growing stronger rather than weaker. Furthermore, as the government stigmatizes the region's population it feels no responsibility toward them, and the resources the state could have spent on caring for the population in that region were now diverted to the war effort or to the benefit of the ruling elite and high-ranking military officers. The international community was roughly split between the countries committed to their business interests that blinded them to the suffering of the Sudanese, and those trying to put morality before money. There was, therefore, no serious pressure on Khartoum or an immediate need to seek a peaceful settlement. Countries such as China, Malaysia, Sweden, Britain, France and Canada, all of which had their oil companies directly or indirectly involved in Sudan, argued that pulling out of Sudan and stopping oil production was not the solution. Instead, they argued that 'constructive engagement' was the better approach. The US, on the other hand, although its approach contained contradictions, and despite its history in Sudanese oil, pushed more vigorously for a 'peace first, and oil production later' policy, perhaps because Washington anticipates a future share in the Sudanese oil industry, but in a more peaceful Sudan.[167] For many years condemnation of the situation in Sudan was verbal, and the people of Sudan were sacrificed for energy and other strategic interests. The biggest partners in the Sudan oil business, China and Malaysia, have scant regard for the human rights of their own citizens:[168] clearly if they cannot be held accountable for the abuse of their own people, it is unlikely that they would give up their appetite for oil in regard for the lives of poor and distant Africans. This question is made particularly pertinent by the veto power in China's hands, which Beijing seems happy to apply against any international action involving Sudan's oil industry, and by the fact that the US has compromised much of its leverage against China due to business interests.

In the face of such international corporate complicity, and given the clear genocide warning from the Committee on Conscience of the United States Holocaust Memorial Museum, human rights groups and activist coalitions called for sanctions against these companies until Sudan was freed from the threat posed by oil development. Such calls fell on deaf ears, except for the US House of Representatives, which passed a Sudan Peace Act in 2001. The act called, among other things, for delisting foreign oil companies from the US stock markets; the act was awaiting a scheduled US Congress hearing on the day of the September 11 attacks on New York's World Trade Center and the Pentagon. This gave Sudan the chance it had been waiting for to endear itself to the US again, and Khartoum immediately condemned these attacks: Washington used this expression as a means to get Khartoum to sign on to the war on terror. In effect, President Bush secretly killed the Sudan Peace Act under the shadow of the war against terrorism, a war in which the government of Sudan began to be regarded as a worthy ally of the US despite many years of hostility over Sudan's role in harboring terrorists and exporting terrorism.[169]

MILITARY ACTIVITIES IN OIL REGIONS

From 1999 to April 2002, the military situation in the oil regions of southern Sudan escalated into deliberate and disastrous destruction. This had devastating consequences for the civilian population, both immediately and in the long term. Oil was clearly implicated in exacerbating the conflict in Sudan, and was now the most significant obstacle to successful peace negotiations. The government of Sudan, gaining in military and diplomatic confidence with its success in bringing foreign national oil companies into the south, remained the obdurate party in the peace process. In addition to the highly significant action by the SPLA against oil infrastructure in western Upper Nile, all reports indicated that a major escalation of fighting was impending. For example, on January 27, 2001, it was reported that the SPLA had attacked the pipeline and made a big hole in it that would take several days to repair before the flow oil could resume.[170] From eastern Bahr el-Ghazal, through the various concession areas of western Upper Nile and across to the Adar Yel concession area in eastern Upper Nile, significant oil-related conflict was imminent and had begun in several places.[171]

What distinguished the fighting during that particular dry season was the intensity of the strategic focus on oil. The government of Sudan was bent on maintaining and extending its security grip on the oil installations and concession areas. The opposition forces – mainly the SPLA but also various local Nuer militia forces – attempted to move to within artillery range of the oil installations of the GNOC (the Unity and Heglig fields), as well as the new drilling sites by Talisman Energy in Concession Block 4 – see Map 1, of the concession areas of south Sudan. In January the

SPLA seized and set on fire three oil wells, destroying the military camps protecting the wells and also destroying an oil drilling rig, thus exerting military pressure on the installations of Talisman Energy and its GNOC partners. Direct attacks on Heglig and Unity were evidence of the distinct possibility of the SPLA's ability to disrupt oil production. It had demonstrated its ability to attack oil facilities north of the Bahr el-Ghazal River, something the government had assured its oil business partners would not happen. This is what proved unequivocally that the oil companies, especially Talisman Energy, had become partners with the government in the war. There was a clear correlation between SPLA attacks on oil installations and the use of Talisman's airfields in the region by the government to stage air raids on southern villages. Every time there had been an attack by the SPLA or by one of the Nuer militia forces, Sudan's forces arrived and attacked civilian villages in the area, so quickly that it was clear they could have only taken off from Talisman's airstrips in the area. Further attacks on the oil pipeline as it approached Port Sudan in the northeast were also a distinct possibility, as the National Democratic Alliance (NDA) forces remained strong in the Kassala region. As confrontations between the government and the opposition armies increased, the government made greater use of oil installations to increase its military efficiency: by allowing themselves to be so clearly drawn into the war the oil companies became partners with the state in human destruction.

As Eric Reeves has observed, the government of Sudan now began several attempts to consolidate its control over Concession Blocks 1, also known as 'Unity,' 2 or 'Heglig,' and 5a, the site of exploration activities by Lundin Oil of Sweden.[172] Such consolidation took the form of removing pro-government Nuer militias and replacing them with the government's regular troops. (The Nuer are the dominant ethnic group in the oil regions.) After the split in the SPLA in 1991, several militias formed in the Upper Nile region. Some were pro-SPLA, others more independent and some were formed and supported by the government as a way to weaken the SPLA. These latter group of militias continued to be armed and supplied by the government of Sudan and were pushed to the periphery of the areas where fighting was most active, in effect creating enmity between the local population groups. More and more Nuer militias in the midst of oil-related devastation grew dependent upon the government of Sudan for logistical support, including food, ammunition, and weapons. In this way, government was able to blame the devastation on what it called 'old tribal warfare between the local tribes,' thus deflecting attention away from itself. This was the defense adopted by Talisman Energy when a class action suit was brought against it for its role in genocide, claiming that the dispute was the work of tribal militias rather than a Talisman-funded government army. In a surprising turn of events, when the alien torts case was allowed to proceed in New York, Talisman hired an English cartographer to produce maps of Upper Nile showing that the areas the legal case had claimed to have been razed to the ground by government troops in an effort to secure Talisman's oil operations had in fact been uninhabited.

This line of argument – that the war-affected southern populations had done more damage to themselves than the atrocities committed by outsiders – has been used time and again in various contexts. Many southerners acknowledge the destruction effected by ethnic militias since the war started. Some of the southern militias were a spontaneous outgrowth of the crumbling political landscape that characterized the period following the split of the SPLA, others were government-sponsored counterinsurgency militias that Khartoum had been recruiting from tribes hostile to the SPLA. Consider the following statement by Chief Ariik of the Lou section of Dinka:

> When we used to fight against the Nuer over cattle or for control of the grazing areas, the actual confrontations were few and far apart, and there were never more than three or four casualties any given dry season. Sometimes years pass without any fighting taking place ... When a man ran away from you, you never chased him for too long, you turned around and let him go ... we never killed the women and children. Our educated children used to call us unciv-ilized for continuing to fight like that. But when these educated

children went to Ethiopia to be trained in the use of guns, we were elated; we thought we were finally going to get weapons to protect our nation from the Arabs, and what we got was Nuer shooting at Dinka, killing each others' women and children and burning villages ... who is more uncivilized now? They will finish one another and their land and resources will now go to their enemy.

In the same vein, the SPLA was considered a Dinka army by some smaller ethnic groups, and the government was able to capitalize on this. At the beginning of the war, Nimeiri used it to recruit tribal militias to fight the SPLA in the name of self-defense. This resulted in increased south-on-south violence, and the government used this to blame all the destruction on southerners themselves, even its own direct military atrocities. More importantly, the government used the south-on-south violence to argue that not all southerners were opposed to the government. A Fertit militia leader in Wau, General Tom Al-Nuer, once said: 'To have a Dinka-dominated SPLA take over the south is worse than Arab control of the whole country, and we the non-Dinka groups around Wau will fight to prevent Dinka domination in Wau.' The Fertit militias went on to become an arm of the government against the Dinka supporters or suspected supporters of the SPLA. Indeed, the government called these allied Fertit militias the Qu'at al-Salam, 'Army of Peace,' and violent conflicts became characteristic of life in Wau from the start of the war in 1983 until the signing of the peace agreement in January 2005. There were similar forces in other regions of the south, including the Mundari militia armed by Nimeiri's government and deployed under the command of Makelele, Anyanya II armed under Abdalla Chuol in Upper Nile, and various Arab militias created and deployed along Dinka Malwal-Baggara border areas known as zones of contact or 'transitional zones.' All of them, whether created by one government such as Nimeiri's and then revamped by the successive governments of Sadiq al-Mahdi and al-Bashir, had the single goal of fighting the war on the cheap: the two most effective ways of using the militias were to thwart the SPLA's ability to create a sense of southern national unity and to disrupt civilian life.

Mention of south-on-south violence, whether by human rights groups, the government of Sudan, or oil companies, was not made in the interest of a balanced reporting of atrocities but as a way to show the southerners in a bad light as people without a cause, and to claim that they are responsible for their own demise. Ethnic wars within the south have now become the single most widely used claim against southern secession and to challenge the viability of the south as an independent state. The oil companies could avert the blame for complicity by pointing to the militias as responsible for all that suffering in the south, implying that it is something southerners themselves need to sort out before pointing a finger at others for the destruction of their country. The government of Sudan has found it the easiest way to impose its will on the southern population under the pretext that they need outside force to prevent them from decimating each other. Human Rights Watch, for example, attempting to report in an even-handed manner, documents a government atrocity with the qualifying phrase 'the rebels are also committing human rights violations,' without specifically explaining what those violations were.

As for the government of Sudan's immediate oil protection policy, its largest strategic goal was to divide areas of SPLA control from one another, and ultimately from their logistical lines to the southern border with Uganda and Kenya. Its locally recruited militias or semi-independent groups that receive logistical aid from Khartoum, like the predominantly Nuer south Sudan Defense Forces (SSDF), and Equatoria Defense Force (EDF), were instrumental in this endeavor. This is why in the dry season from November 2000 to April 2001 the government mounted a major offensive, moving eastward from the garrison towns of Wau and Aweil in Bahr el-Ghazal, and south from Abyei. This put them in a position to seal off the western boundary to Talisman Energy's Concession Block 4, a site where drilling and exploration activities had just begun. The SPLA was, in turn, watching for vulnerabilities in these garrison towns, as they did in the previous dry season when they captured the garrison town of Gogrial, which in 2001 became the early target of the government offensive. It seemed unlikely that the government of Sudan would have an easy time dividing SPLA forces, but the new arms the government had purchased proved far more significant than the SPLA had acknowledged. The government retook Gogrial in 2002.

During this period, there were also a great many aerial bombing assaults by the government of Sudan on the areas along the Southwestern Concession Block 4 boundary, for example in the Twic Dinka villages of Panlit and Turelai in eastern Bahr el-Ghazal. There was also government-supported Arab militia action against civilians further west, including an assault on the medical facility of the International Committee of the Red Cross at Chelkou and on the International Rescue Committee compound at Marialbai, both in March 2000 and carried out by the government-backed Popular Defense Forces (PDF). They were preceded a few days earlier by aerial bombing of Marialbai, an air raid that took place a day after Susan Rice, the US Assistant Secretary of State for Africa, had paid a visit to the village to hear directly from the people about slavery-related crimes that had been frequently reported in the US news media. The local authorities in the south, hoping that this incident would trigger US support for them or a strike against Khartoum, claimed that the raid had been timed to coincide with Rice's visit as demonstration of Sudan's defiance of President Clinton's government. Susan Rice saw the incident as evidence of the brutal nature of Sudan's government, and she called on it to desist from these kinds of actions, but the broader government bombing campaign against civilian and humanitarian targets throughout the south continued unabated for the rest of the year. Indeed, if anything, they became more intensified as the government became ever more determined to increase oil production.

As part of a multifaceted campaign, the government-backed PDF had been and remained an active presence around Panthou, Nyamlell and Akuem of Aweil South, Aweil West, and Aweil East counties respectively, with the express purpose of denying the SPLA the possibility of sending troops stationed in Bahr el-Ghazal to Upper Nile. These were the areas that had been most affected by the slave raiding, another war tactic described earlier. Their activities in these areas were connected with movements of government military trains in northern Bahr el-Ghazal. It also signaled a large-scale, mechanized offensive that eventually targeted not only Gogrial, but Tonj and Rumbek.[173] All of these military actions were preceded by attempts to ban Operation Lifeline Sudan flights to Mapel, the biggest SPLA-controlled airstrip between Wau and Rumbek, and many relief workers who had watched the government's obstruction of humanitarian aid delivery over many years took this ban as a signal that the government intented to embark on military activities, because that was the pattern aid workers had observed over a long period of time.

> Every single time Khartoum tells us not to fly to specific locations, it is always an indication that they will attack that place or some other place in the vicinity ... They do not want expatriate aid workers to witness their evil ... nor do they want to risk a diplomatic nightmare that could ensue should foreign aid workers get killed.
>
> An aid worker who worked in Upper Nile for the
> international medical charity, MEDAIR

The control that the government had over the oil areas only emboldened them into wanting to bring more areas under their control so that they would be able to invite more foreign oil companies to take up new concession areas. The Nuba mountains area was a possible candidate for exploration and an obstacle to other areas within south Kordofan State that could be given out to new companies only after they had been cleared of the possibility of SPLA attacks. There were indications of impending raids with which the people in the humanitarian community were familiar and which had caused the Nuba people to constantly live under the specter of one kind of military action or another. For example, when the commander of the PDF, Brigadier Umar al-Amin Karar, made an announcement in November 2001 that a new PDF brigade – the Homeland Shield Brigade – was to be mobilized, it was followed a few days later by increased fighting in the western part of the Nuba mountains. Though government claims about their immediate military successes were vastly exaggerated, still they eventually achieved much of what they had been best at: destroying civilian villages because the government was planning to extend oil explorations to southern Kordofan. The government achieved an unprecedent success early in the dry season in the Shatt-Kululu area in the weeks leading up to a visit by a host of Asian oil entrepreneurs from India, Malaysia and China in December 2001. However, the previous year had been an exceedingly difficult one for the SPLA in the Nuba region, in part because of the death after a long battle with illness of an inspirational and popular Nuba leader, the Regional Secretary Yussuf Kuwa Mekki. The appointment of a new Secretary, Abdel Aziz Adam al-Helu, who had enjoyed considerable military successes on the eastern front, marked a turning point for the SPLA, which eventually pushed the government back and farther away from the areas under their control.

Even after the success of the oil industry and despite the international condemnation of some of the oil companies, it was still apparent that the government was willing to go to even greater lengths in order to secure militarily the regions around Lundin Oil's new exploratory efforts in Concession Block 5a. The elevated tar road leading sixty miles south from Bentiu was completed, which allowed not only oil equipment but heavy government armor and tanks to move southward, something that offered them unprecedented opportunity to travel south year round and to clear the area along the highway of any civilian population that could pose a threat to oil production. Lundin came back to resume actively exploring in Block 5a after it had been forced out by campaigns of divestment and criticism by civil society groups within Sweden. TotalFina of France was also on the verge of entering into areas close to Lundin's concession area. Furthermore, there were numerous indications that the government was going to repeat on a broad front the scorched-earth warfare that had created security for Talisman Energy, Petronas, and the China National Petroleum Corporation, the partners with GNOC in Concession Blocks 1, 2, and 4. In addition, at that time passive investment partners in the oil project like OMV of Austria were assessing the ability of the government of Sudan's 'security': government troops increasingly became as ruthless as they had been further north in the more established oil concession, with immensely destructive consequences for civilian lives and infrastructure.

As oil became an ever-more promising magic potion for the country's economic woes, more oil concessions were granted. The Adar Yel oil fields, Concession Block 3,[174] in eastern Upper Nile were the next phase in exploration and the destruction of civilian lives that was the norm in the other oil areas. This area, with heavy investment by the China National Petroleum Corporation, received much less attention than has the fighting and civilian destruction in western Upper Nile, but civilian displacement, suffering and destruction were as immense. The government's efforts to create 'security' for this project had sufficient military resources to conduct the kind of scorched-earth warfare that had defined their efforts in western Upper Nile, and in the areas south of Bentiu. In addition to the continuous fighting in the region, it was extended to the towns of Kurmuk and Yabus in nearby southern Blue Nile, which were bombed for the first time since they were taken by the SPLA four years earlier. Speculation abounded with regard to the significance of this move. It was thought that it might be a sign of a new attempt to control the Ethiopian border, as the two countries had been talking about a transportation network to facilitate the sale of Sudanese oil to Ethiopia.

Securing the oil business at its source did not seem to guarantee the security of its export route, whether by pipeline or road. When it became evident that the NDA's eastern front near Kassala was active in ways that threatened the main Khartoum-Port Sudan highway and the oil pipeline as it approached Port Sudan, the government made a major commitment of troops and resources following the temporary capture of Kassala by NDA forces in 2000. This was sufficient to avert the threat but had serious consequences for the civilians, both in terms of displacement of the Beja and other groups in the area and the targeting of specific Beja men who were accused of supporting NDA forces. The arrests of many of these men and their torture during interrogation were reported by Sudan Organization Against Torture (SOAT).

ISLAMIST SOLDIERS AND THE CONDUCT OF WAR

One of the characteristics of prolonged wars like that in Sudan is that although the suffering may be universal, there will be gender difference in the war experience. The war in Sudan has affected women in more and different ways than men, but beyond the usual ways in which such state-sponsored violence affects women and children – through rape, abduction, sexual slavery, and labor exploitation. It is important to focus on how women experience and live with such violence when it takes on religious overtones. Once, in the course of an interview with a group of south Sudanese women, I told them that I was writing on the war and wanted to hear their views on how their communities come to grips with the violent experiences that characterize the relationships between civilians and 'soldiers.'[175] I had also informed them that the term genocide was being used frequently in the media around the world to describe the death and destruction that is happening in their country, and that much debate was taking place on whether or not such a description was accurate. Of the myriad responses that I received, some of which were lengthy and poignant descriptions of the war experience, one particular reaction that remained with me for the past several years was when one of the women stood up pointing her fingers at me as if to accuse me of a crime and said that she did not know why someone would conduct a study about death and destruction.

> What is to study ... is it not obvious how much death has happened at the hands of the soldiers, how many of our loved ones have been carried off into the unknown by the Baggara,[176] does it make fun reading that we are being slaughtered like chickens and no one lifts a hand to prevent it, is it not apparent who should be held responsible for the death of so many people in my village over so many years?

She fired her questions at me in a single breath, as if she had rehearsed them. 'How many people have to die before anyone notices?' another woman shouted.

This response brings several things to mind. One is that there is no question that the communities which have experienced such horrendous violence at the hands of the state have been debating their own ways to come to terms with life under conflict. Some of the questions that come up in such discussions include where the victims' families might bring a case against the perpetrators of violence, how they might be able to escape more of this recurrent violence, and a search for understanding as to why they fall victim to a war that is not of their choosing, a war where they cannot even begin to explain how it involves them.

The second issue is that the communities affected by war are frustrated by series of studies that do not seem to contribute anything to their lives by way of stopping death and destruction. This is particularly the case because the women are more aware of the targeting of the family that the warring parties exercise, but the discourse on genocide only focuses on the consequences rather than the process. 'How does it help prevent future slaughtering if we just focus on reporting how many were killed without learning how they were targeted?' Achol Madut, a young woman activist asked. This is a frustration that those of us who come from these areas can understand, because we know that these studies have been ineffective in spurring the international community to act when it is most needed. It is by now evident that condemnation of the perpetrators of mass murder always happens after the fact, partly because the discourse and the instruments of the genocide convention only seem to facilitate discussions over the applicability of the term during the slaughter and actions against it come later if they come at all – but at this point any intervention is no longer useful for the victims.

It is undeniable that Sudanese women were caught in this conflict and were used as trophies and targets. Targeting women in the conflict must be understood not only as a feature of war in which belligerents target each other's female populations as tools of war but also as a practice that is developed and reproduced within the societies and communities of each side. Therefore, despite the focus of this chapter on the state-sponsored targeting of women in the south, in the west and in other marginalized peripheries, women's rights are subtly and flagrantly violated within the north and other government-controlled parts of the country. It is my contention that the targeting of women by Sudan's military must be viewed as a tactic driven by different projects for different regions of the country, and this is why its manifestation in these regions has taken variable forms according to the nature of each region. In other words, to target women in a specific area as part of a response to a conflict, Sudan's armies employ the perceptions it holds about the people of that region. In the north, as we are currently witnessing in Darfur, the path for the targeting of women was through radical Islamic policies, which have proven intrinsically anti-women. For example, since the NIF came to power in the military coup in 1989, and with the imposition of these radical Islamic policies, women have been forced to wear the veil and instructed to abandon work in public places in occupations that might bring them into contact with unrelated men. It should be borne in mind that although coercing women to veil does not amount to physical violence on the same scale as rape or abduction, it still reflects the state's effort to appropriate women's bodies. It is the starting point of a policy that has contempt for women, and which could escalate into physical violence given the legal requirement for women to be invisible. Of course not all veiled women are coerced into wearing the veil. Many women wear the veil as a means to liberate themselves from daily harassment by Muslim radicals and the state 'morality police.' Others do so out of genuine conviction that it is required of them as good Muslims. But because it represents the reality of women's struggle for visibility, recognition and justice, the state utilizes the Islamic codes to muzzle the voices and to mete out violence to achieve its policies while appearing to be only suppressing dissent. In the same manner that a woman is raped, mutilated and systematically violated in times of war, and caused to disappear from the public sphere, a veiled woman is metaphorically removed from public life. Her body cannot be seen in public and is therefore rendered invisible both physically and in political representation. In other words, even those women who were outside the conflict zone were under severe oppression of the current government, which seems convinced that its ability to remain in power can only be ensured through a systematic and universal pattern of abuse that forces women into invisibility and silence. This is the tool that the state uses to create localized violence against women within the north. I will return in the next chapter to similar processes that, although driven by other ideologies, are taking place in areas controlled by the opposition armies and disadvantageous to women.

Meanwhile, in the south, the ground for targeting of women had already been laid by Islamic and racial ideologies which view southern women who are non-Muslim and non-Arab as lower beings. This image of the southern women is of course very useful in times of counterinsurgency. Northern soldiers deployed in the south enjoy a sense of physical and moral freedom in their dealings with southern women because they are not protected by the same moral and religious codes that might constrain a Muslim man toward a Muslim woman. The Islamic concept of *Hurma* – forbidden or out of bounds – only applies, at least in Sudan's war philosophy in the south, to Muslim women. A northern Muslim soldier would have been more at ease with raping a southern non-Muslim woman than with her northern counterpart. When it became necessary to use military force to suppress dissent within the north, as was the case in eastern and western regions when fighting broke out there in 1995 and 2003 respectively, racial identification replaced religion as the justification for the soldier. If Islam could not provide a rationalization for the act of targeting women in the north as it did in the case of southern women, then explaining this behavior in terms of Arab versus Black was a useful approach.

CONCLUSION

This chapter has used the human rights and humanitarian aid literature and ethnography to paint the picture of the conduct of war by the NIF military. Such behavior was boosted and strengthened by the flow of oil, which in turn has resulted in a renewed sense of military might and conviction in a military solution to state crises. The atrocities committed in order to guarantee security for the foreign oil companies from Canada, China, Malaysia, and Sweden have come under fire from every direction but to no avail, largely because the mother countries of some of the oil companies had no qualms about crushing human beings in order to gain access to material resources, nor were the oil companies and their countries of origin interested in the democratic aspirations of the Sudanese people. Most important was the combination of absolute commitment to tapping the oil at all costs and the military training that imbued its army with Islamic militancy which the NIF government has effectively deployed against the civilian population residing in oil areas. The Muslim soldier who was assured of military might as a result of bigger weapons thanks to oil revenues had also been instructed to see the fight for oil as the defense of a Muslim nation against people who were racially inferior and were not co-religionists. In other words, they were people who could not be spared on the basis of a shared faith. This defense of an Islamic nation meant that the soldier had no remorse for the alleged enemies and was not required to adhere to the internationally sanctioned laws of war, especially regarding civilians. The NIF soldier started his service in the south from the viewpoint that practically all southerners in the oil fields were enemies of the nation and its Islamic project.

The chapter has also offered an extended commentary on the role of corporate greed and the wilful obtuseness of certain countries in facilitating violations and the crimes of genocide and ethnic cleansing in the oil regions of south Sudan. Of major concern was the campaign in the US to force companies that conducted business in Sudan, including the Canadian Talisman, the China National Petroleum Corporation and others, out of the capital markets in the US until peace is achieved and oil revenues could be equally shared. These campaigns were weakened by the objection among some policy makers to the use of capital markets for diplomatic pressures; something they argued could set an unwelcome

precedent. This meant that the campaigns did not stop oil production, therefore the oil money continued to solely benefit the
Khartoum government, as it could only provide services to the
Arab population while the non-Arab populations live in violence.[177] However, the campaigns were instrumental in forging a
strong Sudan constituency in Washington and prompted the passing of a congressional bill called the Sudan Peace Act, which
became the foundation for the US push for peace in the south (this
is discussed further in Chapter seven).

6

INSURGENCY AND MILITARIZATION
OF SOCIETY

If the French experience with the Algerian freedom-fighters in the 1950s, the American war in Vietnam, and the American wars on terrorism in Afghanistan and Iraqi insurgents are any guide, it would be safe to say that counterinsurgency as a military action is as good as the economic incentives that accompany it. Thus Sudan's reaction to regional rebellions, which avoids looking at the economic conditions of people in favor of a pure military option, is unlikely to produce a desirable outcome in suppressing insurgency because the more economically desperate the inhabitants of a dissenting region, the more likely it is that they will choose to support the rebellion rather than succumb to the state's program of destruction. Armed resistance to successive governments in Khartoum has historically been a characteristic of southern opposition on the basis that it has been a North–South affair. This changed in 1983 when the current round of war began. Southern political leaders, especially the SPLA's John Garang, began to frame opposition to the Khartoum government differently. Throughout the 1980s, in his radio addresses from a clandestine base in Ethiopia, he would explain how a minority group of people within northern Sudan were exploiting the North–South divide to further weaken the other marginalized areas that had suffered equal social and economic neglect by the Arab-controlled central government. He called upon various groups inhabiting the Nuba mountains, the population of the Red Sea area, and the vast non-Arab groups of Darfur and Kordofan to join hands in a revolution waged by a marginalized majority of non-Arab Sudanese against the small clique of riverine Arab groups who had controlled the state apparatus for far too long to the disadvantage of everyone else. Garang pointed out to the non-Arab Muslims in the north that sharing the faith with the Arabs had not granted them any recognition as equals. He emphasized the social, political and economic commonalities between all non-Arabs as the basis for a revolution by the marginalized against the center. The opposition in the various under-developed areas of Sudan began to adopt new ideologies and methods of explaining their marginalization. As we saw earlier, many groups joined the SPLA in large numbers, some set up independent opposition groups, others joined together under an umbrella grouping with a national flavor. This chapter will chronicle this history of the use of racial/ethnic identity for the articulation of political interests. It will focus on the early beginnings of the second round of the North–South war and the situation in the Nuba mountains in an attempt to make sense of some of the government's rationale for responding to the insurgencies in the manner that it did. The chapter will also assess the consequences of war for civilians, to paint a picture of how civilians measured the war's impact on their lives.

Because Sudan is made up of ethnic/regional groups that inhabit their own loosely recognized boundaries, the demand for the state to provide even-handed development plans and distribution of services at the same time has been a pressing issue, given that each ethnic region wanted the same services that the government provided everywhere else. The ability of the government to be even-handed depends on the availability of resources and on the development policies conceived by each of the successive Khartoum regimes. Most of these policies have tended to be in favor of the region around Khartoum and Wad Madani, and perhaps a few other centers in the north. The vast majority of the areas that are peripheral to this better developed region have been severely neglected in the most classic sense of bias against rural areas that has characterized development programs in many African countries since independence. But because these neglected regions were inhabited by either non-Muslims in the south or non-Arabs in the west, the far north, the east, southern Blue Nile and the Nuba mountains, this bias has been explained locally in racial and religious frameworks. The notion of ethnic, racial and religious bias of the Arabs or radical Muslims who dominate the Khartoum government against the peripheries is widespread in Sudanese popular political language. It pervades all of the explanations ordinary people provide as the reasons for their poverty. By pairing the rich spectrum of racial and religious diversity found in the country with the perceived abundance of natural resources in the peripheries, which the non-Arab populations think have been extracted for the benefit of the center and to the neglect of the producing areas, racial and religious bias came to be regarded as the only reason why the ethnic regions far from the Arab-dominated stretch along the Nile from Dongola to Kosti are underdeveloped and under-represented in the corridors of power. In this view, the condemnation of the Khartoum government by region/ethnic-based opposition groups is part of the historical baggage that post-colonial states have had to shoulder. However, because the government suppressed this criticism with its usual brutal measures, there has been an inversion of peaceful criticism, which is no longer a platform for dialogue between the government and the governed but a cause for widespread violent confrontation. In the south, it began as a demand for inclusion in the affairs of the state, religious freedom, and representation of indigenous cultures in state structures, but the ruthless response from Khartoum led to the first round of civil war. When the Addis Ababa accord between Nimeiri and the separatist Anyanya movement ended the war after seventeen years, it was hoped that the war had served as a lesson about southern grievances and the potential of the south to set state disintegration in motion, that the rulers in Khartoum would persuade the south by demonstrating goodwill towards its people and would not allow another chance for the south to go back to war. Nimeiri abrogated the agreement in 1983 when he declared the application of Islamic law (shari'a) to be applied all over the country, including to non-Muslim southerners living in Khartoum. This decision opened the door to a new host of factors that led to the resumption of the war. Like the start of the first round of civil war, these factors came again as simple demands that would allow the south to share in the governance of the country. They included opposition to a plan Nimeiri was hatching up to divide the south into three autonomous regions of Bahr el-Ghazal, Upper Nile, and Equatoria because many northerners, including the Islamists, had been pushing him to do so in order to weaken the southern government that the Addis Ababa agreement had stipulated. They also included the decision by Nimeiri that, after the discovery of oil in Upper Nile, the refinery would be built in Port Sudan instead of the region where the oil was found. Nimeiri also attempted to redraw the North–South boundaries in order to carve the oil-rich southern territories into the north such that in case of separation, this resource could not be claimed by the south.[178] For example, Bentiu area, the district in western Upper Nile most endowed with oil at the time, was separated from the south and renamed Unity Province. When southern politicians protested these presidential decrees, a large number of them were put in jail[179] in complete disregard for their constitutional rights to enforce the southern end of the agreement and protect the region. The fact that the constitution prohibited the arrest of legislators and executive members of government before the removal of their immunity was immaterial to Nimeiri's security agents. The arrested politicians were prominent southerners who held public office, including the Vice President of the High Executive Council, Dhol Achuil Aleu, who was also the Minister of Legal Affairs in the south. The Speaker of the Southern Parliament, Matthew Ubur Ayang, was among the politicians detained. They were all interrogated by Umar al-Taib, Nimeiri's chief of security, in contravention of established codes of seniority protocol, a clear disregard for the constitution of the land. Having insisted on re-dividing the south, applying Islamic law, jailing his critics, planning to rob the southern resources for the development of the north, closing down the southern legislative assembly, and dismantling the High Executive Council, Nimeiri had intrinsically ended the autonomous status of the south and had left the people of the south with only one option, to go to war. Students and youth were outraged all over the south and there were massive demonstrations to demand an end to these policies. Nimeiri's security forces were ruthless in their efforts to put down these protests and many students were shot and killed during the demonstrations in Wau in February 1982, and in Malakal, Juba and other towns throughout the rest of the year. The result was the conflict that would continue to rage for the next two decades as more and more of these young people, being hunted down by security agents, fled to join the SPLA when it was established a year later.

Opposition in Darfur began as a demand for the government to revamp its effort to protect the people from armed militias backed by Libya, which were undermining the relative harmony the nomadic pastoralists and the peasant farmers had maintained for centuries. The people of Darfur had also made demands for opportunities of representation in the government, and most of all for Khartoum to respond more efficiently to the droughts that had plagued the region, especially the 1984–1985 drought and the many recurrent droughts thereafter. During Nimeiri's era, these demands were read in Khartoum as a challenge to the government and were usually met with violent repression. When Nimeiri fell in 1985, there was a brief spell of military rule by the Transitional Military Council led by Abdul Rahman Swar al-Dahab until the semi-democratic elections of 1986. When Sadiq al-Mahdi became Prime Minister in 1986, the Darfur demands were met by arming the Baggara Arabs of Darfur and Kordofan, the support base of al-Mahdi's Umma Party. They were armed in attempts to achieve two goals at the same time. The Baggara Arab militias were to aid the regular armed forces in their war against the SPLA in the south as well as functioning as an eye on the non-Arab ethnic groups within Darfur and Kordofan who had been critical of the government for neglecting their region. The Baggara themselves, being unpredictable supporters, had to be appeased by giving them free weapons and free rein to loot, pillage, kill, rape and enslave in exchange for the support of government and for their role as proxy armies. Thus the militias, whose presence on the military scene began long before Sadiq al-Mahdi came to power but whose size and arms increased manifold during what was supposedly a democratic period, were instrumental to the war effort in the south and for the suppression of local dissent within western Sudan. It is this arming of certain civilians to act as lords over others, instead of the regular defense forces enforcing the law, that has led to the chaos that has been unfolding in Darfur throughout the 1990s and reached catastrophic proportions in 2003.

In the Nuba mountains, southern Blue Nile and the eastern region, the same developments, where the local opposition group attempted to initiate a dialogue with the government over questions of neglect that the region had experienced, were often met either with greater neglect, as punishment for speaking out, or with accusations of inciting racism if the realities of marginalization were presented as evidence of a bias by the Arab elite toward non-Arabs. What was common in all these situations was that it was clear the government did not make positive use of its experience with the insurgencies that the country had witnessed before. Instead, it used that experience to better execute more divisive and destructive policies. The earlier opposition exercises, which had initially started in search for a platform on which to express the basic freedom of criticizing the government, had all ended in violent and protracted conflicts, which degenerated into racial or religious wars. The country kept falling into this trap because the ruling elite were not confident enough to allow open democratic competition for power, and this has dragged the nation through bloody confrontation whenever an opposition arose because almost all the successive Khartoum governments have always been bent on the military solution to all political problems.

Once the wars had broken out, the opposition armies in the south and west were nationalist armies who adopted guerilla tactics. They lived among their civilian supporters. While the people may have borne the heavy material brunt of feeding and housing the soldiers, they undoubtedly accepted the nationalist demands and supported these populist opposition armies, protected them and provided young recruits for their ranks. They put the government in a bind. In every case described above the government's military effort experienced difficulties in achieving their goal of wiping out the local nationalist insurgents because the latter hid and relied on local support even when such local nationalism was not a universal reality – not everyone in these regions supports the opposition. Rebel armies have usually proven too entrenched to be eradicated by repression, which meant a military stalemate and the struggle could be nearly endless. Just like Eritrea's three-decade-long war of independence from Ethiopia, Angola's twenty-seven-year insurgency, or Western Sahara's protracted fight for separation from Morocco, Sudan's conflicts have proven nearly unwinable unless a form of understanding was reached by the warring parties. Attempts by Khartoum to repress the southern rebellion, the NDA in the east and the Darfur insurgency have only led to endless struggles because these attempts at repression have either degenerated into direct targeting of civilian populations as a way to weaken the opposition army by weakening its support base, or have caused too much collateral damage in civilian life and property; a fact which has led to failure of counterinsurgency on two counts. First, stigmatizing the whole civilian population as supporters for the opposition has only backfired by leading to further swelling of the rank and file of the opposition army as the youth have either decided to avenge the atrocities and destruction or simply joined the opposition as the only means to escape being targeted by government forces. Second, the government's counterinsurgency measures have failed to fine-tune their tactics. For example, in every single case of insurgency, there was no balance between applying enough force to repress the opposition and measured steps to protect against losing the hearts and minds of the civilians. The government has also deliberately conflated strong nationalist rebels like the ones in Darfur with thugs, robbers or terrorists who have no political cause.[180]

In Sudan, there has been no such thing as a mindless insurgency without a political cause, and the opposition in Darfur had been brewing for two decades before the eventual catastrophic eruption.

Rather than dealing with it as a serious socio-economic and political discontent, various Khartoum governments since Nimeiri have dismissed it as armed robbery propelled by hatred and waged by thugs. The only difference between the various measures employed by successive governments to deal with Darfur was that prior to February 2003, when these political dissenters did not have an organization that grouped them together or represented their ideology, the effort was to find the so-called ringleaders and charge them with specific civic crimes. Since the SLA and JEM were formed, the government has constantly alleged the use of the law to bring to book those who were accused of crimes against the state. Having failed to find the leaders and applying its version of law enforcement, the government decided to engage in counterinsurgency of the worst kind, one that had been employed and refined in the south for years. Villages of innocent civilians were targeted for elimination simply due to their membership in particular ethnic groups where the two rebel movements were thought to have recruited. Targeting these groups was not a mere spontaneous outgrowth of counterinsurgency, but rather an act that has historical, political and economic contexts. Historically, it worked well in the south, not only in terms of recruiting militias from the supporters of the government to attack the ethnic groups considered most dominant in the rebel army, but also in terms of recruiting from within the very marginalized groups as a way to pit them against their own people. This allows a government to explain away its own acts of destruction as a sole responsibility of the specific ethnic group; effecting a policy and then blaming the victims.

Because Khartoum has always sought a military solution, each government that has come to power since the conflicts began has only expected to do the same should there be an outbreak of war. Politically, it maintains the view that the whole region is in a state of war against the government and that the halting of economic development as well as the cutting of services is something the locals can put an end to only if they join the government side in the fight against the rebellion. Economically, such indiscriminate attacks on civilian life in the name of national defense has weakened the economic viability of the region, taking away resources that could have been available to the insurgency. What is clear in all such circumstances is that counterinsurgency, destructive to life and property as it may be, has often worked to the military advantage of the rebel movements because the indiscriminate killing in an effort to disable the rebels simply propelled new recruits into the ranks of the opposition armies.

As the al-Bashir government was receiving the increasing proceeds of oil exploration, as explained in the previous chapter, it began to embrace even more strongly the decision to militarize its response to the Darfur rising. The most important reasons for this move were (1) it had always been the desire of Khartoum to assert itself in the field and win the war in order to legitimate itself as well as prove itself to the northern population as the party most capable of maintaining the unity of the country by all means including the use of force. (2) Dazzled by the new weapons afforded them by oil revenues, both the military and their civilian leaders in charge of policy-making about war or peace such as Ali Osman Taha, the Vice President, and Mustafa Osman Ismail, the Foreign Minister, and Abdalla Gosh, the chief of internal security, seemed to have no realistic assessment of how military operations against an unconventional army plays itself out. The civilian leaders, having no real appreciation of the conditions under which soldiers serve in the southern forests and the deserts of the west, rushed to purchase arms from the former Soviet republics and declared continuation of war. Despite the fact that the targeting of civilian life and property was also seen as a pure military tactic, the practice was also ideological. The military leaders, enticed by the promises of religious rewards in case of martyrdom and material rewards in this life should they achieve military glory and survive the war, and invigorated by their new military tools, became unable to distinguish between real military engagement with real combatants on the one hand and civilian destruction on the other. In other words, their possession of bigger guns was translated into military might, a true example of the concept of the 'fallacy of the instrument – the man with a hammer misinterprets every problem as a nail.'[181]

Likewise, a government that had suddenly begun to acquire a huge military hardware saw its war against the opposition armies of the peripheries in a distorted way: their two-decade-long failure to suppress the rebellions was thought to have been a result of the inferiority of their military equipment. This was one of the most important distortions from the flow of oil money which has damaged the whole country in terms of continuation of war and further destruction, especially of the civilian populations living in oil areas and those in the peripheries where insurgencies have arisen. It gave the government a sense of strength, an impetus to continue a war that they suddenly felt they could finally win. It was also extremely damaging to the country in terms of diversion of oil funds from the services for which people were desperate and toward military equipment and the payment of large salaries to an army much increased in size.

While clearly aware of the threats posed by marginalized regions to territorial unity and unity of identity, the Khartoum governments, especially the al-Bashir Islamist regime, at the time when the citizens of Sudan expected the new-found resources to be used to attract the peripheries into the fold of the state, only vaguely perceived the grievances of the marginalized people. This predisposition to dismiss the claims of the people from the peripheries was reinforced by the government's ideological atmosphere – the Muslim Brothers, the National Islamic Front or the National Congress Party or whatever they will call themselves in the future – had an easier time acknowledging the threats posed by the failure to forge a unitary national identity than the threats posed by, say, secessionist armed struggle. Such preoccupation with defeating the opposition on the battlefields rather than in conference rooms, and promoting the Islamist ideology rather than rethinking the policies that had historically pushed people into armed opposition, have presumably reinforced the institutional interests of the NIF in transforming the most rebellious areas of the country, puzzlingly, into the primary focus of the effort to unite the country.

The elite of the NIF, as can be judged from the proliferation of businesses that they control, seized on the war efforts in the peripheries as an opportunity to streamline Sudan's military structure and doctrine to the benefit of the party's power base. Since NIF ascendance to power, the minister of defense and the head of the army focused on their agenda of purging the army of the elements opposed to the party's policies. This was meant to improve the capacity of the military to perform in the field as an ideology in itself, which was regarded as the only avenue to the success of the broad concept of national defense. The new NIF-controlled military, as its actions in the south, in Darfur and in the east can attest, was so determined on this agenda that they seemed to dismiss the question of causing more people to join the ranks of the opposition armies through their scorched-earth war tactics. They also dismissed the illegal practices that soldiers engage in while serving in the conflict areas. For example, not only were military personnel forced to earn additional income by means of looting or illegal trade because their salaries were not being paid on time or were out of synch with the cost of living at a particular time, but they also had a mindset that the people among whom they were working were all hostile enemies. The military personnel were told that harassing or killing civilians, in the process of interrogation for intelligence information or while searching for the real enemy, was entirely within the confines of the war against the rebellion. Over the years this has been a license for human rights abuses that have clearly translated into war crimes and crimes against humanity, all of which, if not addressed at the end of the war in a reconciliation process, could make Sudan's conflicts unending. These crimes have since prompted the UN Security Council to vote overwhelmingly to indict some of the leading government officials and allied militia leaders responsible for the Darfur atrocities to be referred to the International Criminal Court in The Hague for trial. A list of fifty-one individuals was handed over to the UN in April 2005, but the names have not been disclosed and the case against them has not yet made it to the court as the indictment orders were yet to be issued.[182] Unsurprisingly the Khartoum government was furious about the UN Security Council resolution number 1593 that called for disarmament of the Janjaweed and trial of genocide perpetrators, and has since issued statements in the local media to the effect that it will never hand over any Sudanese citizen for trial in a foreign court, as its own courts are perfectly capable of trying the cases.

The government soldiers' criminal behavior in conflict areas was not a result of lack of training and proper instructions about how to treat the civilians or prisoners of war, but a product of formal training to behave that way. (Human rights organizations must be surprised that in a two-decade-long conflict the government does not hold any prisoners of war: captured enemy soldiers must have been put to death, possibly summarily and without due process of the law.) Training for the rank and file of the national armed forces has been rudimentary and quick – three to six months – in order to turn out more soldiers with as little expenditure as possible. This means they only receive instruction in the operation of the equipment, and almost none in the laws of war or about military discipline regarding civilian-military relations. However, there are myriad indications that the Sudanese soldier's atrocious acts in conflict zones were really a part of their training which emphasized civilian abuse as a means to fight insurgency. It served two immediate purposes. One is that it was intended to terrify the civilians into submission and prohibit them from giving allegiance to the opposition armies. The second is that the wars in the south have been jihadic wars since about 1984, which meant that they were wars to defeat the infidels and their backers, and to convert the unbelievers. These two approaches to training the soldiers were developed in response to a frustration among government officials and the military elite – dating back to the last days of Nimeiri's government – that soldiers who were instructed that the war was about crushing the rebellion or to Arabize the country were found to be largely unconvinced about this cause. The appearance of reluctance among the soldiers to carry out such outrageous policies may have been a product of the fact that many of them were schoolchildren and abductees from the south who were determinedly unwilling conscripts. Some of them could not carry out policies that were clearly against their own people, and even some of those who were Muslims thought that the war tactics they were expected to implement were morally objectionable. Injecting a religious aspect into the war effort, however, was deemed a better and faster way to persuade the larger swath of northern radical Islamic conscripts and volunteers about the urgency of the cause.

In their response to Darfur, for instance, and despite all the talk about the phenomenon of 'armed robbery' that had reportedly become rampant in the western region, only perfunctory preparations were made for measured and targeted assaults on the 'robbers.' And no legal measures were ever planned to deal with the predictable escalation of the phenomenon. Even when the opposition groups of SLA and JEM, who are far more worthy enemies, came onto the field, there were always very limited efforts to confront them directly. The Khartoum government went into western Sudan, as they had done in the south during the previous two decades, with no credible plan for political reconciliation. When it came to confronting the rebels head on Sudan's military was weak, not acknowledging at first that the enemy was not a conventional army. Having discovered this in the field, avoiding direct confrontation with the rebels became the mainstay of its operation, and creating devastation among the civilian support base of the opposition its main tactic. After inflicting military devastation on the ordinary people and their property yet still proving unable to bring political order – as the cases of Darfur, the eastern region, and the south have shown – the military's mood became even more merciless, giving rise to the atrocities that the media has covered over the years. This has led to a widespread politicization of the masses, whose embittered response to the destruction of their lives and livelihoods has caused the growth of ethnic nationalism far beyond its pre-war levels. This has meant that the central government has become largely isolated from the peoples' everyday experiences. Many of those we interviewed in the south as well as the SLA officers we met in Bahr el-Ghazal say that the only contact between the people and the government during these wars was in the military's use of force against them. They say that it will be extremely difficult if not impossible for the government to become acceptable to the people in the peripheries unless it is going to be run with genuine representation of all the political forces in the governance.

During the current wars, most people have both the experience and perception that government, and the idea of the state for that matter, was imposed by a single ideology, race or class. In other words, the NIF's knee-jerk hostility to the idea of a multicultural, racial and religious system of government has contributed both to the rising anti-government sentiment all over the country and the failure of government to assert control over the political process throughout the country. No one in the government seems to have made any plans, in designing their war tactics, for the best way to persuade the populace about their role in governance and how to give the people a sense that when the hostilities have ceased, they will be able to assume their rightful place in the political process. Radicals in the government such as the Energy Minister, Ahmed Awad al-Jazz, who was at one point in charge of military intelligence, do not seem to have anticipated that their insistence on the use of brute force as the weapon of choice in dealing with dissent, however much military edge they may have against the opposition, has also made it difficult for the government to blame the opposition for the escalation of the conflict or the destruction of assets. When confrontation with the opposition began with the show of force and then conciliation later, the government put itself in a serious bind. To try to talk peace only after military setbacks in the field simply made them lose face, and that was why they insisted on war at all costs, even when it meant recruiting more children, wielding the race card, or using religious calls to Jihad as recruiting tactics. To suggest ceasefire while carrying out atrocities, as they did when Nigeria intervened and brought the parties in the Darfur conflict to a negotiating table in Abuja, has only revealed Khartoum's intransigence. The government then tried a two-pronged exit strategy. The first was the increased use of militias so that the government could blame the war on allegations of tribal hatred and claim that the militias were independent groups that were outside government control rather than under its direction. The other tactic was outright military attacks on civilians under the pretext of trying to bring the region under control to prevent civilian deaths and that the civilian casualties were regrettable collateral damage, something no civilians interviewed by human rights groups have been able to accept.[183] Both tactics have proved ominous in the extreme for the civilian population. The activities in the oil-fields of the western Upper Nile, the atrocities in Darfur, the Antonov aerial bombings in Bahr el-Ghazal and Equatoria, and the retaliatory acts against civilians in Kassala after the NDA forces' brief occupation of that town, are all well-known examples of the NIF government's frustration.

People in the peripheries, especially the south, have always sus-pected that the government in Khartoum was not as hated in the north as the northern opposition forces wanted the world to believe. Many in the south believed that the government could not have conducted such a policy of violence against certain classes of citizen if there was no significant support from the other classes of citizen. In other words, without counting on a northern support-base, the government could not have done the things that were done during the hostilities. 'How is it possible that no northern groups were speaking out against the government atrocities in the south in the same way that they are doing right now about Darfur,' lamented James Aguer, a southerner who resides in Khartoum. 'If the war crimes such as those the government has committed in the south were done against Arab northerners, there would have been far more outcry among northerners and the rest of the Arab world,' another young man pointed out. There is in fact a well-documented ignorance among the northern Arab population regarding how the government has always conducted itself in its relationship with the populations of the dissenting regions. This northern ignorance or seemingly deliberate disinterest in the government's abuses in the non-Arab ethnic regions is part of the explanation for their will-ingness to support the government's indiscriminate response to the insurgencies. The other part is to do with the polarized racial and religious set-up of the country; not only because the war has been pitched to them in those terms, but also because there is gen-eral racial prejudice in the Arab communities that biases people's perceptions of the way war is conducted in non-Arab regions. The general impression is that the northern Arab public desires to see an end to the rebellions, and the government wants to meet this desire. But it seems that channeling the war tactic from one of engagement with the rebel armies to one of attacks on civilians who are claimed to support the rebels has been chosen as the quickest way to assert state control and defeating the insurgencies.

Since the northern public has been poorly informed about the nature and structure of political turmoil in, say, the south or Darfur, it had the impression that the government was fighting a just war, as the Khartoum regimes have often described the wars as defense of the nation against enemies of the state who were simply driven by mindless hatred for the Arabs and for the true Muslims who want to hold high the name of Islam. Chief Nyal Chan Nyal of Awan Dinka noted:

> If there was ever a moment in which an Arab child goes without food for a few days, no school for Arab children for years on end, or Arab men seeing their daughters, mothers or sisters being raped right in front of them, northerners would never have been as silent on the war as they have been.

Similar remarks were made by many citizens from Darfur who were living in displaced persons and refugee camps. The government's discourse to the northern population has also been one in which the leaders of the insurgencies were depicted as stooges in the pay of foreign enemies of Sudan and Islam, such as Israel and the US, which were bent on targeting Sudan for destabilization simply because of its Islamic policies. Khartoum has often tried, especially through its media and other programs, to explain to the northern public and indeed to the rest of the Arab world that there is an anti-Arab campaign going on in Sudan, started by the SPLA and supported by the Zionists and the Christian zealots of the Western world. In other words the seemingly uncritical Arab support for the government's folly was not exactly spontaneous; it was to a great extent a product of the government's whitewashing of its atrocities in Sudan's peripheries. But of course it is worth noting that it was not only the northern Arabs who have been oblivious to government actions in the peripheries. As the wars have been prolonged and gradually became a part of life, many developments in the social arena began to detract from the main goals of opposition and the real impact of the war began to reveal itself in the form of the actions by local people, where victims themselves may become perpetrators of the crimes they had pledged to fight, something akin to the process Mahmood Mamdani has described in Rwanda regarding Hutu and Tutsi wars against one another despite the knowledge that the Belgian colonizers had taken advantage of some historical squabbles, magnified them and concretized them as a mechanism to augment their rule over both factions (Mamdani, 2001).[184]

The social impact of Sudan's two-decade long unresolved conflict manifests itself in the relations that had formed between civilians and the various armies in all conflict zones. In the south, the opposition armies expected the civilians to pay the cost of war, and the civilians had to reconcile the efforts to protect their property to fears of being accused of disloyalty. Such demands have undoubtedly had a serious negative impact on the lives of the non-combatant populations. These relations have presented themselves over the years of Sudan's civil wars, especially in the south, in the northeast, and in Darfur, in three ways. First, the day-to-day interaction between the civilians and the soldiers, especially regarding the problems of feeding troops and meeting many other demands that they make. Second, the economic consequences of military recruitment of young men and boys and the forcing of women and girls to act as porters for the armies, especially how these new roles affect agricultural production, which was largely done by women. Third, the social consequences of war, especially the reconfiguration of sexual relations, gender relations and the near erosion of social control mechanisms as a direct result of the conditioning of young men to violence.

MILITARY–CIVILIAN RELATIONS AND CONTESTED NATIONALISM

When the current round of the North–South conflict began in 1983, it ended a ten-year hiatus after the first civil war. The news about the war starting again in south Sudan caused a great deal of anxiety, particularly in the rural areas. The immediate reaction was to question the necessity of going to war again so soon after the nation had just experienced a mere decade of relative calm. For rural inhabitants like Nuer and Dinka, among the largest ethnic groups in the country and whose territories were the first recruiting fields for the new southern opposition army, it was necessary to think about what life was going to be like having to deal with an unpaid local army. They became concerned about how best to prepare, how to protect their livestock from being confiscated to provide food for the armies of both sides. The memories of the previous war were still fresh in the minds of many people, especially the arbitrary government attacks on villages under the guise of looking for the 'rebels' that the previous governments favored. Rural people were immediately concerned about where they might take refuge if such practices were repeated. For the Sudan government, it was also a time of hasty action, preoccupied as it was with how to contain and keep the guerilla armies of the south from attacking the towns. As had been the case in the first round of war, the government immediately accused the entire population of south Sudan of dissidence and resorted to either declaring war and destroying the villages, or arranging for appeasement of the civilian population of the south in attempts to turn them against 'their own cause.' Appeasement was always hard to achieve so the former nearly all too often prevailed.

> I was in my last year of secondary school when the little village of Luonyaker, sixty miles east of Wau town, where I had attended primary school was attacked by the government regular army and was burned to the ground under the allegation that the people of the village were sympathizers of the rebellion and that they had been hiding and feeding the rebel forces. Large numbers of civilians were killed, including a prominent schoolteacher, Mayom Thiep, who had taught generations of Apuk section of Dinka including myself. The attack was so sudden and shocking to the inhabitants that it prompted the youth, many of them from my own school, who had not even made up their minds yet about the war, to join the rebel force out of fear and anger over the destruction of their village and the killing of innocent people. This was the manner in which more

and more youth throughout south Sudan were propelled into joining the opposition armies, that despite their nationalistic reactions,
some of their reasons were to do with the government's blunt
counterinsurgency that targets innocent people.[185]

Most people in the rural areas and some in urban areas immediately felt the anxiety of the economic consequences of war, as the
civilian population has always found itself caught at crossroads in
such situations of the sudden outbreak of violence. To house, feed
and reinforce the guerilla army meant both unaffordable expenses
and serious government retaliation. To be opposed to the 'people's
army' was to be short-sighted about the large-scale and long-term
effects of Arabization and Islamization that the government of
Sudan was accused of pursuing vigorously. Civilians may also find
themselves labeled as enemies of the people if they fail to support
the opposition army, a suspicion or accusation with dire consequences. Failure to support the opposition provokes negative consequences for one's physical well-being as well as social status in the
community. The onset of this phase of the war led people to invoke
the past – that their villages, property and lives would be destroyed,
as was the case during the previous war. I remember hearing people express the fear that things may get worse during the current
war, because they had noticed the much larger and better armed
rebel army. The size and the equipment of the new army was something that could be positive if the rebels' priorities were set right, i.e.
with national interests at heart, but could also be ominous if they
lost sight of the initial goals for forming the opposition front.
However, the many civilians were almost automatically conscious
of what their responsibilities were going to be. They knew
what they would end up having to provide, whether or not they
were willing to do so. Ten years of a fragile peace (1972–1983)
had given rural folk some hope and opportunity to rebuild their
lives. During the years of relative calm, people had begun to accu-
mulate property, mend the war's social wounds, and tried to be part
of the political structure of Sudan's polity. Indeed, the ten-year
hiatus between the wars produced many dividends as a generation

of southerners who made up the opposition during the next round of war was educated during this period. Now their future could be easily wiped out by yet another round of hostilities, and 'only God knows how long these hostilities will last this time,' as one popular Dinka song that emerged around this time said.[186]

Like all human societies, the south Sudanese dreaded war because it threatened their lives and livelihoods. Although the failures of the successive Khartoum governments to live up to their responsibilities drove the southerners to arm themselves and start the war, no one made the mistake of forgetting what war means. The opposition groups from south Sudan may have started the war by taking up arms, and of course they had many disagreements among themselves over how to approach their opposition to the Arab government: the specter of war's destructive nature hovered above everyone like a gathering storm, but no one had ever suggested that liberation was without suffering. 'It is not that we prefer war and life in the bush over peaceful opposition, but we do this because we have exhausted all other possible means to resolve our differences with northerners,' said one former police sergeant who had just joined the new rebel movement when I met him in August 1983. The civilians, despite their apparent support for the rebels, were not happy about the presence of troops who, even though their own, camped in their villages, slept in their houses, expected to be fed, and demanded to be cared for in many other ways. In other words, it was feared that war and the presence of large armies in the villages would affect all aspects of everyday existence. The presence of troops caused overwhelming social, cultural and economic disruption. The need to feed them was a heavy burden, and this became evident throughout rural south Sudan regardless of the level of prosperity of different regions. Every rural inhabitant felt the weight of the war. When the troops were moving, whether to training camps, or on a military action, they expected the civilians en route to pay the cost of war. A popular phrase, 'we pay our blood to defend the nation, contributing to the upkeep of the volunteer army is the least we can expect of the people of this nation,' was a slogan used by rebel soldiers during the early days of the current war. It was not only a question of how much logistical support the civilian population could offer, but also the sympathy and tolerance it could extend toward the army's behavior and social misconduct.

Like all societies undergoing rapid transition, the resumption of war brought a cleavage over the many pressing social, cultural, political and economic issues between the military and civilian population. The making of war by conventional military personnel differed a great deal from the old established traditions that used to govern the making of warfare. It is this conflict that determined the perception of war which this section of the chapter describes. This was a period of a powerful sense of change, when the demands of war-making contradicted the traditional moral fabric. On one hand, the government war machinery was that of a modern state with a growing scale of sophistication in warfare tactics and weaponry, which made the southern traditional system of war-making nearly obsolete. On the other, the traditional social and economic system of south Sudan, being unable to cope with the powerful state-launched war, modified its organizational aspects of military life. The tools of war (both human in the form of youth and material resources) underwent a transformative development in strategy, organization and purpose. They became separate entities from all other aspects of daily living. Traditionally, war was made in conjunction with production, the image of individual warriors, and knowledge about the enemy. Now, the soldier was solely an object of war whose daily worry was how to win a battle. Given the attitude that the civilians should look after the soldier, the soldier's worry was no longer how to secure his daily meal; he was not concerned as to who should look after his family. He was no longer expected to worry about preserving the social norms of the community. These were roles to be assumed by the civilian population without question. Some people came to interpret the attitudes of the soldiers as 'If the civilians responded to the war demands, well and good, if they did not well and good, we will serve ourselves.' The soldier's mistakes were to be excused and his demands tolerated. His success and safety at war were no longer contingent upon pleasing the ancestors or religious leaders or agreeable everyday behavior as in the old days, but rather on perfecting his military skills. This change in the mentality of war-making, from being tied to the supernatural powers to being related to worldly perfection, is key to understanding the behavior of soldiers during this second round of war. In the past it was believed that war was the perfect occasion for supernatural repri-mand for social misconduct. The warrior was therefore expected to adhere to basic moral codes in an effort to avert any war-related misfortune. This belief became nearly obsolete during this war. The impact of this change was evident in the everyday problems of feeding and housing troops, which the people of rural south Sudan felt in many ways. Despite the fact that the people had to conform to avoid the wrath of the soldier, this did not stop them from using what was intrinsically a license given to them by the new ideology of warfare to rape, rob or steal, all in the name of nationalism.

The people of wartime south Sudan have constantly provided explanations as to why they were anxious at the advent of war in the early 1980s. Needless to say, they knew that war was no simple busi-ness. The many local wars between and within ethnic groups that they had gone through for generations and the seventeen years of the first round of North–South conflict had shown them that war was violent, painful, costly, and fatal. They knew the mere fact that the SPLA was their own and was needed for defense against the government-sponsored Arab militia raids did not ameliorate the fact that sometimes the officers were unable and sometimes unwilling to control their soldiers. People were expected to under-stand the reality that once out of control, a soldier was a soldier, whether a people's soldier or that of the enemy. War was a trade that did not always conform to the rules of rational thinking. The people of south Sudan were constantly asserting that the SPLA sol-diers could talk about their sacrifice for the nation, although they have undeniably sacrificed a great deal, but that the violent experi-ences of war all too often spill over into civilian life as well. In other words the soldiers had little to be proud about, something ordinary civilians could not be proud of. They had both paid the cost of the search for freedom. The very definition and the destructive nature of war applied to both civilian and military. Many years later, when the war was well into its first decade, I had a chance to travel to south Sudan, worked as a humanitarian aid worker, and interviewed hundreds of people about the war experience. One Dinka elder commented:

> These young men go to Ethiopia on their own account, they come back with guns and some military training, we welcome them back, we support them in order to fight and protect us against the Arabs, but they keep acting as if they can do it without us. They think of us as backward and unconscious of our rights, but they have nothing, they are nothing if we stop feeding them our grain and livestock.

Many people talk about how everyone shouldered the burden of war, except perhaps for many of the commanders whom the people accused of confiscation of property, cowardice, and whose wish to involve everybody in the war was considered almost as a law which no one could oppose.

CIVILIANS AS FODDER OF WAR

In Sudan's war people became an important resource to be controlled and appropriated. Some of the important tools of war that have most characterized the conflict have included massive killings of civilians, bombing of refugee camps, forced population transfers, separation of families, sexual abuse of women, and herding of population into controlled areas in order to manage them more efficiently with regard to the Arab state's racial and religious program. These tools were employed as low cost counterinsurgency measures. They were supposedly to guard against rebel attacks, but in reality they were meant to prevent the southern civilian population from giving any support to southern resistance armies. Southern civilian populations were randomly accused of abetting the SPLA and other southern opposition forces, and that perception gave the government a license to use all means of terror to pre-empt any decisions the civilians might make to support the SPLA. This assault was for the most part because the majority of northern Sudanese politicians, especially those who seized power in the 1989 coup d'etat, want Sudan to become an Arab and orthodox Islamic nation.

WOMEN AND WAR: A TRIPLE BURDEN

In the studies of wartime violence, gendered violence represents an old argument that violence in wartime affects men and women differently. Activists worldwide have invoked the phrase 'gendered violence' to recognize a wide array of abuses: the use of violence by one warring party against the women of the other; the reproduction of violence within families and communities after many years of militarization; demands on women to increase childbirth in response to wartime high mortality rates (demands that sometimes translate into marital rapes); forcing women and girls to produce food for the belligerents; sexual violence associated with young men's new-found power of the gun; and so on. Much of the literature on wartime violence tends to focus on the use of extreme violence by the warring parties against civilians under each other's control as a way to fight the war by proxy, i.e. to destabilize the support base of the opposing group. The use of rape as a weapon of war has been unequivocally documented in the south and more recently in Darfur,[187] and we have seen how the government has often used it to humiliate the 'enemy.' However, as important as it is to document such abuses, equally important and more insidious is the way in which violence is reproduced and carried out within the communities by members of armed groups who hail from these same communities, as such violence is hard to stem long after the hostilities have ceased.

The war in Sudan presents a good example of a situation where individuals and communities grapple with the consequences of a militarized situation by creating new strategies of coping in place of the old norms that governed behavior in the past (Jok, 1999a). In using this idea of looking at the violence as an outgrowth of individual efforts to come to grips with the changed world, it would be useful to analyze gendered violence as the continuation of an ongoing dialogue between people of a shared past who hold common ideas about power. By the time the civil war was about to wind down after twenty-two years of fighting, Sudanese women had established strong roles in household and family decision-making as a result of the war. These experiences influenced the thinking of the military elite and community leaders, for example, in western Dinka when, during the humanitarian relief intervention years (1989–present), they became increasingly preoccupied with women's negligence of their national duties. Relief supplies were becoming the backbone of the SPLA in the wake of the deadly split of the rebel army and the fall of the Mengistu government in Ethiopia in 1991. In their concern to continue a national struggle with a hungry population, the military tacitly suggested a few solutions. Of concern for us here was the effort to redefine women's roles in the struggle with the expectation to increase women's contributions to the revolution, not only in order to release men for more strict military activities but also to find women's resources that were previously untapped to be set in motion for the purpose of liberation. This effort, actively propagated between 1991 and 1997, was a failure both because the goals and means were not well defined, and because it translated into violence against women on every level of society. SPLA officers and many other ordinary men were heard randomly suggesting the need for people to urge the women to hold up their reproductive front (i.e. make themselves more sexually available and have more children). This policy, which I call nationalization of the womb, has become an almost normative expectation, and it is the area in which women have paid a heavy price in simply trying to play their role in the national struggle.[188] Such emphasis on reproduction as a part of the war has produced a subculture of violence when young men read it as a license to sexual aggression, whether in domestic settings or elsewhere.

CONCLUSION

This chapter examined the nature of counterinsurgency in all the regions of Sudan that have taken up arms to assert their political opinion. Two points are raised in this chapter. The first is that the more indiscriminate the government armies were against the civilians in their attempt to suppress the rebellion from its alleged roots, the larger the ranks of the opposition forces swelled, with the predictable result that the relationships between the ethnic and region-based uprising became polarized beyond reconciliation. The wars, therefore, became militarily unwinable, and naturally so prolonged that they simply reached a permanent stalemate. The second point is that the longer the wars continued, the more likely it was that violence would develop as a subculture and as a part of life, and the result was that violence went beyond the usual atrocities that were committed by soldiers against the civilian support base of their opponents. It was possible that violence would be reproduced within the communities from which the soldiers hailed, and even within the families, as more and more young people were conditioned to violence as a part of their day-to-day experience. More insidious in this was the development of gender-based violence for reasons to do with attempts to control women's reproductive roles and with the contestation of nationalism: men were nationalists and women were not necessarily capable of contributing to liberation or defense, and therefore women had to be appropriated to support this cause.

7

SUDAN AND THE REST OF THE WORLD
The Search for Peace and Security

Since independence, Sudan, like many countries in post-colonial Africa, has suffered from a crisis relating to the question of whether the country should maintain the colonial configuration it has inherited or redefine its ethnic and geographic frontiers. One major factor that complicated the resolution of this crisis was the interest of neighboring countries. For example Egypt, a country with a colonial past in Sudan, has consistently maintained that Sudan's inherited colonial boundaries must be kept unaltered. Since 1963, Egypt has constantly made references to the charter of the Organization of African Unity (OAU) that prohibited a return to pre-colonial political geography. That this insistence on unity at all cost risks continuation of war is immaterial to Egypt: its interest in ensuring maintenance of the 1959 Nile water agreement was paramount. The emergence of an additional country on the Upper Nile appears to threaten Egyptian guarantees to a free flow of the Nile. Other countries such as Ethiopia, Eritrea, Chad, Uganda and Kenya, although sympathetic to the political interests of the Sudan's peripheral regions such as the question of self-determination for the south and the demands of the rest of the marginalized regions for inclusion in the political process, have had their own reasons to support the unitary existence of Sudan, not least of which is the presence of several tribes on each side of the border. For example, because some Darfur tribes straddle the Sudan–Chad border areas, the war in Darfur is as much a Chadian problem as it is Sudanese. Some of the ethnic groups that make up Darfur, such as the Zaghawa, are also represented in Chad. The situation with Eritrea is the same. This has meant that Sudan's wars variously affected these countries, sometimes only in terms of refugee spill-over with enormous economic and environmental consequences, at other times in terms of Sudan's sponsorship of opposition groups in these countries, or in terms of Sudan's role in exporting militant Islam to the neighbors. As may be expected, the African-Arab racial question and the issue of political Islam within Sudan are also apparent in these inter-state politics. Furthermore, recently many countries neighboring Sudan have expressed interests in buying Sudan's oil and by so doing have risked alienating the south and other marginalized regions. It had been the hope of the south that the African countries would stand by the African Sudanese in the same manner that the Arab countries support the Arab north.

This chapter will examine the regional impact of Sudan's civil wars and the efforts of the neighboring countries to restore calm to Sudan as a matter of national security for all the countries in the region. It also evaluates the various peace processes from the per-spective of the ordinary Sudanese as well as the views of smaller opposition groups that were excluded from the negotiating forums. The material for the section on the regional impact of Sudan's wars comes from the documents issued on peace talks, interviews with the participants in these talks and from reports by human rights groups. The rest of the material on the responses of the Sudanese people to the efforts for peace is derived from inter-views and group discussions within Sudan and in the diaspora. I was also able to make frequent telephone calls to individuals in Sudan, particularly Khartoum, Nyala, al-Fasher, Kassala, Kadugli and Damazin. Through basic research methods of data collection in the field like participant observation and personal discussions with a wide variety of consultants, I have been able to gain an understanding of ordinary people's perspective on the peace processes. During the summers of 1998 to 2005 I spent time in many rural communities, partook of many communal events, including the so-called 'people-to-people' peace initiatives, and explained and discussed my research objectives with prominent personages and the community at large. My ultimate aim was to develop a nuanced understanding of local responses to conflict and mediation by cross-fertilizing these perceptions and interpretations of the role of mediators with the personal testimonies and experiences regarding peace talks from a representative cross-section of the communities that I have studied.

In terms of the regional and international implications of the war and the interests of the neighboring countries, just to give two examples at the outset, it will be recalled that the success of the Lord's Resistance Army in northern Uganda to destabilize that region has to do with Sudan's provision of arms and training camps as retaliation for Uganda's hosting of the SPLA. In relation to the war in Darfur, a complicating factor is that the porous nature of both sides of the Sudan–Chad border has enabled Chadian dissident politicians and oppressed ethnic groups to count on their kin on the Darfur side for assistance in their opposition to the governments of Chad. For example, the incumbent president of Chad, Idris Déby, came to power with the help of ethnic militias partially based in Darfur. Likewise, Chad's Zaghawa pressured Déby, a fellow Zaghawa, not to support Khartoum's counterinsurgency measures against Darfur rebels. Furthermore, several SLA and JEM fighters had fought in Chad with their kin and returned to Sudan when the conflict erupted to defend their people against what they saw as a racially motivated targeting of non-Arab Darfurians by Khartoum and its allied Darfur-based Arab groups.

Countries neighboring Sudan, including Chad itself, have also felt the impact of Sudan's war in a variety of other ways, not the least in terms of the burden of hosting a large number of refugees fleeing the Sudanese conflicts, increased insecurity at the borders, or the economic upheavals of the war in terms of lost trade. They have also been exposed to political destabilization created by Sudan's moral, material and financial support to various rebel groups that have historically been opposed to the government in N'djamena. Northern Uganda in particular has been hardest hit.

The Lord's Resistance Army has for several years maintained headquarters on the government's side of the front line in Sudan, reportedly at one point in Juba, the capital of the south. Their activities in the Acholi territory of northern Uganda have forced the country to remobilize more than 3,000 of the soldiers who had been demobilized after the civil war that brought the ruling National Resistance Movement under Yoweri Museveni to power. The conflict has also stopped development efforts and curtailed service delivery in the affected areas of the Acholi people, and has caused a humanitarian catastrophe spanning a period of more than twenty years. Sudan has wavered between denial that it supports the LRA and claiming that its support of the Ugandan rebel forces was in self-defense against the neighbor's support to the SPLA.

Sudan has also supported the operations of extremist Islamic groups within Ethiopia and Eritrea in retaliation for support these countries have allegedly given to the SPLA and NDA respectively. It will be recalled that the SPLA had enjoyed a great deal of support from the former socialist government of Ethiopia under Mengistu Haile Mariam, but the current government of Melese Zenawi, although not openly hostile to the SPLA, has ceased direct supplies to the south-based opposition forces since 1991. Also within the period leading up to and during the wars in the Democratic Republic of Congo, the regional conflicts of interest have openly been displayed in that country, with Sudan and its neighbors supporting different groups in the Congolese civil war. For instance, Sudan attempted to rebuild its relations with the DRC when the late President, Laurant Kabilla, made the gesture by visiting Khartoum in 1998, to the dismay and outrage of the SPLA. 'Kabilla's visit to Khartoum is a most regrettable gesture toward a government accused of terrorism and it sends the wrong signal,' one SPLA member declared in Nairobi. But it was not until the intervention of many African countries, notably Uganda, Rwanda and Zimbabwe in what was the first and largest Pan-African effort to break up the Congolese civil war that Sudan took advantage of the chaos in the DRC to launch attacks against the SPLA from the rear bases it had established inside that country's northern borders by 2000.

Fearing the possibility of becoming a further cause of regional instability, some of these neighboring countries decided to mediate in an effort to bring a peaceful solution to Sudan's conflict. A regional group consisting of Sudan and its eastern and southern neighbors, the Inter-Governmental Agency for Development (IGAD) was formed in 1989 and attempted to negotiate a peaceful settlement of Sudan's North–South conflict. Other countries had made similar attempts in the past to no avail. For example, Nigeria had agreed to host talks between the SPLA and the government of Sudan in its capital Abuja in 1992 and 1993, but the negotiations always collapsed, partly because of the bad faith the negotiations demonstrated on the part of Khartoum, and partly because the SPLA and other southern groups could not agree on a unified position *vis-à-vis* the north.[189] Many issues regarding the governance of SPLA-controlled areas, ideological rifts between the leadership and rank and file, and the diverging views on the goals of the movement regarding unity or separation have all caused serious tensions within the SPLA. As stated earlier, when the SPLA split occurred in 1991, the breakaway group called itself the SPLA-Nasir.[190] It was later renamed SPLA-United, which in turn broke up again and a new group called the Southern Sudan Independence Movement/Army (SSIM/A) was set up under the leadership of Riek Machar Teny, one of the leaders of the initial breakaway group. SPLA-United remained under Lam Akol Ajawin and Kerebino Kuanyin Bol and stayed poised to fight the SPLA, and although both groups were separatist movements, they received their military supplies from the government, as Khartoum used them to weaken the main SPLA, which remained its biggest and most formidable foe. The existence of so many factions that were partly with government and partly alleging to fight for the south made it difficult for any peaceful negotiations to proceed in an environment of uncertain alliances. The Abuja talks collapsed in the end.[191] In 1995 IGAD took one of its most significant steps toward brokering peace in Sudan, and reached an initiative called the Declaration of Principles (DOP), negotiated in Asmara, Eritrea. It included points accepted by all parties to the

North–South conflict as common ground for a peaceful settlement such as abandoning the military option as a solution, unity of the country, religious pluralism and the right of the southern people to self-determination through a referendum. The DOP was hailed as a promising step toward peace, and despite the fact that southerners are always suspicions toward the north, many southerners were quite jubilant about this initiative. However, the government of Sudan was able to stall the project for many years by wavering between slowly implementing the DOP and dropping them all together, and hunting for other more favorable initiatives in the region.[192] The Islamists were particularly unhappy about the concept of self-determination for the south. Much like the previous governments, the NIF considered autonomy and the right to self-determination as only a step toward southern secession, an eventuality they have been determined to prevent by any and all means.

Instead, the NIF government launched what it called a 'peace from within' initiative. This was intended to achieve a peace agreement with the small breakaway factions of the SPLA mentioned above, particularly Riek Machar's SSIM, which had been renamed yet again as the Southern Sudan Defense Force (SSDF), but without involving the northern opposition parties or the main SPLA. Khartoum wanted to appear interested in peace, talking the language of peace with some southerners with a view to portraying the SPLA as a war-mongering party for refusing to join the process. 'Peace from within' culminated in what became known as the Khartoum Agreement of 1997, and included provisions for a referendum to determine the future of Sudan, but it was unacceptable to the SPLA because it contradicted some of their key demands and principles agreed upon in the DOP and had been agreed and signed by representatives of smaller opposition groups representing a minority of the people of the south. As the war was entering its twentieth year, the parties to the conflict had put the entire country in a bind; it seemed that political settlement was even further away, and a decisive military victory by any one side almost unforeseeable.

It was not until the coming to power of George W. Bush in the United States that the IGAD initiative got a boost. Bush, under the influence of a very strong Sudan constituency in Washington as well as pressure from a coalition of Christian right organizations and other advocacy groups, went from having been thought to be one of the US presidents least interested in international affairs to being one of the most involved in a drive for global democratization. On the issue of war and peace in Sudan, he began on September 6, 2001 by appointing John Danforth, a former senator from Missouri as a special envoy on Sudan and charged him with responsibility to broker a peace deal.

The North–South war was at that time the world's most devastating ongoing conflict. Raging with varying degrees of intensity even before the country's independence in 1956, the conflict was now also the world's longest running conflict with an estimated death toll of over two million, mainly in the south. Numerous attempts had been made to broker reconciliation since the IGAD declaration of principles but these failed for a number of reasons, including the increasing mistrust between the parties. Furthermore, the main warring parties, i.e. the northern Islamist government and southern opposition the SPLA had shown little commitment to a serious search for a peaceful solution of the conflict. Until Bush's interests came into play, there had been an equal lack of political will and commitment to a solution on the part of the international community, especially among the dominant countries in the West as well as within the region. The US Secretary of State, Madeline Albright, responding to a question about what the US was doing regarding the question of slavery in Sudan, had said in 1999 that 'the human rights situation in Sudan is not marketable to the American people,' suggesting the importance of the American public in pushing the executive and the legislative branches of the US government to act on an issue.[193] The US government at the time did not see that there was a strong constituency to justify an American involvement in pushing for peace in Sudan. Likewise, many western European countries insisted on the position that Sudan's conflict was an internal affair and that 'constructive engagement' with the government was the best approach. The weaker party in this conflict, the southern opposition, had sought out the assistance of the US and looked to the American people for help either in mediating a peaceful settlement or extending assistance so significant as to grant them a decisive victory. They looked to the Christian West from the viewpoint that since the Islamist regime in Khartoum was receiving help from the Islamic world, the south should naturally be helped by the Christian world. Indeed, any statement by an African or a Western country pointing out the government atrocities in the south was read by the south as a positive gesture long overdue and by the north as evidence that the southern rebellion was instigated by foreign countries that were plotting to stop the Islamist project. If an African country made a statement mentioning the tragedy of the south, such remarks would be enough to cause the Sudan government to plead with the Arab countries that Sudan was under the threat of disintegration due to an African coalition and due to threats of Western invasion because of a Christian and Zionist coalition. For example, the vice president of Sudan Taha, Ali Osman declared in August 2001 that 'Whether through the Libyan-Egyptian Initiative or IGAD, anyone who believes that the government will accept peace that dilutes Islam is deluded.'[194] Nevertheless, when Sudan's human rights situation became a concern for a growing constituency in the US, some three years after Secretary Albright's statement and shortly after a new president took office, the US Congress passed the Sudan Peace Act by a vote of 359 to 8, condemning Sudan's human rights abuses in south Sudan.

But despite the high profile that Sudan's war had always maintained, especially in the United States since President Clinton's two terms in office, the war and its attendant devastation continued unabated. The US Committee for Refugees under Roger Winter, Human Rights Watch, Christian Solidarity International, United Nations Special Rapporteur on Human Rights, Christian Aid and many others kept issuing estimates of Sudan's death toll from the war as increasing and about to exceed two million. According to many of these agencies, the war had resulted in more casualties than any conflict since World War II. Yet it remained one of the most misunderstood conflicts on the entire continent, and that misunderstanding was reflected in the lack of interest in a political solution that the international community exhibited on the pretext that it was a complicated war for anyone to tackle. It was often described as a conflict between the Arab Muslim north and the Christian African south, mainly because of statements from Khartoum and different regions of the country that emphasize racial and religious divides. These two concepts were picked up and used in the media and elsewhere without the explanation of their meanings or how they operate. They have since emerged as powerful factors in the search for easy and even lazy explication of the conflict. Such an explanation proved terribly misleading to would-be peace brokers in the international community. As I have shown in earlier chapters, I cannot say that Arab-African racial and Christian-Muslim religious categories are non-existent in Sudan. On the contrary, race and religion, as has been demonstrated earlier, have been the most important and clear manifestations of other types of conflicts. In other words, even though the role of resources is evident in these conflicts, race and religion have become the tools with which the confrontation is fought out. They have become the national guide for development plans, service provision, maintenance of security, as well as how the marginalized explain their subjugation. Regardless of scientific or biological notions of race, the Sudanese maintain racial ideas that have been ingrained into the politics of nation building. Nevertheless, to focus on race and religion as if they were fixed factors and without explaining how they work is to miss what makes the south and north such bitter opposites. To begin the search for peace with race and religion as if they are characteristics of ancient social relations is a reductionist approach, and suggests that the conflict between the two parts occurred as a racial–religious conflict within relatively homogeneous cultures torn by different communal histories of racial and religious choices. There are other layers that make the situation slightly different. Racial and religious differences are never sufficient cause for conflict, but rather are the tools for achievement of other ends. What accounts for this bitter divide in Sudan is also a matter of basic political, cultural, economic and social choice where race and religion have acted as a manifestation of the conflict over basic needs. It is a situation where dominant groups have attempted to use racial and religious indoctrination as a condiment to neutralize the bitter taste of history. The south and north of Sudan have never been one society. They are now more than ever at loggerheads over racialized resource distribution, sharing of power, and self-determination for the south. More recently, because of the north's effort to impose Islamic or shari'a law, and Arab culture; the government's resolve to end the disputes by military means, and pitching the conflicts to the Arab and Islamic world as African-Arab confrontations beyond Sudan, race and religion have taken on the size and scope that now dominates the characterization of the wars in Sudan.

Like the rest of Black Africa, the Sudanese state is the anomalous product of a colonial history, but unlike the rest of post-colonial Africa, such colonial history has proven to have more deadly consequences than anywhere else on the continent. What distinguishes Sudan from the rest of Africa is its position as the microcosm of African-Arab relations. This lack of historical oneness has over the years manifested itself in the control of the Arab-dominated north over power and wealth to the disadvantage of the peripheries. It has also revealed itself in the long history of slave raiding that continued until 2002 and enslavement of southerners by northerners, which is still going on for a large number of currently missing abductees. Above all, a half-century of brutal military confrontation has sharpened the place of race and religion in the conflicts. To reduce this war to a recent phenomenon of a politicized Islam was to look for quick-fix solutions that have certainly proved ephemeral. Further, mediators in the conflict seem to have understood this at last. By 2002, and in response to this tragic conflict, there were many diplomatic players in Sudan. In addition to Nigeria's numerous attempts to mediate in the 1990s, Libya and Egypt have also sponsored a more recent initiative.[195] The Nigerian peace efforts reached an impasse, and the Libyan–Egyptian initiative was not trusted by southerners on suspicions of bias of Libya's Gaddafi and Egypt's Mubarak toward their Arab brethren in the northern Sudan. The Americans also regarded it questionable on the basis of Libya's 'terrorist' status as far as Washington is concerned, and Egypt's conflict of interest due to her historical links with Sudan that made Egypt an unsuitable mediator. But as mentioned above, the most important of all the initiatives was the IGAD, a coalition of governments from the east and northeast Africa region that had been attempting to broker a peace deal in Sudan since 1995. Equally important were the IGAD Partners Forum led by the US and Norway. The IGAD process, despite the fact that a number of IGAD members have diplomatic problems among themselves, gained credibility and momentum because of considerable investment of political will, funding and a good deal of patience by the IGAD countries and their international partners. Yet no scholarly research has been done to chronicle their successes and failures so as to apply that knowledge to the Darfur problems or to systematically present what past mistakes to avoid and what accomplishments to build upon to promote similar processes in the other embattled regions of the country.

Even more problematic in the search for peace was that it focused on the warring parties, the biggest ones, with very little acknowledgement or solicitation of the opinions of the people who actually live with war, the affected communities and the smaller armed groups. As stated earlier, a lot of work has been done on Sudan's conflict, especially in relation to the documentation of human rights abuse by both sides of any given conflict. There has been a lot written on the suffering that war has inflicted on the civil population such as displacement and famine,[196] violence against women, the collapse of civil structures and breakdown of sociocultural norms in the face of the protracted crumbling of the political landscape.[197] Other studies have looked at the localized ethnic-based confrontation and factionalization of opposition forces, which draws civilian populations into conflicts that are essentially none of their choosing.[198] Studies have also been conducted on how humanitarian relief operations may fuel the conflict through appropriation of relief supplies by combatants.[199] Many of these studies are illuminating, providing the necessary context for anyone wishing to understand why and how Sudan's wars drag on.

What they do not show, however, is how the Sudanese people regard the possibility of a long-term solution; how the international diplomatic community might have mediated; what difficulties outside mediators encountered in approaching the Sudanese; and what the Sudanese found problematic about how mediators behaved. It would have been more instructive to the peace process to cross-pollinate the ethnographic material from the war zone with the thinking about peace negotiations at the international level. Mediators conducted the peace process for south Sudan, as well as in the other regions in turmoil, in an environment of poor contextual information and in a milieu of mutual misunderstanding. It should be the aim of researchers and mediators to gain an understanding of the changes in the functioning of the many peace initiatives to broker a just and lasting peace. Specifically, it is crucial to examine the role that influential countries such as the US could play in taking advantage of this ripe environment to get the peace process going. This needed to involve a consideration of the multifaceted nature of peace initiatives, the Sudanese people's response to them, and the resulting confusion and multiplicity of Sudanese negotiating camps. Top-down peace deals that focused on the main warring factions and not involving the people who had actually been the fodder for the burning conflict have proven unworkable. Because they excluded the very people whose livelihoods were most affected by war, such deals have been unsustainable. It would have been important, therefore, to explore the views of the ordinary Sudanese, the civil society groups, and the many factions in Sudan's conflicts, as well as their relationship to the wider regional and international contexts. Drawing on cultural knowledge of Sudan, and using the war-related ethnographic research material that has been collected over the years, the mediators needed to develop a comprehensive assessment that focuses on local, regional and international issues of one of Africa's longest, most deadly, most politically and diplomatically nuanced crises for which a solution must be found.

I have based this conclusion on the observation of recent historical events. When the Addis Ababa peace agreement was reached in 1972, between Nimeiri's government and the southern opposition group at that time, the Southern Sudan Liberation Movement, one of the tricks used to attain a quick agreement was to sweep under the carpet all of the atrocities and crimes against humanity committed during the first round of war, to prevent the peace negotiations from getting bogged down on issues of seeking justice for the victims of the seventeen-year-long war. It was argued that focusing on such issues would only derail the negotiations: the best solution was to try to forget these crimes and violations and focus on reconciliation. As became clear soon afterwards, people never forget such crimes: they are most likely to avenge their loved ones and destruction of their property. In other words, wishing the problems away did not build peace. It only served as a spoiler of what was already a fragile peace. This issue became one of the main reasons why Sudan was back at war after a short hiatus of ten years. After all, a variety of views among the Sudanese people indicated that they do not remember war in abstract and collective terms of victory or defeat only. Individuals and families remembered the kinds of experiences they had during the war, 'the real scars of war,' as many people have described them.

Other critics have widely denounced these peace processes because of their huge cost, lack of ingenuity, and lack of real headway. They were frustrating to the mediators because the parties clearly came to the talks not in good faith but to create a façade of interest in peace. One report described them: 'none are peace *processes* in the sense of continuous negotiations; in fact, there is no real negotiation in any of them, only a trading of well-worn positions and the obligatory release of dueling press releases.'[200] The main criticism was that since this was a chronic conflict, disingenuous diplomatic efforts to end it had brought with them notable dangers, which needed to be carefully weighed against the successes that they may have brought. Critics saw these on-and-off peace talks as encouraging the warring parties to masquerade as being interested in peaceful solutions, which allowed them to avert their constituents' demands for commitment to peace in addition to creating an alibi for the mediators' lack of political will. They gave the mediators a sense that they were doing what they could and that it was the warring parties that failed the Sudanese people, not the international community. This was more so especially for the wealthier countries of Western Europe and North America that had been paying the cost not only of the peace talks, but also of the huge humanitarian operations. The donor countries that had funded OLS for over sixteen years and continue to do so, referred to the amount of money they had paid when cornered about their lack of will to help resolve Sudan's crises as if throwing money at Sudan's conflicts was going to put out the flames of war.

Another element to the perceived weakness of these peace talks was the exclusion of smaller factions and civil society groups from the process. This undermined local institutional capacity to bring and maintain peace. It also weakens the willingness of the Sudanese people themselves to take responsibility for failed peace deals. It is important to consider the possibility that the multiplicity of Sudanese peace initiatives may be fueling conflict – particularly when soldiers scramble for more military gains on the eve of the talks in efforts to boost their negotiating positions. This said, however, lest we rush to write off these peace initiatives as harmful, it is important to weigh the harm and the benefits affected by mediated negotiations. The large number of countries and private NGOs interested in peace in Sudan may have very well increased the benefit of the peace talks by keeping war-induced tragedies in the media limelight, but due to their intractable nature, mediation responses may simultaneously increase the 'harm' by giving the warring parties the impression that pressures from the international community to reach an agreement were business as usual.

Based on this premise, it is my view that a chronic conflict such as this required different levels of analysis and understanding from the short-term narrowly based mediating initiatives that had been the model for much diplomatic effort in Sudan. It has been clear that owing to the lack of coordination and a unified position on the part of mediating countries, interventions have failed to prevent many deaths. Although important in keeping the issue on the agenda, the restriction of mediation efforts to the warring parties has completely marginalized the rural populations and the urban poor in whose name I think the interventions were initiated. Compared with the high-level politics of peace, the immediate, peace concerns of ordinary folk appear both mundane and more fundamental – namely, to defuse the dangerous mixture of deteriorating local economies, high mortality rates, collapsing civil structures, and limited access to the forums where their fate is being discussed. Such exclusion has caused failure of peace deals in the long term and has promoted localized violence.

Although the failure of the international community to press for peace in Sudan was portrayed in decontextualized media accounts as a result of the SPLA's unclear demands and negotiation in bad faith, the historical reality of mediation was much more fluid and complex. First, the processes creating and asserting any approach to peace were always culturally contingent and politically contested. Whereas, for example, the SPLA found unacceptable such concepts as 'human rights' and 'democracy' in an environment where the government of Sudan commits daily acts of brute terrorism, the mediators pushed for Western democratic ideals. In situations such as this, the crucial questions to ask were: In whose image and whose interests were these peace approaches formulated? When, why and how did these concepts become the sole measurements for commitment or indifference to a peace process? Where and when does the responsibility of a mediator for ensuring success begin or end?

The international concerns and the fate of conflict resolution in Sudan lost sight of the political dimensions of the rise of inter-ethnic violence, resistance to the state through local religious beliefs and prophecy, and the impact of rivalry among the educated class over their own constituencies. These issues have hampered an inclusive and sustainable peace deal. Unless there were ways to identify measures of local peace building, a national peace process would not only be difficult to achieve, but also nearly impossible to sustain long-term. There have been numerous opportunities to coordinate and balance all the initiatives in order to develop a more comprehensive, in-depth vision of the local impact of these regional and international peace efforts. Mediators needed to focus on the changing patterns of peace initiatives; the delivery of diplomatic assistance and how it was received by the warring parties as well as the Sudanese civil society groups; and how the search for international peace (including the war on terrorism) impacted on some mediators' ability to be trusted by both parties to Sudan's conflict. It appears not to have been an immediate mediators' goal to identify ways of potentially reducing current levels of misunderstanding and mistrust between warring factions on the one hand and the mediators on the other. This may have been accomplished through familiarity with the basic local perceptions Sudanese people held about the mediators and informing the Sudanese about the inner workings of the Western and regional diplomatic environment.

As for the fate and problems facing the apparent US commitment to bringing peace to Sudan, it is important to examine those obstacles that derived from the complexity of Sudan's conflict that impeded US peace efforts. It was equally important for the mediators to make known to the Sudanese the problems that emanate from Washington. While the US has often expressed concern over the escalating violence and the attendant human catastrophe in Sudan, the degree of commitment in Washington has been wavering at best and superficial at worst. American Sudan lobbyists and the Sudanese people have called upon the legislative and the executive branches of the American government to save Sudan. A host of binary opposites, however, were clouding the vision of Washington officials working on Sudan. There were as many factors that have militated against outright US involvement, as there were factors that have kept Washington's interest in a peace process alive. Some of these were mere assertions made by observers and others were supported by evidence. They include: (1) Sudan's sponsorship of international terrorism for which Washington imposed sanctions and trade embargoes on Khartoum in 1995 set against the backdrop of strong trading interests with Sudan, especially in gum Arabic, which means that Washington's commitment to sanctions had been watered down considerably. (2) The north's challenge that

Washington maintains its neutrality in the Sudanese conflict. Given the huge humanitarian assistance that the US was offering to organizations in south Sudan, despite Washington's claim of neutrality, the north saw the US as an improper mediator in the conflict. (3) In the same vein, when oil began to flow to the north from southern oilfields, the proceeds of which the government has used to boost its military position, US capital markets were under pressure to de-list foreign oil firms operating in Sudan as punishment for their complicity in human rights abuses. Such firms as the Canadian compnay Talisman Energy Inc. stood accused of facilitating the Sudan government's attack against civilians inhabiting the oil areas. Since US oil firms could not do business in Sudan's oil enterprise due to the trade embargoes mentioned above, pressure mounted on Washington either to work harder to bring peace so that oil companies can compete freely in Sudan, or deny the government of Sudan the oil profits that make it uninterested in peace. In addition, the US government argued that this must be viewed from the perspective of the overall international business environment. Using capital markets as diplomatic tools was regarded as setting a precedent that could easily get out of hand. (4) Furthermore, the strong US-based constituency that has grown among church groups, some senators and representatives and civil rights leaders in support of the Christian south has forced both the executive, especially the State Department and the White House, and the legislative branches of the US government to pressure the government of Sudan to improve the human rights situation, grant humanitarian access to famine-stricken areas, and to seek peace in good faith. Nevertheless, pressure from the Christian right was overplayed in Khartoum as amounting to direct material assistance to the south, and provided a tool that the government of Sudan used in its search for help from the Arab and Islamic world against the south. (5) After September 11, 2001, the government of Sudan issued statements condemning the attacks in New York and Washington, DC and vowed to support the US in its war against terrorism. This seemed to signal a potential thawing of diplomatic relations between Washington and Khartoum, and the south Sudanese began to view such developments with suspicion, again painting Washington as an untrustworthy mediator. Civil society groups in the south complained that Khartoum (which had hosted Osama bin Laden between 1991 and 1996) was taking the US for a ride, and if US intelligence could not see that, then Americans could not be trusted to negotiate a just settlement. In sum, America's ability to bring peace to Sudan, at that time seen by observers to be the only hope, was desirable to the warring parties and at the same time mistrusted by both. The mediators' poor contextual understanding and their ambiguous relationships with both sides of the conflict exacerbated such mistrust.

Over the past several years, therefore, Washington has put its weight behind local and regional peace proposals, more so since George W. Bush took office as president. The Sudan Peace Act mentioned above brought together various political forces in a cohesive effort on behalf of the Sudanese in a fashion few other issues have been able to accomplish in Washington. The process gathered momentum when John Danforth first arrived in Khartoum and initiated the discussion by giving the government of Sudan a list of steps to take as a way to test its genuine interest in a negotiated settlement. Danforth called them 'confidence-building measures,' and they included a cease fire in the Nuba mountains, halting of aerial bombing of communities in the south, agreeing to resume the IGAD peace talks, and granting unfettered humanitarian access to war victims. With the pressure mounting on the government of Sudan, the gains it had made in the war over the oil fields, and the US war on terrorism, the government of Sudan was able to come back to the peace talks in 2002. The US influence on the peace processes culminated in the signing of a very hopeful protocol mediated by Kenya under the auspices of IGAD signed in Machakos in July 2002. The Machakos Protocol, as it was called, was negotiated by a number of delegates whose instructions kept changing and whose mandates were limited. This required frequent halting of the talks so as to allow the delegates to consult with their superiors back in Khartoum and at SPLA headquarters. The delegates were able to reach agreements on the least controversial issues and deferred the trickiest points to a face-to-face negotiation between the Sudanese Vice President Ali Uthman Muhammad Taha and the SPLA Chairman John Garang de Mabior. The two men, using the Machakos Protocol as a foundation for their talks, were able to negotiate successive deals in Naivasha, Kenya, which culminated in the comprehensive peace accord that was signed in Nairobi on January 9, 2005, and the implementation of which has been complicated by the sudden death of John Garang on July 30, 2005. The implementation is also made difficult by the NIF/National Congress Party's unwillingness to adhere to the basic clauses of the agreement, notably the security arrangements, movement of troops, and the distribution of the most important sovereignty ministries like energy and finance, which the NCP continued to control. And despite the criticism that the agreement was not inclusive enough to work, a criticism that is true, the populations of the war affected regions were quite jubilant about the cessation of hostilities.

For southerners, the agreement may not contain everything they had fought for, but it includes the one issue most people have agreed upon, and that is the right to self-determination. The agreement called for a six-year interim period during which there will be two governments, one for the south to be called the Government of Southern Sudan, and another for the north, which includes southerners, and is to be called the Government of National Unity. After the interim period, the south will hold a referendum to decide its fate between unity with the north or separation from it. The other questions that form the pillars of the agreement include wealth-sharing in which the oil revenues would be divided down the middle between north and south; power-sharing whereby the head of the government of southern Sudan will also be the first vice president of Sudan, and some of the so-called key sovereignty ministries will go to southerners; and finally the security arrangements that will govern the relationship between the armies of the two governments. Criticism of the agreement was based on two important issues: the exclusion of smaller political forces from the agreement, and the fact that it had no conception of how to resolve the conflict in Darfur. In the case of the latter, it was argued that it is short-sighted to end war in one side of the country only to plunge into a similarly challenging war in another part, and that the southern peace will be threatened by the continuing hostilities in Darfur. This was especially a problem because the head of the government of southern Sudan became a partner with Khartoum in dealing with Darfur, and the SPLA will have to decide whether to continue its support to Darfur rebels or to fight them as part of its new capacity.

THE DARFUR CRISIS AND THE PEACE PROCESSES

It has been stated earlier that although the Darfur crisis had been brewing for quite some time, the eruption into an all-round war at the particular time that it did was probably related to the progress that was being made with the North–South peace process. The peace talks were being criticized for not taking a comprehensive look at the Sudanese conflicts as state-wide crises that would not end by solving only the problems of one region. The deal between the government of Sudan and the SPLA was regarded in other areas of the country as creating two autocratic governments who will monopolize the state power, to the continued marginalization of all the other political forces and regions. The exclusion of other aggrieved regions from the negotiations threatened them and perhaps the opposition movements in these regions reasoned that fighting was the only way to get them noticed and given a seat at the national reconciliation talks.

Nevertheless, it will be recalled that war on terrorism, and the blemished reputation the US under George W. Bush was gaining for its wars in Afghanistan and Iraq, seem to have prompted Washington to regard Sudan as a test of its ability to restore its eminence through bringing peace to an Islamic country, which would be a major foreign policy achievement offsetting the failure of earlier missions. This, coupled with the civil society pressures being mounted on Western European countries to end the long and deadly war in the south, caused the US government to put its weight, perhaps rightly so, behind the effort to bring peace to south

Sudan, with the view that peace in the south could translate into peace in all the other regions. To this end, not only did the US revamp its support of the IGAD process, but also talked its European allies into a concerted effort, leading to an increase in the activities of what was known as Partners of IGAD Forum, made up of the US, Britain, Italy and Norway. Against the advice of various independent agencies such as the International Crisis Group and Center for Strategic and International Studies to merge the efforts for the resolution of the Darfur crisis into the IGAD-led negotiations on the south, both the mediators and their above backers were convinced that the southern peace process must proceed independently of the other crises. They thought they were too close to reaching a deal to risk losing it by attaching the Darfur crises to it.

The search for the resolution of the Darfur problem, therefore, had to begin somewhere else. In the face of this ever-increasing humanitarian calamity, pressures were mounting on the UN to take action on Sudan. At the end of July 2004 the UN Security Council passed a watered down resolution threatening unspecified consequences if the government of Sudan did not disarm the militia and restore order and security by 30 August. The deadline came and went with no consequences. Indeed, destruction, displacement and death worsened in Darfur and apart from the huge humanitarian effort from Chad, no one did anything as far as a resolution to protect the civilians was concerned. For example, the UN reported that the Sudanese police charged with restoring calm in Darfur were sexually abusing women in IDP camps. Reporting the continued involvement of the Sudanese authorities in abuses against civilians proved some of the most damning indictments by aid groups. Interviews with IDPs revealed that the women could not venture outside the camp to collect firewood out of fear of Janjaweed attacks. Instead of protecting them, the police exploited their vulnerability by collecting the firewood for the women in exchange for sexual favors.[201] Human Rights Watch reported that 'some police officers had followed the women to the forests and threatened to beat them unless they succumb to their demands.'[202] There was outrage from across the international human rights spectrum about the absurdity of making the forces that were committing the killings, rape and looting part of the forces meant to restore security and protect people. They regarded the mass killings as the government's own project and thought it was preposterous to expect Khartoum to stop itself from executing its program.

Campaigns in human rights circles to get the situation declared as genocide were to no avail. It was not until US Secretary of State, Colin Powell, stated that the crisis in Darfur was 'the worst humanitarian crisis in the world today,' that the UN began to exert a benign pressure on Khartoum. The UN envoy to Sudan, Jan Pronk, declared just a few days before the deadline expired that Khartoum was not cooperating. In a press conference he said, 'In Khartoum, we hear a lot of fine words, but the situation in Darfur has not changed much. The UN doesn't want promises, but their fulfillment.' Pronk reminded the authorities in Khartoum that they had to fulfill four conditions by the end of the month to avert UN sanctions: disarming and confining the pro-government militias and providing lists of those guilty of crimes against humanity in Darfur; keeping regular soldiers, apart from police, away from the camps for displaced persons in the region; no hindrance to the work of humanitarian organizations operating in the camps; and continuing negotiations with the Darfur liberation movements for a political solution to the crisis 'whatever the difficulties' and 'whatever the conditions.' But as the case had been all through the years of the war, the government of Sudan probably once again made, or at least promised, just enough progress to give the international community the excuse to back off. The UN had neither the political will nor the mandate to impose sanctions on Sudan when the deadline expired. Even if sanctions were imposed, they would have been more symbolic than practical, with little impact on Khartoum's actions. Many Sudanese in the affected areas supported the sanctions idea, and the Sudanese diaspora thought that sanctions might have little practical value, but would affect Sudan's international respectability, in which case the sanctions would be better than doing nothing. It was suggested that the UN endorse an African Union peace-keeping force of at least 3,000 troops with a robust mandate to protect civilians. The international community would also have to commit significant financial resources to the logistical support of such a force. But Khartoum has been able to wield its oil wealth and oil prospects in whatever fashion and was most likely to secure international protection, probably from China, Sudan's biggest oil investor. The regime has also used its new-found wealth to restore its international image, especially its relations with both the Arab League and the Organization of Islamic Countries, and the continuing support of both these international organizations only emboldens Khartoum in its most savage internal policies of civilian destruction.[203] This makes any concerted international action against it almost impossible.

A multitude of foreign interests in Sudan militated against any unified international position on the best approach to ending the tragedies of Darfur. A combination of oil interests, international Islamic fraternity, and Arab relations seemed to have prompted the Chinese and the Pakistanis to abstain from the UN resolution on Darfur. Arab countries like Syria and Egypt made it clear that foreign intervention was not acceptable in dealing with the Darfur crisis. Despite acknowledging that there was a crisis in Darfur, the Arab League has continued to oppose outside intervention saying it cannot under any conditions accept foreign interventions, 'since such intervention aims at partitioning Sudan and seizing its wealth ... The territorial integrity of Sudan is a national interest concern for the countries in the region,'[204] a clear demonstration of the African-Arab alliance on a larger scale beyond racialized relations within Sudan.

As was the case with the south, many Arab countries echoed the Sudan government's accusation that Israel has been trying to take advantage of wars in Sudan to develop a foothold in the region. Accusing Israel of supporting southerners was probably under-standable because of the popular politics which suggest that the south is anti-Arab and that Israel could see in southerners potential allies, but such indictment was made so frequently, and without any evidence, that the claim could only be interpreted as intended to elicit support from Arab governments. However, undocu-mented allegations of Israel offering support to the liberation movements in Darfur spoke to Khartoum's desire to internationalize the conflict only if Islamic and Arab countries got involved, but the presence of Israel and the US was regarded in Khartoum as a Zionist design, something Sudan's rulers think all the Arab countries should protest. Israel dismissed the claims as 'crazy accusations.' The only thing linking Israel to Darfur was an Israeli press announcement that it was planning to send aid supplies to Darfur and a medical team to the refugee camps in Chad. But the involvement of Israel was bound to be charged with other regional politics. As Eric Reeves wrote:

> Given the high level of feeling about Israel within the Arab world, and the tendency of all sides in the Arab-Israeli conflict to politicize events for their own interests, Israeli assistance in Darfur may prove to be a mixed blessing. The Governor of Kassala State in eastern Sudan recently linked 'global Zionism' to armed opposition groups in that region as well.[205]

There is no evidence supporting Khartoum's claims of Zionist involvement in Darfur, which indicates that such allegations are part of Khartoum's usual policy of raising the specter of Israeli interference as a way to galvanize Arab support.

It was not until 2005 that the UN began to move slowly. The UN Secretary General, Kofi Annan, established a commission to investigate whether acts of genocide have occurred in Darfur and who might be responsible for them. The commission was headed by Antonio Cassese, an Italian jurist who has done similar work on crimes committed in the former Yugoslavia. The commission presented the possibility, perhaps, of some justice being carried out to bring those responsible for the Darfur disaster to account for their acts. But the commission concluded that although horrendous atrocities amounting to war crimes and crimes against humanity had been committed in Darfur, they had not become genocidal.

Negotiations to end the war in the south pushed forward independently of the war in Darfur, but some negotiations began to be conducted between the government and the Darfur rebels concurrently with the south-related IGAD talks. There have been a number of significant initiatives, but as yet no real progress toward stabilizing the situation on the ground nor on achieving a just and enduring political solution to the conflict. Attempts to find a resolution began when the Chadian President convened a meeting between the Khartoum government and the rebel groups in the Chadian border town of Abéché. Although the JEM refused to join the talks due to suspicion of Chadian bias, the meeting resulted in a ceasefire agreement on September 3, 2003, that committed the warring parties to a forty-five-day cessation of hostilities as of September 6. A second round of talks, again mediated by Chad, followed when the government and the SLA met again in Abéché from October 26 to November 4, 2003, but they quickly reached an impasse over trading of accusations of ceasefire violations.

> The rebels conditioned their substantive participation on adoption of internationally monitored protocols for civilian protection and unhindered access of relief supplies and workers to areas under their control; disarming of the Janjaweed; and the presence of international observers at the negotiations.[206]

The government objected to the internationalization of the Chadian peace process. 'The most that could be done was to renew the ceasefire for another month.'[207] The final Chadian attempt at peace in Darfur was convened in the capital N'djamena in December 2003. Each party went to meet with President Déby separately, but the talks collapsed and the secretary general of the SLA, Mini Arko Minawi, hinted in a press conference that the talks were called off because the government of Sudan had learned of the rebels position in advance: the rebels had demanded direct talks with the government in the presence of international observers. The talks collapsed and Chad's interior minister told the press that the negotiations had broken down due to what he called 'unacceptable rebel demands,' and that the 'talks have been suspended; it's a failure.'[208] The failure put the Chadian authorities in a bind. For Idris Déby, who came to power through assistance from Khartoum and cannot afford to anger them, to maintain loyalty to the government of Sudan was to risk losing his Zaghawa constituency within Chad;

but to support the Darfur rebels at the behest of Chadian Zaghawas who want to lend their weight to their kin across the border, is to stir the wrath of Khartoum. Such are the issues that make Sudan's neighbors nervous about instability in Sudan.

The matter was then taken up by the African Union (AU), and the warring parties have since had several rounds of meetings in Abuja, Nigeria under the auspices of the AU. Building on the ceasefire agreement of August of 2003, they conducted a number of mediated discussions on possible political solutions to the Darfur grievances and to allow humanitarian aid to reach the hundreds of thousands that were displaced by militia and government aerial attacks. At the height of atrocities and the international cries, the AU resolved to send monitors to report on the targeting of civilians and violations of the ceasefire agreement, but substantive discussions were difficult to start. When they finally got underway, the liberation movements walked out in protest at the alleged killing of sixty-four civilians by government forces on August 25, 2004 in Yassin, near Nyala, in violation of the ceasefire accord. AU monitors were instructed to investigate the incident. The movements were worried by initial government attempts to exclude from the discussions a political solution to the conflict and concentrate only on a ceasefire and humanitarian and human rights issues. They also had concerns about the confinement of their troops as part of any ceasefire agreement, believing that this would benefit the government militarily. They eventually at least agreed on an agenda, but the attention of the AU and African governments was distracted by many other events across the continent, including the efforts to consolidate the peace process in Burundi and the evermore disastrous humanitarian situation in the Democratic Republic of Congo.

It had become clear that nothing short of foreign military intervention, at least in a peace-keeping capacity or protection of civilians, would save Darfurians. The tragic problem was that a few observers, military or otherwise, in such a large territory, where there are virtually no roads, a fragile ecology and where the old order has broken down, was not going to be enough. And what country or countries would send the kind of force the situation in

Darfur required? After much debate and pressure from the human rights and advocacy community as well as the initiative of African governments such as the Rwandese, the African Union troops began arriving in Darfur in early summer of 2004 to the relief of all concerned. They were too few, with too limited a mandate to prevent the slaughter, and with inadequate logistical support. Their mandate was to protect the AU monitors, not to protect Sudanese civilians. There were initially 150 from Rwanda, followed by the same number from Nigeria by the end of August. However the Rwandan president Paul Kagame said, 'Our forces will not stand by and watch innocent civilians being hacked to death like the case was here in 1994,' referring to UN troops who did not intervene as genocide unfolded in Rwanda because they did not have a mandate to stop the slaughter. 'If it was established that the civilians are in danger, then our forces would certainly intervene and use force to protect civilians ... In my view, it does not make sense to give security to peace observers while the local population is left to die.' This force was, however, too small to be effective. While it is not possible to compare the situation in Darfur to that of Iraq, the analogy may be entirely possible as a way to gain perspective on the difficulties that awaited the African Union mission in Darfur. If the 160,000 US and allied troops cannot control Iraq, it is hard to imagine how the 150 Rwandan troops could have been expected to make a practical difference in Darfur, which is nearly the same size as Iraq. Still the statement of the Rwandan President had great symbolic value as it set a precedent in the long-awaited commitment of African leaders to solving 'African problems.' A number of African countries, Rwanda included, have been pushing to give the troops a formal mandate to use force to stop attacks on civilians. Nigeria also agreed to an expanded mandate with up to 3,000 troops, and made gestures that it will offer as many as 1,500. Algeria, Egypt, Kenya, Libya, Tanzania and Uganda have all indicated that they were willing to offer troops. Despite the small size of the force currently in place, and despite what is essentially an overwhelming tragedy, nearly two years later, it seemed to have managed to reduce violence, at least in the IDP camps closest to the force's headquarters. But the vast majority of Darfur IDPs continue to live under terror while the government of Sudan vehemently objects to increasing the AU force's mandate.

The government of Sudan rejected any foreign peace-keeping force and instead suggested that it would handle security itself, and that remains as Khartoum's preferred position. It was not until the end of August 2004 at the Abuja talks that the government relented slightly and agreed to accept peace-keepers under certain conditions. The head of the government's delegation in Abuja, Majzoub al-Khalifa, announced their agreement to increasing the AU forces and that these forces may be granted more room for protection of monitors as well as 'civilian protection from the rebels.' However, the government continued to drag its feet, did not formally agree to any enlargement of the force, and still objected to the use of foreign troops to protect civilians and humanitarian aid. Human rights and advocacy groups such as Human Rights Watch kept pushing for international donors and African countries to boost support for the AU mission in Darfur, to ensure that more AU troops were deployed quickly to protect civilians.[209] The size of the AU force has since been increased to some 7,000 troops at the time of writing, but violence against IDPs continued, albeit sporadically, and there are now demands for the replacement of the AU force with one from the UN, a proposition Khartoum continues to object to, but which pressured it into another round of talks in Abuja in March and April 2006.

Because gross human rights abuses continued in Darfur throughout the first half of 2005, where government-sponsored Janjaweed militia were attempting to consolidate 'ethnic cleansing' long before the international rescue intensified, and which they were executing by attacking IDPs, mostly farmers who tried to return to their homes, the matter became so disturbing that on May 26, 2005, the UN Secretary-General Kofi Annan and AU Chairman Alpha Oumar Konaré met in Addis Ababa to host a conference, which brought together officials from the US, the European Union and African nations to increase support for the African Union Mission in Sudan (AMIS) for Darfur. NATO's

Secretary-General, Jaap de Hoop Scheffer, also attended. They may have finally felt that they had a duty and a critical role to play in rapidly boosting protection for the people of Darfur. Observer groups such as Justice Africa, International Crisis Group and Human Rights Watch urged donors and troop-contributing countries to agree on a firm timetable for accelerated deployment of 12,300 AU troops. The AU mission of 2,400 troops was at that time too small to protect civilians proactively throughout Darfur (current AU plans call for 12,300 troops on the ground by spring 2006). The human rights observers said that this was far too slow to curb the destruction and that an urgent transfer of the mission to the UN is the only immediate life-saving option.

In a press statement, Peter Takirambudde, Africa director at Human Rights Watch said: 'If African countries contribute more troops and donors provide needed technical and logistical support now, it should be possible to speed up protection efforts in Darfur ... The people of Darfur can't wait until next spring for the African Union to reach its planned troop deployment.'[210] The Sudanese government at the national and state level has taken no serious steps to rein in or prosecute those forces, despite several UN Security Council resolutions since July 2004 demanding such action, and the security situation remains clearly dangerous for the whole population. Even by early summer 2005, six million people in Darfur were faced with banditry, militia attacks and a devastated economy, two million Darfuris were already displaced and living in the confinement of the camps, while the farmers among them were unlikely to be able to resume planting crops outside their villages. All this was happening in an environment where an estimated 3.5–4 million people in Darfur were not going to have enough to eat in the remaining months of 2005. Instead of facilitating the humanitarian relief effort that was attempting to help millions of Darfurians, the Sudanese authorities stepped up a bureaucratic war on relief workers. Since December 2004, the Sudanese government continually attempts to intimidate some humanitarian agencies in Darfur through refusal to renew visas, arbitrary arrests, detentions and other more subtle forms of harassment. In May

2005, for example, the country director of Médecins sans Frontières (MSF) for Sudan, having just announced that rapes and other violent assaults were still rampant in Darfur despite government assurances to protect its own citizens, was arrested for 'propagating lies against the state.'[211] Although MSF is one of the many NGOs to insist that the government atrocities in Darfur and south Sudan fall short of genocide, it admits that racial/ethnic cleansing motives drive the actions of denying relief to civilians.

The high-level conference on AMIS mentioned above was a good opportunity for human rights groups to voice their concern. Just as Human Rights Watch did, the International Crisis Group President Gareth Evans wrote a letter addressed to world leaders, including those who were meeting at the Addis Ababa conference, in which he urged much stronger international intervention to stop the ongoing killing in Darfur.[212] He highlighted two areas in particular that immediately demanded a bold new approach: the mandate of the international troop presence, and its size and capacity. The existing mandate of AMIS, as authorized by the African Union Peace and Security Council, had focused on monitoring and verification, leaving to the Sudanese government the basic responsibility to protect civilians and humanitarian workers. But Evans said that 'Khartoum has utterly failed in its responsibility to protect its own citizens ... And AMIS's own protection role is so highly qualified as to be almost meaningless.' For world leaders to suggest that the Sudanese government can provide security is a slap in the face for the victims and their entire communities: the perpetrators cannot be expected to go against their own project of racially targeted elimination or creation of conditions that result in mass starvation.

Most observers would have agreed with ICG's President that the force's mandate needed to be strengthened to enable and encourage it to undertake all necessary measures, including proactive action, to protect civilians in Darfur. While everyone was clearly tiptoeing around the Khartoum regime due to diplomatic issues, trading interests and sovereignty matters, it was undeniable that its reluctance to accept an expanded mandate must be met with a decision to commence deployment of a fully mandated protection force whether or not Khartoum agreed. Although the AU might have had the best will in the world, by early 2006 it had become apparent that it was unable, without substantial further international support and a stronger mandate, to deploy an effective force of the magnitude and time-frame required. International Crisis Group suggested that African personnel with strong international support would be ideal, but that if this proved unworkable in the short time available, a multinational bridging force would be the only solution to tackle Darfur's most urgent protection needs. NATO was asked by the AU as the best-equipped organization to provide, and lead, the additional troops required in the necessary numbers and within the necessary time-frame, but in an interview on National Public Radio in the US shortly after the Addis Ababa conference, the Secretary-General of NATO declared that he did not foresee the involvement of NATO troops, but that together with the European Union, they were most likely to provide the basic logistics such as flying in the troops and supplying them as requested by the AU.

After its commission's report on war crimes and a Security Council resolution, and despite US opposition to the idea of the International Criminal Court, the UN finally agreed to refer the Sudanese war crimes case to the ICC in The Hague. A list of the accused perpetrators of the crime of genocide and other war crimes was compiled by the State Department in June 2004. Musa Hilal tops a list of seven supposed Janjaweed commanders accused of war crimes: rather than go into hiding, he assumed a very public presence in Khartoum and made himself available to Western journalists, even inviting them along on trips to his tribal homeland in north Darfur. In what must have embarrassed the Sudanese government, which habitually denies any ties to Hilal, the sheik was usually traveling home aboard Sudanese government aircraft.

But it appears that sheik Hilal knew how to play his cards. On one hand, it seems highly unlikely that the Khartoum government will move against him because he knows too much of what has really happened in Darfur. He hinted at this on many occasions when he met with foreign journalists in Khartoum. He once declared that the government approached him and many of the other sheiks and asked for their help in fighting the Darfur rebels, and that they had gladly agreed because they were suffering from these rebels too. He said that the sheiks recruited young men to help in this fight, but that mistakes or crimes that they had not foreseen took place, and laid the blame for these mistakes squarely on the government's doorstep. 'It is the government's responsibility, not ours.'[213] He declared that the Blacks had also killed the Arabs for years over grievances about land and water, which had given rise to bitterness among the latter. 'When the government put forward a program of arming all the people, I will not deny, I called our sons and told them to become armed,'[214] Hilal continued. On the other hand, it appears Hilal did not have much to fear from those in the international community who suggested that he might be arrested; his name appeared at the top of the US State Department's war-criminals list in June 2004, but the State Department met with him in the following month in Khartoum. That meeting epitomized the transformation that has occurred in American policy toward Darfur and it explains Washington's vehement opposition to the referral of Darfur crimes to the ICC in the early part of 2005. From having led the charge for international involvement in the region and first raising the specter of genocide, the Bush administration became noticeably reluctant to lend importance to the declaration of genocide unanimously passed by Congress. What explains this shift is that the Bush administration was caught between salvaging the progress it has made with Sudan in recent years – most notably the North–South peace settlement that American diplomats were instrumental in forging – and the risk of losing it all by pushing too hard on Darfur. One State Department official expressed the dilemma this way. 'The Sudanese will bend to a certain point, but beyond that they just won't. The real danger here is that if you go too far, it derails the North–South deal, and you're back to another 22 years of war.'[215]

This situation reveals how adept the Khartoum government has proved at playing one part of the international community off the other. At the same time that they have assumed a conciliatory stance toward the UN's demands, they have played to their Arab neighbors and more militant domestic constituency by darkly warning of an Anglo-American invasion. Khartoum authorities tell their followers that the Americans, the British and the Zionists are gearing up to invade Sudan as they did Iraq and that the regime's supporters should prepare to turn Sudan into 'another Iraq' if the invasion happens. The two-pronged strategy has worked satisfactorily for the Islamists in Khartoum. For example, on August 4, 2004 the al-Bashir government announced full cooperation with the UN while an estimated 100,000 of its supporters were in the streets of Khartoum denouncing foreign meddling in Sudanese affairs. The latest phase of peace negotiations in Abuja, Nigeria, which took place during March and April 2006, collapsed at the end of that period as the mediators' deadline given to the parties ran out on April 30. The government's top negotiator, Ali Usman Taha, returned to Khartoum in protest at the unwillingness of the rebel movements to sign the protocol that had been reached. Darfur opposition movements had made renewed pre-conditions in the areas of power sharing and security arrangements, including the demand that the position of Sudan's vice president be permanently given to a Darfurian. They also demanded that Khartoum withdraw its troops from Darfur, something the government cannot do, nor can it be expected to agree to. It was also understandable that opposition groups made such a condition given that no Khartoum government since independence has ever signed a single agreement it was willing to keep and therefore Darfurian representatives were suspicious that Khartoum was going to use this agreement to buy time while it planned to launch renewed attacks when it suited it. This leaves the mediators in a serious quandary as to how to proceed and reveals one more important weakness in the international peace-making system: the conflict between various national interests of the mediating countries. The missing link in Darfur's peace process is strong coordination among the countries involved in the search for peace. It will be recalled that it took ten years before IGAD was able to achieve the shaky North–South peace agreement, and that should function as a warning to both the warring parties and the mediators in the Darfur conflict that they must try to avoid falling into the same pitfalls that prolonged the southern process. Further protraction would be gravely detrimental to more Darfurians, as the UN World Food Program announced that it was cutting in half the food rations to the IDPs and refugees due to lack of funding, and to cohesion of the nation as protraction of the conflict could frustrate the Darfurians into seeking separation as an alternative.

CONCLUSION

This chapter was aimed at addressing the East African regional implications of Sudan's wars, and the search for a mediated settlement, beginning with the Abuja peace talks between the NIF government and the SPLA up to its culmination into the IGAD peace initiatives. When these peace efforts produced what became known as the Naivasha Protocol, an agreement signed in Kenya, there was a widespread feeling of jubilation, but this sense of triumph was quickly dampened by two events. The first was the untimely death of SPLA leader, John Garang, the immediate consequence of which was the suspicion throughout south Sudan that there had been foul play in his helicopter crash while returning from a visit to the Ugandan president, Yoweri Musevini. A more damaging development that resulted from Garang's death was the slow pace which the NIF government took in the implementation of the so-called 'Comprehensive Peace Agreement.' There were immediately strong signs of NIF unwillingness to hold up its end of the agreement. Instead, it seemed that it used the period between January 2005, when the agreement was signed, and the end of the year, in order to regroup and revitalize its hold on power. For example, the wealth-sharing agreement was surrounded with such secrecy that the government of southern Sudan did not even know how much money was coming in as oil revenue, 50 percent of which was supposed to go to Juba. This has raised the ever-present specter of 'Arab exploitation' among southerners, a sentiment detrimental to the peace process. It has also aroused the usual fears that the north has never been known to respect peace agreements. The power-sharing agreement had stipulated that some of the sovereignty ministries such as defense, finance, energy, and the interior would go to the SPLM*. This was not the case and the SPLM was left to make an unpleasant choice between pushing the peace process to a point of a referendum to be held on unity or southern separation after a six-year interim period, or to drop the whole process alltogether and return to war. So far, the former seems to prevail. The reality is that the NIF continued to control the whole government after the peace agreement. Even where southerners were given a position of power, as in the Ministry of Foreign Affairs under Lam Akol, shadow ministers like Mustafa Osman Ismail continued to hold the real power. The NIF has deliberately watered down the agreement and there are no strong signs of its implementation anywhere in the south. Whether it is the withdrawal of its military from the south, disarming its proxy militias in the oil regions of Upper Nile, accepting the findings of the Abyei Boundary Commission†, dispensing the funds for rehabilitation of infrastructure in the south so the Government of southern Sudan can begin to function, or assistance with the repatriation and resettlement of the millions of IDPs who are desperate to return home, the NIF has failed to meet the obligations it has made in the agreement.

The second event that nearly submerged the joy of peace was the Darfur insurgency. This latest phase of war has engendered unprecedented state-sponsored violence and catastrophic famines and has in turn led to a multinational peace-keeping effort by the AU. However, this internationalization of the conflict has not produced quick results by way of preventing suffering and death. This chapter looked at the logistical and financial problems faced by the

---

* The SPLM is the political wing of the southern opposition SPLA.
† An International Commission set up soon after the signing of the peace agreement to look into the history and possible solutions to the disputed Dinka territory called Abyei that was placed in South Kordofan in the 1972 Agreement.

AU mission, their limited mandate in protecting civilians, the intransigence of the Sudanese security forces, and the latest UN Security Council Resolution to indict prominent figures in the NIF government, including President al-Bashir; Second Vice-President, Ali Osman Taha; the head of Khartoum's viciously efficient security and intelligence services, Major General Saleh Abdallah Gosh; former Minister of the Interior and current Minister of Defense, Abdul Rahim Mohamed Hussein, and many others in the administration at both local and national levels, for trial in the International Criminal Court in The Hague.[216]

The tragedy of the Darfur crisis is that the world community continues to watch the continuing violence and genocidal destruction powerlessly, and seems to have resigned itself to the whims of the NIF – that the mediators in Abuja can only hold the meetings when Khartoum wants them to, and that there is no mechanism to force the warring parties to the negotiating table. There is also a danger that the SPLM should strive to influence the NIF military policies or negotiating platform in the ongoing Abuja peace talks, now that both have become partners in the government of national unity. The failures of the international community to bring those accused of crimes against humanity to book indicate Khartoum's ultimate genocidal victory. It also tells us a lot about the weak nature of the genocide convention. Despite the clear evidence that genocide has taken place, Human Rights Watch, for example, contradicted its own report because of the question of intent in the arguments about whether genocide can indeed be verified to have taken place.

> Whether [National Islamic Front] policy [in Darfur] amounted to genocide remains unclear. The International Commission of Inquiry into the crimes in Darfur concluded that there was no government policy of genocide, but that crimes may have been committed by individuals with genocidal intent and that this question should be resolved in a court of law. Determining whether there was genocidal intent requires access to government documents and to those in the leadership who planned and coordinated the campaign in Darfur.[217]

The surrendering of responsibility for peace in Darfur to the SPLM was a tragedy on two accounts. The first is that the SPLM is certainly incapable of stopping genocide in Darfur as it does not have any leverage within the NIF-controlled government, nor does it have capacity to influence regional politics that could be rallied to pressure Khartoum. The second is that there is not even a strong constituency within the south that is concerned with Darfur, one which could pressure the SPLM into making peace in Darfur a priority, as the people of Darfur are viewed in the south as the killers of yesterday becoming the victims of today.

8

CONCLUSION
Which Way Sudan?

The problem of racialized and religious violence makes the question of national unity in Sudan a burning issue today as it has done since independence. More than fifty years after independence, the Sudanese remain divided on the issue of what the country's cultural outlook, its racial self-perception, its system of government, the citizens' loyalty to their ethnicity or region versus loyalty to the state, and above all, whether ethnic, racial, and religious diversity is to be embraced as a source of strength or to be attacked and eliminated as a source of weakness and disunity. The ruling elite, self-identified as Arab and insisting that everyone else should become Arab as well, remain fearful about the consequences of sharing power and resources with the non-Arabs in the peripheries. They fear that making concessions to the regions in revolt will simply lead to the latter demanding more, so the dominant group keeps it all or risks losing it all; and they seem to have made the decision to keep most of the power and resources in a society that is deeply divided along racial and religious lines. The consequence of this decision is a nationwide sense that the inhabitants of Sudan are divided into state-favored citizens and the marginalized subjects, to borrow Mahmood Mamdani's phrase. The results of such a divide have included deadly confrontations between the state and the aggrieved regions, and squabbles between the Sudanese government and many sections of the world community, a situation that is increasingly reminiscent of the dilemma that was faced by the Afrikaners in South Africa in the descending years of apartheid. The more divided by this racialized distribution of power and wealth the country becomes the wider the split in world opinion and actions regarding the Sudanese state. Like apartheid South Africa, there is a raging debate between the countries that are heavily invested in the Sudanese oil industry and those opposed to conducting business with a rogue regime. The former have turned a blind eye to the human rights crises engendered by oil exploitation and are not willing to entertain the concept of socially responsible business. They continue to give the Khartoum government the profits it needs to boost its position in the war against the dissenting regions. Other countries that support economic sanctions against Khartoum, while they wish to have access to the Sudanese market, attempt to force the government to make reforms and reduce abuse of human rights before it can expect to join the community of respectable nations. Which side wins in this duel depends on how long and at what cost each side is willing to hold onto their position, whether the investors in Sudan can withstand the blemishing mark of assisting a genocidal government, and whether the sanctioning countries can withstand the pressure from their corporations to open the doors to their involvement in Sudan.

This chapter summarizes the study by picking out key points that function as manifestations of Arab-African, Muslim-non-Muslim, center-periphery confrontations that have torn at the fabric of the nation for five decades. It will attempt to read the recent past as a way to think about the future. If reconciliation is reached, and in the face of the long history of oppression and devastation wrought on the non-Arabs by the manifolds of racism, religious persecution, slavery, ethnic cleansing, and genocide, what form of recompense could possibly set Sudan on a path to peaceful coexistence? If Sudan is to build a national policy that reduces discord and promotes unity, cleans up its human rights record, allows basic liberties, eliminates inequality on the basis of race, religion, ethnicity, gender, and ceases exporting militant Islam to other countries, what would it have do in order to achieve this? Three basic issues have dominated the national unity debate for over fifty years: (1) the racial policies that facilitate the control of power by the Arabs of the northern Province, the riverine populations who live along the Nile from Dongola to al-Jazirah, (2) the use of militant Islam and Arab cultural nationalism as mechanisms for cultural homogenization of the country into an Arab-Islamic state, and (3) the silencing of the marginalized non-Arab majority of populations that occupy the remote regions peripheral to the centers of power. These are not issues unique to Sudan, and the experience of other countries that have a similar set-up could have functioned as a guide to the Sudanese, if the country had been open to a civil debate about its identity crises.

Unfortunately, the state was quick to militarize the debate. Instead of responding to the grievances of the peripheries in measured nationalistic steps, the leaders of Sudan allowed themselves to be blinded by racism, cultural nationalism and religious zeal; and the prism through which they looked at the question of national unity was therefore tainted by prejudice, perhaps also intoxicated by greed and power mania. They deployed radical armies imbued with Islamic militancy and trained in unremorseful human destruction. They resorted to a deployment of weapons purchased with the resources of all the peoples to strengthen the Arabs' posture in order to limit, reduce or eliminate the elements they have deemed obstructive to the image of Sudan they intended to build, i.e. an Arab-Islamic cultural project. The result, as may be expected, has been that the peripheries have been in turn equally radicalized, and the country has been polarized almost to a point of no return, and the wars attest to this polarization. This extremism on both sides has undoubtedly set the nation on the path to disintegration. Many Sudanese now say the few options left for Sudan to choose from include either a break-up, a blind insistence on this brand of unity, which forever embroils the country in endless conflicts, or to reform its ways so as to allow every citizen to feel a sense of belonging without any prejudice.

While the south's unrelenting attempt to break away has often been blamed on colonialism, that the Europeans were responsible for creating a divisiveness among the Sudanese who would have otherwise headed toward a unified national character, many of the informants I have talked to wonder who the Arab rulers and their apologists in academia and diplomatic circles were going to blame for Darfur, the Nuba mountains, the southern Blue Nile, the eastern province, all of which have been up in arms against the Arab-controlled state for reasons that emerged long after the departure of the British colonial officials. These other regions were considered by the ruling elite in the past as part of a cohesive 'north,' that they were nearly on their way to becoming absorbed into the Arab fold, and that the colonial impact on them had not been as anti-unity as the south was instigated to be. But these regions have also increasingly been feeling excluded from the type of union the Arab elites have tried to forge. If the situation continues as it has for five decades, a break-up of the traditional north is unavoidable. The south has already edged a step toward separation and is now waiting impatiently to hold a referendum to chart out its own future, but the Nuba mountains, the southern Blue Nile, the eastern region, and now Darfur will surely all seek opportunities for self-determination. While the peripheral areas that formerly made up the 'north' like Darfur and the eastern region have not yet started talking about separation, the militarized reaction of the state to their grievances, a response which has deliberately targeted the civilians as Khartoum's means of fighting the opposition by proxy, and if the situation persists into the foreseeable future, Darfur and other regions will most likely be frustrated into heading toward self-government if not a demand for total independence.

RESISTANCE, RESOURCES AND WAR IN THE SOUTH

This study has also attempted to highlight the rise of political Islam as the successive regimes in Khartoum have tried to unify the identity of the nation on the basis of forging racial and cultural homogeneity, but instead caused further polarization, which in turn threatens the nation's territorial unity. The Islamic and dictatorial regime of General Abbud (1958–1964), produced no solution to the 'southern problem' through his military adventures, nor did the civilian government (1964–1969) that assumed the reins of power in the wake of the October 1964 popular revolution, and in spite of all efforts, proposals and recommendations of the Round Table Conference on South Sudan as a priority issue. The question of south Sudan, especially with regard to the issues of racial identity of the nation and of the secular versus Islamic constitution, has remained a thorny and intractable dilemma for the Sudanese state. It has increasingly been intensified by state-sponsored violence, and has now reached a stage where it does not seem to lend itself to an easy solution in a united Sudan. The socialist regime that signed the Addis Ababa accord, while acknowledging unity-in-diversity and the principle of a secular constitution and system of government in Sudan, also became the target of scathing attacks by the anti-socialist traditional Islamic and sectarian political forces such as the Umma (ansar al-Mahdi), Democratic Unionist Party (DUP – Khatmiyya Islamic sect), and the fundamentalist Muslim Brothers who later evolved into the currently ruling National Islamic Front. They led Nimeiri toward self-destruction by pressuring him to do away with the Addis Ababa accord and apply Islamic law.

The opposition posed by the Islamic sectarian and fundamentalist alliance over time, and their constant attacks (supported in many cases by key Arab states) on the 'May regime,' as Nimeiri's government was often called, almost proved fatal for Sudan. This later led to a national reconciliation deal between Nimeiri and the Islamic political forces, Umma, DUP, and the Muslim Brothers, at the expense of the consensus reached in the Addis Ababa agreement regarding a secular constitution and system of government for the state. The suspicions of Africans in south Sudan were to be proved right again when, in September 1983, the President of the Republic Ja'afer Mohammed Nimeiri decreed the formal introduction of shari'a, or the Islamic laws, the declaration of Sudan as an Islamic state, and the preparatory measures adopted to promulgate an Islamic constitution with the president appointing himself as Imam or Islamic spiritual leader. The Addis Ababa accord itself no longer enjoyed validity and was rendered useless by the new measures and presidential decrees that violated the constitution with impunity. The balance of power had shifted from center to right, so that the engendered political crisis leading to instability in the relations between the north and south sparked off another rebellion in south Sudan that led to the formation and birth in Sudan's political landscape in 1983, of the Sudan People's Liberation Movement and Sudan People's Liberation Army.

The emergence of SPLM/A into the Sudanese political scene marked the beginnings of another phase of a devastating conflict and instability in the political history of the Sudanese state, which raged on for twenty-two years before it was ended in a fragile peace agreement that is yet to show dividends in the eyes of the war affected communities in the south. That period has seen several governments come and go, starting with the demise of Nimeiri's regime, followed by the Transitional Military Council (TMC) under General Abdul Rahman Swar ed-Dahab, the short spell of Sadiq al-Mahdi's premiership, followed by the dictatorial military regime of Omar al-Bashir in 1989 backed by the fundamentalist NIF. The NIF regime, like Abbud's dictatorship of 1958, is unashamedly Islamic extremist, advocating as it does the institution of an Islamic state in the Sudan to be governed by an Islamic constitution and implementation of Islamic laws, with the exemption of the south and the capital Khartoum according to the current agreement. The principle of an Islamic state and constitution espoused and advocated by the NIF in northern Sudan is one which the two main sectarian parties; the DUP and Umma, would also find difficult not to advocate if given and allowed the opportunity.

Almost all of the confrontations between these successive regimes and the southern opposition are as much resource wars as they are ideological. The southern resources, whether assumed or real, are the main reason for northern insistence on keeping the country united, a policy in the interests of the country but not in the humanity of the people who inhabit it. They are also among the reasons that south Sudanese felt cheated. In addition, the racial and religious ideologies were also the primary driving force behind the government's refusal to treat all ethnicities and cultural practices as equal, with a view to an eventual emergence of an Arab-Islamic national identity. Needless to say, such ideologies polarized the country and set it on the path to self-destruction that has made it the location of some of the worst humanitarian crises in the world today.

It is more than eighteen years since the NIF-backed regime came to power, and it has not shown any signs of moderation on a secular constitution and system of government, bent instead on continuing the war and the imposition of its model of the Sudanese state. And so it signed a peace deal with the SPLM only to get embroiled in another equally brutal conflict in Darfur and in the east. The narrative does not bode well for Sudan. It reveals and betrays a history not of optimism, but a sad one, bitter and littered with intense conflicts of identity, and threatening to break apart the very foundation of the state, the pride of its people in their citizenship. Furthermore, the divergent views of the parties to the conflict, the theocratic Arab-Islamic trend on the one hand, the African-secular dispensation on the other, increasingly appear to admit no solution in a united Sudan. Fundamental disagreements and differences exist about the nature of the state, its constitution and system of government. The gap appears increasingly unbridgeable and there has been little chance of agreement and shared definitions on the fundamental questions of the state, the laws governing it, and conventions by which a modern state abides. This realization has begun to set a new trend: as all indications show, the remaining options are limited, the solution to the problems of the 'Sudanese state' increasingly lie nowhere else but in partition. On balance, partition would bring to an end the vicious cycle of violence, intractable civil wars and questions of identity, the state, and the unresolved constitutional problem in Sudan since 1956. However, while this picture may be crystal clear in regard to North–South relations, it is complicated by the risings in other regions of the country, and perhaps it is important to think what other scenarios the conflicts in Darfur, the Nuba mountains, southern Blue Nile, Nubia, and the northeast region present. If Sudan is headed toward an inevitable disintegration, it is crucial to think of the possible alliances and the lines of separation beyond North–South, i.e. which other regions are most likely to form a separate state together and which areas must not be merged. I phrase this issue in this manner not only to complicate the picture beyond simple calls for a break-up, but to also point out that those of us who are opposed to the concept of unity-at-all-costs are not, I take it, pro break-up, in the sense that I think disintegration a wonderful thing and hold that the sooner the break-up the better off the Sudanese people; I am against unity-at-all-costs for quite other reasons, including the fact that real decentralization has not been tried. Being anti-unity does not necessarily make someone pro-disintegration.

OTHER PERIPHERAL REGIONS

The conflicts between the northern elite, particularly those who have controlled the state apparatus since independence, and the peripheral regions have not just been a local affair. They were influenced by and have influenced the debate over the regional Afro-Arab politics as well as the rising debate on the role of Islamic radicalism in world politics and international relations. The numerous disagreements between Khartoum and various regions of the country, before they escalated to a state of violent conflicts, were often based on different types of grievances presented by each dissenting region and on the responses that emerged from the central government. These disagreements have been escalated by the interests of other radical Islamic states such as Iran and by the changing geopolitical developments in the neighboring countries such as Chad, Egypt, Eritrea, Ethiopia, Libya, and Uganda. These international and regional concerns, as this study has demonstrated, have implications that either protract the wars or could aid the search for peace, depending on how Sudan's woes affect these countries and what their positions in the conflicts are. Those impacted by both refugee spill-over and insecurity produced by Sudan's support for opposition groups are more invested in what becomes of Sudan.

Over the past several years, Sudan specialists in academia, advocacy groups, and policy analysts have almost all suggested that the only possible solutions under these circumstances were to fold Darfur and other regional conflicts, including that in the northeast, into the IGAD-sponsored North–South peace talks that were negotiated in Machakos, Naivasha, and Nairobi, Kenya, and deal with the nation as a whole in an inclusive and comprehensive arrangement. But given the treacherous past, I contend that there was another possible solution, and that was for Khartoum to reconsider the notion of a unified Sudanese state, which requires the use of brutal force, and start thinking about the ways that could divide up the country in the most peaceful fashion. After all, it has been part of the NIF government's rhetoric to entertain the possibilities of break-up and this has been articulated by the regime's own representatives in various forums.[218] If autonomy for the south has finally been agreed upon only after a long struggle spanning fifty years of demands for self-determination, it is possible to think that the other regions will eventually end up on the same path, especially as long as the Khartoum governments insist on war crimes as the method with which to force different regions into the polity and achieve national unity. Instead of ending up fighting them for another fifty years as it did in the south, it would be best that Khartoum spares itself and the people of northern Sudan continuous bloodshed by granting self-determination for all. After all, what was appropriate for one area, such as the right to self-determination granted to the south, should have been considered a possible solution to similar problems in all the other regions. If the Sudanese regime agreed to suspend its narrow interpretation of Islamic shari'a law in order to accommodate one region, it should be appropriate to do likewise for all the other areas that objected to that shari'a. Otherwise, a bloody and messy break-up of Sudan may no longer be a distant prospect for those who are serious about ending the recurrence of slaughter in Sudan. The government's own representatives have remarked that 'it would be better to have more states with good relations than one state torn apart by war.'[219] After all, the trend for break-up has already been set in motion by the acceptance of a referendum on the south's political status six years down the road. If Sudan cannot exist as a pluralistic society, as the ruling elite have tried to culturally and racially homogenize the country, it may have to do so as several states.

PEACE AGREEMENTS AND THE FUTURE

This study has examined the tools used by the government of Sudan to execute its various wars, some of which have been labeled and verified as genocidal policies, whether the oil-related destruction in Upper Nile or the counterinsurgency activities in Darfur. It has also addressed the justification for these actions. I have attempted to show how, although the destruction is universal, the techniques of mass murder have affected some sectors of the rural populations more than others. Like all wars, although Sudan's conflicts appear to have affected every sector of the rural populations, the way it was experienced by individuals and groups has racial, religious, ethnic, and gender differentials to it. Without a doubt, it has affected women in different ways than men, and some ethnic groups and regions more than others.

> [And] this is why the Arab government keeps fighting, as the Arabs in the north do not know what it is like to live under protracted conflict ... if it were the case that Arab children could experience the hunger, disease and lack of education as the rest of Sudan's children have, northerners would have rallied against the war a long time ago

asserted one southern informant. But since these actions still served the government's end goal, which has been to carry out speedy regrouping of populations, reallocation of resources, genocide and ethnocide, it did not matter whether the destruction was through immediate physical elimination or through the type of dispossession that leads to death, such as the 1988 and 1998 famines in Bahr el-Ghazal and the 1984 and 1988 famines of Darfur, some of which the government had denied for a long time, and when it finally admitted that there were humanitarian crises, it blamed them on natural causes such as droughts and crop failures. In the name of national pride, Khartoum is always unwilling to admit that the famines are more man-made than natural. The 1998 Bahr el-Ghazal famine, for example, killed 100,000 people in a course of four months, and the main causes of famine were Murahileen Arab raids, the military activities of a warlord called Kerebino Kuanyin Bol whom the government of Sudan had armed as a way to placate the SPLA, and finally by drought, the consequences of which would have probably been averted had the Sudanese authorities not been prevented by national pride from issuing early warnings.[220] These actions resulted in the destruction of family networks through displacement and stripping of assets. Other actions included prohibition of certain ethnic groups from their religious worship and other cultural practices, and suppression of certain linguistic and cultural groupings through the national educational system, the government-sponsored media, and jihadic wars that targeted specific groups for elimination or absorption.

Given religious, racial, ethnic and gender dynamics within the affected regions and due to the intentions of the Khartoum government, Sudan's wars have proven more insidious to women, children, non-Muslims, non-Arabs, and ethnic regions that have made demands for equality. Almost all the weapons used by Khartoum to enforce its policies were intended to displace the civilian population, which is regarded as the most subtle but effective approach to defeating the opposition armies and to executing the policies of regimentation of the nation's citizens. The cumulative effect of all military activities throughout the war period was a state of chronic insecurity and poverty in the marginalized rural areas of the country. This in turn has led to a chronic population drain from the peripheries toward specified locations where they are made most vulnerable to the Arabization and Islamization designs, where they are captive and impoverished, where they function as a reservoir for cheap labor. For example, the raiding in northern Bahr el-Ghazal that displaced southerners into the so-called transition zone (the border areas between southern Kordofan and Darfur in the north and Bahr el-Ghazal and Upper Nile in the south) was not only effective in removing the support base from underneath the SPLA, but also subjected these IDPs to enslavement and other forms of abuse while they had neither room to reject the ill-treatment nor the ability to return home. The same has been the case with northeastern tribes such as the Beja and Beni A'amer who were collectively accused and punished for allegedly supporting the NDA opposition forces and were herded into camps and shanty towns around Kassala with the intent of rendering them incapable of lending their support to the opposition armies of the NDA or the Beja Congress. More glaringly the case of Darfur where, in addition to the drought and poverty-induced displacement that has been going on for nearly two decades, the conflict and its attendant humanitarian catastrophe of the last three years, have forced nearly 2.5 million Darfurians into IDP camps scattered across the western region and further north up to Khartoum where their vulnerability to cultural, economic, and social pressures were many times increased. The north and westwards movement of the displaced has created other types of humanitarian problems such as the risks of being raped by both the police that were supposed to protect them and the Janjaweed militia that were constantly lurking to prevent them from ever thinking of a return home. It has also caused both the forced and preemptive migration of Darfur non-Arabs into government-controlled camps within the north, which fulfills the government's plan to keep them captive and susceptible to the cultural engineering designs of Arabization. Flight into refugee camps in Chad has been another alternative, which fulfills the government's plans of depopulating the non-Arab areas for the express purpose of redistributing their land to Arabs and the allied militias. Thus, for example, the displaced in the transitional zone were often exposed to economic exploitation by local landowners, and a modern form of slavery has emerged from this whereby slavers can continue to practice their vice while looking like employers.

In the Greater Khartoum area large numbers of displaced persons have always been considered illegal squatters.[221] They are constantly under the threat of forced relocation to settlement sites lacking the necessary infrastructure and distant from city amenities. As recently as May 2005, the police attempted to forcibly relocate the IDPs of a camp called Soba Aradhi, south of Khartoum, to another location that was said to have no basic services such as schools, clinics and the markets, and a harsh desert environment not suitable for human habitation. The new site had no public transit system and once relocated, the IDPs did not have access to the basic services, which were centralized in Khartoum some forty kilometers away. The pretext for relocation was that the area had been just legally zoned and that the inhabitants could buy plots so as to build better houses and provide services, knowing full well that the IDP families could not afford to buy any of that land as the capital city's real estate prices had been rising tremendously and were well beyond their means.[222] A violent confrontation ensued when the IDPs resisted the relocation and the police shot into the crowd, killing about 18 people, wounding close to 300 and destroying their property. The IDPs were reported by the government to have killed about fourteen policemen, the evidence for which has remained unverifiable. The UN special representative of the Secretary General for Sudan, Jan Pronk, expressed concern about this incident and urged the government of Sudan to exert maximum restraint in handling situations like this in the future to prevent loss of life. Many other officials of the international agencies in Khartoum have appealed to the government emphasizing the need to respect the rights of IDPs as called for in the international conventions, the protection of civilians, respect for human lives, and to treat people in accordance with the law. But no matter how much resistance they put up, and despite the UN condemnation of forced relocation without notifying the IDPs far ahead, they were eventually forced out just like other IDP camps around Khartoum that had to succumb to similar measures in the past. Without concerted and systematic efforts to create more stable conditions for them, they risk remaining in a state of vulnerability and dependency, especially as the new locations they are transferred to are usually far from the centers of employment in a city where public transportation is scarce and costly. It is also here that women are most susceptible to rape, labor exploitation, and children are subject to recruitment into the army to fight against their own people or are blackmailed into the Muslim faith. It is here that the cultural front in Sudan's conflict is most active in favor of homogenization into Arab and Islamic identity. For non-Arabs to live in Khartoum, refuse conversion to Islam, and above all, demand services from the state, is something that the Khartoum government does not tolerate. What underpins this sentiment is that these people are viewed as subjects rather than citizens or as citizens of a lower degree than those who have adopted an Arab culture. The fact that non-Arab Sudanese displaced persons from the peripheries are not accorded the respect enjoyed by all other citizens is a common worldview among public officials in Khartoum. Several diplomats working in Khartoum have heard this from people as high up as the president. A diplomat from Norway once told President al-Bashir, in the context of trying to negotiate humanitarian access to the Nuba mountains and some other no-go areas of the south, that Norway and other members of the international community were also looking after 'your people in refugee camps in Ethiopia,' and the president reportedly said 'those are not my people,' suggesting that all southern refugees were against the government, and therefore did not enjoy the same protection and welfare that the state provided to others. They were not regarded as equal citizens with the riverine Arabs or other Arabized Sudanese who did not question the policies of racial and Islamic regimentation.

As for the populations that braved the onslaught and remained in their home areas, in the south, the northeast, the Nuba mountains and Darfur particularly, the overall military situation that emerged against them was complex and portentous, but with a distinctly twofold character. In areas where government of Sudan military forces and their militia allies confronted the main forces of the SPLA, the Sudan Liberation Army, the Justice and Equality Movement, the NDA forces, and other organized forms of resistance, there was intense fighting taking place in the context of rough strategic parity. In the south, before the 2002 ceasefire agreement and the subsequent Machakos peace protocol, this was chiefly in the more westerly parts of Upper Nile and Bahr el-Ghazal provinces due to the government's efforts to exploit oil reserves in these areas. Civilians, of course, continued to pay the heaviest price for being the natural owners of the land and for refusing to move on government orders of relocation without compensation. For example, aid agencies estimated that these resource-related wars have resulted in the displacement of 200,000 civilians and the death of thousands more in the year 2001 alone. They have caused disruption of relief services such as child immunization campaigns and feeding programs for under-nourished children; and by extension produced more death and long-term harm.

On the other hand, where the government of Sudan did not encounter major military resistance from the various opposition armies, their rapidly growing ascendancy became clear. Here the military situation was ominous in the extreme for the civilian populations in an extension of the scorched-earth fighting that had been creating displacement of populations around the oil concession areas since 1998, and which has created massive civilian population displacement that was extensively reported by human rights groups and aid agencies in the Bentiu area in 2001.[223] The fighting in oil regions south of Bentiu, and in eastern Upper Nile, particularly produced human displacement and destruction unprecedented in this region.[224] This has all happened amid protests by NGOs, religious groups, human rights agencies, and other civil society organizations, but without any initiative from any government to intervene on behalf of the civilians. Because these cries from south Sudan were not taken up by any foreign government beyond lip service, the government of Sudan continued to regard condemnation of killing by a handful of NGOs as business as usual. It was easy to silence them by means of threats of expulsion or detention of aid personnel.

In the peace talks, it seemed that history was about to repeat itself. More war crimes and crimes against humanity, as this study has described, have been committed during the current round of the North–South war than all the previous conflicts, especially by the government and its militias, but no mechanism was built into the peace process to deal with these atrocities and destruction in order to establish accountability for these crimes and to restore justice and effect recompense. While so many people throughout the country were caught in the euphoria of the prospect for a peace accord that was reached under the auspices of IGAD, both the mediators and the parties to the conflict wrote off the atrocities as inevitable occurrences in a prolonged conflict that should not be revisited during peace negotiations, lest they take away the focus that should be concentrated on reaching a quick peace deal. Therefore, the negotiations have deliberately avoided the writing of a mechanism of restitution into the comprehensive peace agreement. It is understandable that parties to the war could not agree to the establishment of a system that could come to haunt them. The dilemma that mediators faced in this regard was severe. If they had pushed the issues of accountability for atrocities and war crimes tribunals to take place after the peace agreement, they might not have achieved an agreement; having avoided them in order to safeguard the peace process, they have risked overlooking the question of justice for the victims of war. The two were clearly incompatible. One thing became clear, however: there could have been no illusion that bringing a peace deal that did not address the issues of restoration of justice was bound to wreck any accord in the long run, especially because the war affected communities have neither received justice for the crimes committed against them nor have they realized any other immediate peace dividends. For example, the issue of slave raiding by the Baggara against the Dinka, which has gone on for over two decades since the beginning of the second North–South war, remains a searing wound on North–South relations and is bound to remain so during peace-time, possibly waiting for one powerful event to trigger either revenge by the Dinka upon the Baggara, or the Baggara reverting to their old ways when circumstances allow. Many Sudanese and outside observers have suggested that a peace accord that does not address this issue is one that has no regard for future human security and cannot be guaranteed to be respected by all in the long term.

There was also the question of the denial of food to the civilian populations by the warring parties as a weapon of war. This has been pointed out many times by human rights organizations, the UN and foreign governments. This has led to the death of hundreds of thousands of people in the south, in the Darfur region, the Nuba mountains and other parts of Kordofan, and the responsibility for the loss of these lives lies squarely with the government. Surely, something had to be done within the peace agreement to account for this tragedy, if only to enable the people of these regions to trust the government once again in a post-war Sudan. The absence of such trust remains a threat to the peace agreement and the territorial integrity of the country.

In the south, there was one most pressing issue, the question of militias in Upper Nile and the militarization of ethnic identity, which had been disastrously fanned by the state as a counterinsurgency tactic between 1991 and 2004. Most of these groups of armed men were sponsored by the government of Sudan for the sole purpose of wrecking any southern unity so that the south would fail to present a unified voice during the search for settlement of the conflict and possibly during the forthcoming referendum for southern self-determination. The immediate consequences of their activities were the destruction of their own communities, the deprivation of their own people, and the overall weakening of the southern cause. For example, in April 2006, a member of the Upper Nile State Assembly for Lungechuk County issued a statement accusing Salah Abdalla Gosh, the head of Sudan's internal security, of arming some groups from SSDF to attack the SPLM positions in the county.

It should also be borne in mind that a protracted conflict such as this has led to a phenomenon of reproduction of violence within communities and families throughout rural Sudan. Staggering statistics of rape and sexual abuse that both government and opposition armies have been accused of, are important in their own right but were not given serious attention both during the search for peace and in postwar reconstruction plans. A more sinister development to reckon with has been the fact that years of conditioning youth to violence has led to a growing use of violence domestically, within families and communities. This is something that lives on and it affects families, especially women and children that are now living in households where domestic violence is widespread. Now, with peace on the horizon and no plans being made to deal with the large number of soldiers who will be demobilized without proper preparation for civilian life, the situation remains one of continued and total insecurity, especially for women and children. This was something that both the opposition armies like the SPLA and the government of Sudan needed to be aware of, and were expected to embark on plans to remedy long before they started setting up the institutional structures of a post-war nation. Solutions to these issues needed to be built into such institutions at the outset, something that seems to have been a priority to neither side during the peace talks.

During the implementation phase, parties to the agreement are said to have not been cognizant of the long history of mistrust that had developed and continued to magnify not only between the armies, but also between the populations of different parts of the country. To reconcile this mistrust, they needed to pay attention to the power of symbols. The question of shari'a in Khartoum, for example, and the way non-Muslims have historically been treated had continually given non-Arab and non-Muslim citizens a feeling of insecurity in what was supposedly their own country. Other symbols mentioned by different Sudanese included the use of Islamic colors such as the color of the passport cover, or the Islamic symbols on the national currency and the names given to things and places such as the river Kiir, which the Arabs call Bahr el-Arab. The use of these terms or application of these colors may not have had any ill intention behind them, but they were usually read differently by different peoples, and therefore became a part of the whole identity question and the contestation of the nation's cultural and racial character. It was important for a state interested in building a multicultural union to look for more neutral symbols if all the citizens of Sudan were to feel at home in every corner of their country. The point here is that having no mechanism built into the agreement to deal with these questions was a mistake, and waiting for an implementation phase of the comprehensive peace agreement without the tools to deal with them was an even bigger mistake. It did not bring human security and not all the citizens were able to experience the rewards of peace.

PEACE AND GENOCIDE

The prospects of a successful peace agreement between Khartoum's NIF or the National Congress Party and the southern opposition has muted international criticism of the regime's genocidal wars in other arenas, such as the far western province of Darfur, the Beja's Red Sea hills and the Shilluk Kingdom in Upper Nile. At the time of writing, the southern peace was still so fragile that the mediators and other actors, especially the would-be implementers, were treading carefully on the issue of continuing problems in other parts of the country so as to not lose the momentum gained in the south. Some actors believed that although the comprehensive peace agreement was likely to end one conflict, it could escalate conflicts in other parts of the country, as one US diplomat involved in the Sudanese peace processes noted, 'You cannot have peace in one part of the country while war continues in other parts.' The focus on seeing the southern peace through before turning to the other areas has worked to limit the world's understanding of the scale of catastrophe in Darfur. But when Darfur's genocide finally began to come into view, despite Khartoum's contrivances and obstructionist attitude, this in turn led to the perverse effect of obscuring the intense human destruction and displacement that accelerated in south Sudan and Upper Nile province in particular, in the months leading up to the signing of the peace agreement, while everyone was either looking toward Darfur or focusing on the southern peace agreement.

The militias were a potential problem for the implementation of peace in south Sudan. Closely aligned with the government and high-ranking officers in the Sudanese army, they remained a serious problem for the new southern authorities in the Government of Southern Sudan. Although these armed groups are relatively small, they have the potential to destabilize the regions in which they are active, and if the Government of Southern Sudan cannot quickly control them or persuade them to join its forces, the civilians in those regions will quickly lose faith in the peace agreement. Since early March 2004, there has been intense destruction, and between 50,000 and 150,000 people have been displaced by a series of militia attacks in the Upper Nile area known as the Shilluk Kingdom. Most of the displaced have moved to government garrison towns, the Nuba mountains, the Panaru area, a group of islands in the swampy region between the White Nile and Lol rivers, and northern Sudan. This area was largely inaccessible and the information that came from the area at the time of peace negotiations was so sketchy as to be downplayed by both the government that caused it and the international community that failed to insist on ending that deliberate destruction before continuing with the peace talks. Complicating this situation was that the area had few humanitarian actors on the ground, and the scale of the problem, the whereabouts of the displaced, and the exact character of the perpetrators, remained uncertain for a while. It was later learned that some Nuer militias, feeling left out of the peace agreement and abandoned by their commanders who had gone to Khartoum and then switched back into the SPLA fold, had to fall into the pay of Khartoum, but were wreaking havoc as a way to get themselves noticed as potential spoilers of peace if the peace agreement did not grant them a piece of the pie. Three international NGOs, Tearfund, VSF-Germany and World Vision as well as the UN had to pull out of the area in 2004. Their field staff was able to fill the information gap about what was going on there.[225]

It was this sort of militia activity that made many people worried about the viability of the peace agreement. Such an agreement, as the Sudanese were headed toward implementation and the world community was about to deploy peacekeepers, was still meaningless unless the international peace support operation was so robust as to be unlike any deployed before in the region. If the other similar missions in the region, in Somalia, Congo and Rwanda in the days of genocide were anything to go by, the Sudanese situation did not look any different given the large number of armed groups that had no or little loyalty to any side that could bring them under control. Such a peace-keeping force, if it were to be effective in Sudan required adequate manpower, transport capacity, communications gear, security arrangements, and personnel knowledgeable of the terrain and subcultures of the area. That did not seem to be evident anywhere as the country headed toward implementation of the agreement while the killing and destruction continued. The problem was that the UN resolution that mandated the peace-keeping force had allowed for a time-frame of 240 days for the troop deployment, which eventually proved too long, given that it did not take long for destruction to be effected and the massacres to be carried out. And many people were worried that peace monitors did not have the mandate to rein in the remaining militias in the south. Of particular concern was the Nuer-dominated South Sudan Defence Force (SSDF), whose allegiance to Khartoum had been a source of much instability in the greater Upper Nile region. Khartoum was well aware of this lack of preparedness of the peace-keeping missions, and was likely to use the SSDF and other militias to its military advantage in the ways we saw in Upper Nile in 2004, whether in the Shilluk Kingdom or in the Akobo area of eastern Upper Nile, where civilians were also victims of frequent attacks by these Khartoum-backed militias.[226] There was also the Equatoria Defence Force (EDF) in southeastern Sudan. Although the EDF joined the SPLA in December 2003, a small group, which calls itself EDF-2, remained loyal to Khartoum and posed a potential threat, especially if it were to join forces with the northern Ugandan rebels of the Lord's Resistance Army. Such threats became evident in October 2005 when the LRA, under the guidance of EDF-2, attacked several convoys heading to Juba, including an attack on a mine removal team in which a Swedish anti-personnel landmine expert was killed. The incidents disrupted the much needed cleaning of the Yei-Juba road, and with it went the potential for the resumption of trade between Uganda and south Sudan, something the southern population was very much in need of and was anticipating with pleasure.

If the agreement was both threatened by the political and economic dynamics within south Sudan as well as failing to end localized violence, it was even unsettling in relation to the conflict in Darfur. Indeed, it already appeared that the Khartoum government had trumpeted the signing of the comprehensive peace agreement in order to use that as a sign of its belief in peaceful negotiated settlement, and by doing that it kept the international pressures at bay through its rhetoric about its ability to bring peace, while carrying on with its military option. This attitude had already been demonstrated by its actions regarding its promises of humanitarian access to Darfur, which came so late and with so many restrictions as to be totally absurd. As it used the charm offensive over the years to frustrate the world community, the regime was able to yet again go on charming but not delivering.[227] Unfortunately, the response of many in the international community to Khartoum's mere promise of expedited humanitarian access, which came much too late for many tens of thousands of civilians, was probably going to repeat itself in the current optimism about peace negotiations in Darfur.

Having signed the agreement with the south, the regime expected the international community to reward it with an opportunity to go on destroying the non-Arabs of Darfur under the guise of a genuine seeker of peace demonstrated by its good faith in achieving the peace deal for the south. But the regime needed to be confronted with the clear prospect of concerted international action, both in enforcing the terms of the southern agreement and in securing fully adequate humanitarian relief in Darfur as well as verifiable commitments to a negotiated settlement in Darfur. Falling short of this was a signal to the regime to go on behaving the same way it had done for years. It lied, talked peace with Darfur tribal leaders and then reneged. It promised to control its militias only to continue killing the non-Arab peoples of Sudan in vast numbers, escaping blame by alleging that the militias were out of its control and characterizing the carnage as part of an age-old tribal feud that has nothing to do with Khartoum.

At the time of writing, there was still a lot of concern among many Sudanese and outside observers about the level of commitment from Khartoum to the comprehensive peace agreement. The ruling NIF or National Congress Party, as it now calls itself, had made compromises on its Islamist ideology after pressure from the international community in the aftermath of the September 11, 2001 terrorist attacks in the United State. But a degree of skepticism was still warranted, as no Khartoum government had held its peace commitments in the past. The government has always been slow in delivering on its promises on various issues. The limited commitment it had made to the international community to stop the militias in Darfur, which it did not carry through, and its intransigence in the latest Abuja peace talks were clear evidence of this pattern. Given its response to the fighting in Darfur, it remains to be seen how soon the government will fulfill its promises of power and wealth-sharing and self-determination for the south, especially since the adoption of a UN resolution, on 31 March, 2005 which called for those implicated in Darfur's crimes to be tried by the International Criminal Court. There is no question that the Security Council's decision to refer Darfur crimes to the ICC is a landmark in the solution for Darfur, as it promises to provide accountability for the atrocities. As things stand, such accountability is the only way to break the cycle of violence in Darfur, as the victims and their families may be able to take comfort in restitution instead of revenge down the line. It might also be the way for the nation to move forward and maintain its unitary existence. The many efforts to submit people to a national identity designed by a few have neither resulted in the desired national unity nor total Arabization. They have not produced a fully Islamic state either. On the contrary, they have proven the more divisive because of the violent wars these efforts have engendered and the destruction the wars have effected in many parts of the country.

NOTES

1. There were a lot of murmurs from different corners of the meeting about the chief's audacity to speak of such matters as defecation with such straightforward language in front of a prominent foreign visitor, but there was an approving laughter.
2. This is my translation from Dinka. It was excerpted from a much longer speech in which the chief gave many more reasons why southerners and northerners do not belong to 'one race.'
3. In 2005 Khartoum, the capital of Sudan, was chosen as the 'capital of Arab culture,' even though government estimates of ethnic breakdown of the population indicate that only 39 percent are Arabs. *New York Times*, March 20, 2006.
4. There has been a great deal of mixing of people from Arabia, the Nile Valley, and other parts of Africa, there is no question that the phenotypic expressions found all over the Sudanese landscape are a product of this genetic mixing.
5. For a clear theoretical framing of race and attachment to nature, see Moore, Pandian and Kosek (2003).
6. The recrutiment of militias by the central government to fight the southern insurgency and offer the Arab herders, who were facing environmental challenges, the capacity to encroach as far south as they could in order to graze their livestock, began in 1983.
7. See Human Rights Watch (2003). Human Rights Watch has six book-length reports on other aspects of human rights abuses by the government of Sudan and the opposition armies since 1983.
8. Having come under fire for abetting human rights violations a major Canadian oil company, Talisman, also brought the government of Canada into the limelight as complicit in the acts of civilian devastation, and in turn prompted the Canadian government to send a high profile fact-finding team to Sudan. The team then produced a lengthy report in which Talisman was indicted as complicit in the Sudanese government's acts of ethnic cleansing. See Harker (2000).

9. The International Crisis Group (2002), the Center for Strategic and International Studies, and the Institute for Security Studies of South Africa also wrote long reports highlighting the atrocities and recommending the halting of oil production until such time as security has been established and a peace agreement secured.

10. A particularly damning report about oil-related genocide was issued by Christian Aid (2001). Another was written by Ryle and Gagnon (2003) on behalf of a coalition of Canadian NGOs.

11. Upper Nile and Eastern Bahr el-Ghazal, which are the oil-producing areas, lie within the Sudd region, one of the biggest swamps in the world. This makes it impossible for the government army to be mobile during the rainy season as the terrain becomes impassable to military trucks, but the hard-topped roads built by the oil companies facilitate year-round access for the army.

12. Christian Aid's (2001) damning report used first-hand and eyewitness accounts to detail how these atrocities were carried out with no respect for human life and without remorse.

13. See the report by Ryle and Gagnon (2003), written on behalf of Sudan Inter-Agency Reference Group (SIARG).

14. It would take a few more years before the pressure on Sudan to seek peace with the south yielded any results, but the government could not succumb to this pressure and stop the oil-related atrocities. Both the killing and the revenues flowing to Khartoum continued. The killing has since subsided, but the oil money is still flowing into the hands of the Islamists.

15. See African Rights (1997) and de Waal (1997).

16. See the *Fact Sheet on Access Restrictions in Darfur and Other Areas of Sudan* issued by Office for the Coordination of Humanitarian Affairs in Khartoum on April 20, 2006. This is the body that coordinates a massive relief operation carried out by more than 14,000 national and international relief workers assisting the conflict-affected population, working for 84 NGOs and Red Cross and Red Crescent Societies, as well as 13 United Nations agencies.

17. As we will see in the chapters that follow, smaller armed groups and political parties as the South Sudan Defense Forces (SSDF), Equatoria Defense Forces (EDF), the Umma Party, Democratic Unionist Party (DUP), and others were outraged that peace negotiations were focusing on the NIF government and the SPLA/M.

18. The estimates of IDPs and refugees were made by United Nations High Commission for Refugees. See UNHCR (2006).

19. Neither Khartoum nor Washington ever made public what the purpose of this visit was, but the Islamist government was among the first countries after the September 11, 2001 attacks on the US to offer help with the war on terror.

20. This fear became reality as the Darfur tragedy continued unabated well into 2006.

21. As the implementation of the North–South peace agreement progresses so slowly as to be ineffectual, the ability of the SPLA to bring an end to the Darfur tragedy gets more remote. The SPLA seems increasingly focused on negotiating the implementation process, leaving little time and political will for Darfur.

22. There is much anticipation and likelihood of separation in 2011 as there is a well-founded fear that the Khartoum government, whichever party will be in power then, would do its best to thwart the southern referendum. It is almost impossible for the north to let go of the south without a fight, and if the process is not internationally monitored, Khartoum is surely capable of wrecking it.

23. See Fadlalla (2004) and al-Agab (1987). Both texts, by focusing on the policies that could keep Sudan united, gloss over the issues that have forced the populations of the remote regions into secession. See also Holt (1966) Fleuhr-Lobban (1990).

24. This kind of representation of Sudan is also more common in journalism and literature. Many daily newspapers and magazines in Khartoum as well as in many Arab capitals publish widely on Sudan's unity as unquestionable.

25. One of the problems of ethnography in contested political entities is that one cannot be entirely certain about how generalizeable are the views of ones' informants.

26. There is a huge amount of 'grey literature,' much of which was produced by the High Commission for Human Rights, especially its Human Rights Rapporteurs, and by the UN Department of Humanitarian Affairs. Both agencies maintain an active website, where these reports are easily accessible. Operation Lifeline Sudan, the UN-led consortium of aid agencies delivering relief to Sudan, has also produced assessment reports. See for example Minear (1991).

27. Harker (2000).

28. Examples are: Amnesty International (2000), African Rights (1995a, b), Human Rights Watch (1994, 1996), Africa Watch (1990).

29. See Ryle and Gagnon (2000).

30. The phrase 'infidel West' is usually reserved for the United States.

31. Humanitarian relief operations, which have been carried out through a tripartite agreement involving the government of Sudan, the United Nations, and south-based Sudan People's Liberation Army, started in 1990. The effort, known as Operation Lifeline Sudan (OLS) with northern and southern sectors, is estimated to have cost about 4.5 billion US dollars since it started. These estimates are based on the annual global appeals for aid in Sudan that are prepared by the European Community Humanitarian Office (ECHO), UN, and independent NGOs.

32. The phrase 'southern problem' is commonly used in the northern popular discourse, and is often heard in political speeches, in the local newspapers, in academic conferences, and in ordinary conversations. It continues to create

serious tensions between northern and southern students on university and school campuses.

33. Readers may find this reference to 'northern opinion' vague, but it is gleaned from the scholarly writing by northerners, interviews, and from the editorials and news in Arabic language papers published in Khartoum and other Arab capitals. There has also been significant written source material, both grey literature and published work, mainly in the area of conflict and its causes, the peace processes, and the role of the international community in supporting a lasting settlement of the conflict. These sources have been instructional to me in understanding the debates surrounding the causes of civil wars and how to end them.

34. Fadlalla (2004).

35. The Arabic language print media exhibits much of this approach in the way the Darfur crisis is reported. Daily columns and editorials written by well-known academics and commentators have dismissed the single most common factor between the wars within the traditional north – the issue of race – and the wars are often depicted as unrelated to one another.

36. See Beshir (1975).

37. Wai (1981), Deng (1994), Ruay (1994) Garang (1987), Alier (1990), Malwal (1981).

38. Lesch (1998).

39. Warburg (1992, 2002).

40. Johnson (2004).

41. Prunier (2005), Flint and de Waal (2006).

42. For example, this debate is evident in the anger that many northern Sudanese families feel and express about the conscription of their young boys into the Sudanese army for the war effort in the south. Many in the dissenting regions also express unhappiness with their leaders' timing of the decision to go to war against the government, and their war strategy.

43. Research into the causes of Sudan's conflicts has already been conducted by a prominent historian of Sudan, Douglas Johnson in his authoritative *The Root Causes of Sudan's Civil Wars* (2003).

44. It is worth keeping in mind that Sudan is home to the world's largest number of internally displaced persons (IDPs). Many of them have been escaping droughts, famines and conflicts in Darfur since 1983. Others, perhaps the largest group of IDPs, were displaced from the south into the north by the twenty-two-year-long war between the government of Sudan and the SPLA. These IDPs, approximately 4.5 million people, are to be found everywhere around government-held towns both in the south and north, but most of them have taken up residence around Khartoum. For concise studies of the situation of IDPs, see African Rights (1995a) and Harir (1992).

45. Beshir (1979).

46. For details of this opinion, see Deng (1994).

47. See Sharif Harir's (1992) description of this process.
48. Detailed examples appear in Harir (1993). See also a well-argued position on race in Idris (2001).
49. It is worth pointing out that although the northern region represents only 5–6 percent of the population, it has maintained a representation of more than 50 percent and occasionally exceeded 70 percent of the constitutional posts. For example, since independence, not a single president has come from outside the northern region.
50. These two parties have rotated in power or have formed coalition governments during Sudan's democratic periods.
51. Although a full control of the government by Muslims came into being only after the NIF-backed military coup d'etat of 1989, this group of militant Muslims began showing their power in the last few years of Nimeiri's reign when their ideologue, Hassan al-Turabi, became the Attorney General of Sudan. See Warburg (2002).
52. The interview with Achol Malek in Aweil West was conducted by the author in the summer of 2001. This women's organizer attempts to highlight the gender differentials in the war experience.
53. De Waal (2004).
54. Of the local groups that have highlighted the atrocities, the most prominent and consistent is the Sudan Organization against Torture (SOAT). Established in the wake of the ascendance to power of the National Islamic Front, SOAT has issued reports and statements documenting and condemning the flagrant abuses committed by government agents since 1989. These abuses include torture of opponents or suspected opponents. See Lesch and Fadl (2004).
55. Warburg (2002).
56. Sudan's political development has been characterized by military autocratic governments, usually overthrown through popular uprising followed by a brief democratic period in which a government is elected. For example, independence was followed such an interlude only to be reversed in 1958 by Ibrahim Abbud, a military dictator. Abbud was then deposed in a 1964 popular movement and an elected government ensued until 1969 when Ja'afer Nimeiri, a young military officer, took power in a coup, and ruled Sudan for the next sixteen years through a brutal dictatorship. He was then deposed in a popular rising in 1985 and a democratic period followed in 1986 under Sadiq al-Mahdi who was in turn overthrown in a military coup led by the current president, Omar Hassan al-Bashir, in June 1989.
57. Khalid (1990).
58. Sudan's popular political discourse is awash with stories about how the Arab elite always describe military coups carried out by officers from the peripheries as racist coups, a characterization that would not normally be given to a coup staged by Arab officers.

59. Abdel Aziz was wounded during a fight between his Sudan Liberation Army and the government forces in the summer of 2003 and was transported to northern Bahr el-Ghazal, an area controlled by the south-based opposition SPLA, for treatment.

60. The term 'political Islam' has been defined in many different ways. It is used in this book to mean the use of Islam both as a ladder to political office and as a drive to base the system of government on the teachings of Islam and the establishment of a theocratic state.

61. For a clear and concise opinion on the relationship between political militant Islam within the Islamic countries and the form it takes in relation to the United States, see Munson (2004).

62. See Rethven (2002).

63. Of course, the reverse has also been argued, that governments in the Islamic world also use growing anti-West sentiment to deflect the attention from their own democratic and social service failures. For this argument, see Gerges (1999).

64. The term fundamentalism is used in local Sudanese discourse to refer to the local wish to revive the old Islamic way of life as the scripture dictates. I do not use it here in the sense that it is commonly employed in Western literature, where fundamentalism equates with violent militancy.

65. Slavery in its modern form resurged as a tool for counterinsurgency between 1983 and 2002, and continued to pose a threat to North–South relations. It threatens unity of the country to this day.

66. Between 1920 and 1946, the British had instituted a policy called 'the closed districts ordinance,' which was designed to prevent the influx of Arabs and Muslim missionaries to the south as a way to preserve the southern cultures from Arab-Islamic influence. Northerners could only travel to the south by means of a government-issued permit.

67. In a puzzling and unusual move, the NIF government took a full page advertisement in the *New York Times* (February 20, 2006) in an effort to promote Sudan as an emerging market for foreign investment. The government listed its own estimates of racial/ethnic and religious breakdown of the country's population, in which the percentage of Arabs was put at 39 percent. The current government usually tries to steer clear of such statistics, focusing instead on the rhetoric that Sudan is an Arab country.

68. A detailed and clear description of this complex period can be found in Johnson's *The Root Causes of Sudan's Civil Wars* (2003).

69. Of course the force of the previous powers – the Turkiyya and the Mahdiyya – was felt by the people, but this contact was strictly in terms of the authorities wanting them to give things, above all slaves and porters to carry ivory or timber to the centers of power in Khartoum or Cairo.

70. Phrases of this kind were enough to annoy those Sudanese who self-identify as Africans/Blacks. One young Nubian man I interviewed in Cairo in 1998

expressed his wonderment as to why it was an 'Arab breadbasket' and not simply an African or Sudanese breadbasket. A phrase like this is construed as turning national resources over to the Arab world.

71. See Jok (2001).
72. The Sudan's branch of the Muslim Brothers later became the National Islamic Front (NIF). They changed their name due to circumstances in Egypt that had led to the mass arrest of the Muslim Brothers by Nasir's socialist government. The NIF became the National Congress Party in the 1990s.
73. Note that the name al-Ashiqqa is Arabic for 'the brothers,' which in this sense refers to Sudanese and Egyptians being brothers, a part of the old northern Sudanese effort to become Arabs.
74. O'balance (2000).
75. See Bashir (1968).
76. There are no written reports on the death toll, but having interviewed so many former Anyanya fighters, civil servants, and politicians, I estimate that 500,000 people fell directly and indirectly victim to the war.
77. Johnson (2003).
78. Sadiq al-Mahdi remains obtuse to this day in emphasizing religion as the basis for popular support for his party.
79. Ansar (the defenders) were the riverine Arab people of middle Sudan who claim to have been the defenders or followers of the Mahdi and, therefore, more deserving of leadership in Sudan because of their religious connections to the pious Mahdi and their historic victory against the foreigners of the Turkiyya overlordship.
80. This was a widespread story traded by word of mouth throughout Sudan in the 1970s. I remember my elementary school teacher talking about it in class. Unfortunately, I have never come across any written evidence to document it.
81. I overheard Nimeiri talking about this in a hospital room in Egypt when he visited my uncle, the late Lawrence Wol Wol, who had been a cabinet minister in Nimeiri's government. This was in 1990 and Nimeiri had been in exile in Egypt since his overthrow in a popular uprising against him as explained below.
82. Note that schools had been closed down in 1964 as Prime Minister Mahjub escalated the fighting.
83. Mayen had been a member of a faction of southern opposition called Azania Liberation Front, later renamed Southern Sudan Provisional Government in 1967 under the leadership of Aggrey Jaden.
84. This was from a diary entry of April 19, 1982 that Collins, a prominent historian of Sudan, wrote after listening to southern friends who filled him in on the happenings following the dissolution of the southern regional government in October 1981. See *Sudan Studies Association Newsletter.* Vol. 24(2): February 2006:6.

85. Public pronouncements by Nimeiri said that shari'a was only applicable to Muslims, but the written constitution said nothing on this matter, so that when it was applied, the courts did not make such a distinction. I recall that many of the first few convicts whose limbs were amputated, were Christians from the south or from the Nuba mountains.
86. See Toulabor (1994).
87. See Bayart (1991).
88. The interview with Lualdit, as he is affectionately known, took place in Wanjok, Aweil East County headquarters in June 2003, where we were both attending a joint meeting of independent agencies and the SPLM authorities on the issue of abduction and slavery.
89. O'balance (2000).
90. Chief Faustino Ngot made these remarks in 1995 in the context of a long interview by a visiting delegation to his compound outside Lietnhom east of Gogrial. The delegation was made up of United Nations and Save the Children Fund staff and I was the interpreter.
91. See Malwal (1981).
92. For details, see Johnson (2003).
93. Policy statements coming out of the United States Department of State and European Union countries almost all invariably speak of the importance of keeping Sudan as one country. In fact, they promise this much to the government of Sudan as a way to lure it into peace talks; that its fears of break up should not hold it back from engaging with the international community regarding the troubled regions of the south and Darfur as the world community will ensure that unity is maintained.
94. In 1952, the chiefs of the Bari people of Equatoria made a statement addressed to the colonial authorities in which they objected to the way the British were intending to hand over power to northerners. See the Sudan Archives at Durham, document marked as SAD 696/8/1-105.
95. See Johnson (2003).
96. See Jok (2001).
97. Johnson (1998).
98. See Collins (1999).
99. See Johnson (1998b).
100. See Deng (1999).
101. United States Refugee Committee (1998).
102. For a more detailed discussion of these complaints, see Patterson (1999).
103. Informal conversation with John Ryle, August 2003.
104. Ali Askouri quoted by John Ryle in a review of a British Museum exhibition of ancient Nubian artifacts. See Ryle (2004a).
105. *Al-Rai al-A'am*, a Khartoum Arabic daily newspaper (2005).

106. Several reports have been written on behalf of the International Rescue Committee, New York.
107. Crummey, Miller, Ireton and Dalmau (2006).
108. Amuom speaks fluent Arabic and was felt to be more suitable to command a force that includes Arab-speaking northerners.
109. The London-based opposition publication *Sudan Democratic Gazette* covered the Kassala massacre extensively.
110. Communication with Beja people living in Kassala and Port Sudan in 2003 has revealed that a large number of Beja youth are in jails and other detention facilities called 'ghost houses' in these towns.
111. For a concise history of the region, see Young (2004).
112. See also the Scandinavian Institute of African Studies (1994).
113. For a concise history of the Nuba, see Nadel (1947).
114. See Sagar (1950).
115. R. C. Stevenson has classified Nuba languages and dialects as a way to argue that the term Nuba may not have originally been an indigenous term, but perhaps a word given by outsiders who wanted to group all the non-Arabs of the region into an ethnic entity. See Stevenson (1984).
116. See Meyer and Nicholls (2005).
117. The footage of the bombing was made part of a documentary about the Nuba and their survival and rise of Christianity during this war entitled *The Hidden Gift: A Journey of Faith and Survival.* Los Angeles: The Windhover Forum.
118. For more recent accounts of the disaster, see Polgreen (2006).
119. Sudan has, in recent history, been comprised mainly of north and south as distinct entities, and Darfur has been part of the 'north' not only in terms of the confrontations between north and south in which Darfur was part of the north, but also a major geographical part of the entity 'north.'
120. Yousef Takana quoted in International Crisis Group (2004).
121. O'Fahey and Salim (1983).
122. O'Fahey (1980).
123. Ibid.
124. For the humanitarian consequences of the 1980s drought, see de Waal (1989).
125. In the 1980s, Colonel Gaddafi dreamed of gaining control of Chad, starting with the Aouzou strip in the north of the country. He mounted a succession of military adventures in Chad, and from 1987 to 1989 Chadian factions backed by Libya used Darfur as a rear base.
126. See Ryle (2004b).
127. See the report of the United Nations fact finding team on Darfur's crisis. The report was co-authored by a six-member team led by an Italian jurist, Antonio Cassese (United Nations 2005).

128. It is worth noting that although Sudan has not signed the 1948 Genocide Convention, developed in the wake of the mass atrocities of World War II, it has signed the Rome Statute, which defines the crime of genocide in exactly the same language as the convention.

129. Eric Reeves, 'Khartoum Triumphant: Managing the Costs of Genocide in Darfur.' See http://www.Sudanreeves.org. Report dated December 17, 2005.

130. The silence of the army was attributed in part to the fact that Nimeiri was away visiting the United States to solicit more funds for the war in the south and to renegotiate the country's debt service plan as the economy was at a standstill.

131. Anderson (2004).

132. International Crisis Group (2004).

133. Sudan had been under United Nations sanctions sponsored largely by the United States because of Sudan's sponsorship of international terrorism, a label that prompted President Clinton to order a military strike against Khartoum in the summer of 1998.

134. In early 2005, al-Turabi's family issued a press release on his suffering health, the way he was being treated by the prison guards, denial of medical attention and the inadequacy of the food he was given, and demanded his release or trial in court.

135. De Waal (2004).

136. al-Haj (2003).

137. Dr. Van Rooyen made this statement in the context of his consultancy for Physicians for Human Rights. See Physicians for Human Rights (2004).

138. For updates on the continuing violence both within Darfur as well as in refugee camps inside Chad, see *New York Times*, February 28, 2006.

139. Sudanese governments have historically taken to this idea of hiding humanitarian crises from the eyes of the international community, partly because of national embarrassment, but mainly because of suspicions that aid workers are spies of their governments. There is also a sense that the influx of foreigners gives dissenting regions some international recognition, which the government does not want granted to them.

140. Apart from the worst deliberate human destruction of our time, the Jewish Holocaust, most Western European countries could easily be found guilty of genocide if the convention on genocide was applied retroactively, whether in reference to the slave trade, the destruction of the native populations of the Americas or the violence of colonization.

141. Inter-Regional Information Network (2005).

142. I interviewed this old man afterwards and told me that he was happy to talk to me about the future of the country on condition that I do not publish his name.

143. Spear masters in the Dinka religion are most revered for their perceived wisdom and their role as the priests that mediate between humans and the supernatural world. For details on these beliefs, see Lienhardt (1961).

144. I was able to videotape this speech and the entire event, and this excerpt is my translation from Dinka.

145. It is said that most southern IDPs in Khartoum simply profess Christianity in response to the threats of Islamization. Access to humanitarian aid provided by church-based relief organizations is another possible reason for the increasing church attendance. They have become the staunchest defenders of Christianity in Sudan as an affront to Muslim radicals. For details of this politically motivated growth of the Christian faith, see Barsella and Ayuso Guixot (1998).

146. Prunier (1996).

147. Turabi is the ideologue of the Muslim Brotherhood and at one time the spiritual guardian of the current Islamist regime until the political falling-out with president Bashir in 2000, after which he was removed from the post of Speaker of the National Assembly. He was jailed for conspiracy to overthrow the government and remained in detention until his release in May 2006.

148. See Bona Malwal's (2005) critique of the government-SPLM peace agreement of January 9, 2005.

149. For more information on the Republican Brothers, see Warburg (2002).

150. See Human Rights Watch (1996).

151. In its report Christian Aid focused particularly on how Sudan is using oil revenues to sustain its military campaign. In these efforts Sudan is being supported by its overseas partners through a consortium made up of oil companies from Canada, China, Malaysia, Sweden, and the United Kingdom.

152. Roger Winter had been a strong advocate on behalf of the people of south Sudan and the Nuba mountains while heading the Refugee Committee, but was appointed the Director of Office of Foreign Disaster Assistance (OFDA) when George W. Bush took office in 2001.

153. The traditional concept of Jihad – holy war – extends beyond forced conversion to Islam. It also includes vigorous efforts to win the minds and hearts of the unbeliever, even blackmail by witholding the use of resources unless the population convert to Islam.

154. In 1989 a military coup overthrew Sudan's democratically elected government and brought to power Lieutenant General Omar al-Bashir and his National Salvation Revolution Command Council, an Islamic militant government.

155. Mahdiyya is the period between 1881 and 1898 when a revolutionary group of Islamists overthrew Ottoman rule and took control of Sudan until the British conquest and colonization of Sudan.

156. John Garang, SPLA commander, who first articulated the dominance of the Arab minority clique in public speeches on Radio SPLA, has been described as anti-Arab racist.

157. Because displacement may not be a result of rational thinking, people may try one place and then change their minds and move to another location once life becomes untenable in the place of first choice. Southerners displaced to government-held towns rarely have such options.

158. The term transitional zone has been used, especially by aid agencies, to refer to the border areas between the north and the south where displaced persons first move to before deciding which northern towns to settle in.

159. Although the imposition of sanctions had been discussed in Western capitals for some time, what eventually triggered it was the assassination attempt on Egyptian President Husni Mubarak by Sudanese security operatives in 1995 while attending the Organization of African Unity annual summit in Addis Ababa, Ethiopia.

160. See for example, Human Rights Watch (2005a).

161. The exception of course is the rising wealth of the ruling Arab minority elite as the national economy has grown faster than any other in Africa for the past three years.

162. See Ryle and Gagnon (2003).

163. See Deng and Morrison (2001).

164. Ibid.

165. Harker (2000).

166. See Reeves (1999).

167. Despite the sanctions, the US turned a blind eye to the importation of gum Arabic, a substance which is used as an additive in soft drinks. Because Sudan is one of the leading producers of this crop and there is a high demand for it in the US, they could not but violate their own sanctions: 'If we did not get it straight from the primary producer, we will be forced to buy it from a third party such as France at triple the price,' in the words of one Congressional leader. The US spent millions of dollars to Sudan every year purchasing gum Arabic: money which was put to ill use by the Islamists in Khartoum. Other problems in the US policy on Sudan were the oscillation between sanctions that bar US companies and lack of concerted pressure to get Khartoum to change its anti-reconciliation behavior.

168. See Reeves (2001a).

169. See Reeves (2001b).

170. See Inter-Regional Information Network (IRIN), a UN-sponsored news agency, January 27 2001.

171. See Reeves (2001c).

172. Reeves (2001c).

173. Rumbek became the provisional capital of the new government of southern Sudan in 2005 as stipulated in the IGAD-sponsored peace agreement that it is hoped will end the North–South civil wars.

174. The government gives oil concession areas either numbers or different names, such as 'Unity.' The idea dates back to Nimeiri's reign, and serves to strip the areas of their history and do away with the possibility of the inhabitants claiming them as their own. After some time, when people have been displaced without title deeds and the history of settlement of the region has been altered, the state will have freed itself from any responsibility to the civilian population and no royalties would be paid to them.

175. The word soldier is almost exclusively used by south Sudanese to refer to the government army, and it is used here in that sense. Most people in the south use Anyanya or SPLA when they mean southern opposition armies.

176. This was a reference to the slave raiding that had gone on for over fifteen years in which the Baggara Arabs of Darfur and Kordofan have captured women and children and dragged them into slavery in the north. See also Jok (2004).

177. The non-Arab people who were displaced by war and had moved to Khartoum and other northern cities, were deliberately excluded from the sharing of resources. Normally stationed in unhealthy slums on the outskirts of the city, millions of IDPs were denied most public service programs and protection available to the Arab communities.

178. The act of redrawing the boundaries within what is supposedly one nation was in itself an indication that the north was well aware of the south's potential or eventual break away.

179. Southern members of parliament or the national assembly and a number of southern regional assembly members were imprisoned in 1983.

180. Both the SLA and JEM were organized and run by well-educated men and women, many of whom are professionals who left comfortable lives in order to fight on behalf of their masses who have suffered marginalization for long.

181. *The London Review of Books*, February 2004.

182. See Human Rights Watch (2005a).

183. See the reports by Physicians for Human Rights (2004, 2005b).

184. In his ground-breaking work *When Victims become Killers* (2001) Mahmood Mamdani has described the racialization of the Hutu–Tutsi ethnic difference under colonialism, which pitted the two groups against one another, and how that led to civil war and genocide instead of them fighting colonialism collectively.

185. I have been conducting an inquiry into the lives of my schoolmates who had joined the SPLA, and it has turned out that nearly half of the 300 of them who were in my class have perished in the war. The lists will become part of a memorial that I hope to help establish in the town of Luanyaker.

186. South Sudanese popular concepts about social relations and subcultures have changed considerably since the war, and songs and poetry have now come to include common references to the war, its social ills, the weapons and the morality of community members.

187. A very persuasive document produced by Physicians for Human Rights (2004) for the US Agency for International Development has shown the government-allied militias various uses of rape in the Darfur conflict as a way to weaken the enemy. See Physicians for Human Rights (2004).

188. See Jok, Madut Jok (1999b).

189. For a detailed description of these Abuja peace initiatives, see Wöndu and Lesch (2000).

190. Nasir is the name of the town in central eastern Upper Nile where the coup against the SPLA leader John Garang was first staged.

191. Wöndu and Ann Lesch (2000).

192. This 'forum hunting,' as SPLA leader John Garang called it, threatened further widening of the views on a possible settlement. The SPLA was satisfied with the IGAD process, but Khartoum wanted more Arab involvement, and was hoping that a more favorable initiative involving Arab countries would arise.

193. Mallaby, S. (2000).

194. Quoted in Johnson (2003).

195. The Egyptian–Libyan Sudan peace initiative, although expressing unprecedented desire to end the Sudanese conflicts, fell short of mentioning the right of the southern people to self-determination, and was therefore rejected outright by the SPLA as a pan-Arab coalition against the non-Arab Sudanese. It was not continued because it was rejected by some parties.

196. Deng (1999).

197. See Rolandsen (2005).

198. Johnson (1998b), see also Hutchinson (2001).

199. Karim, Ataul *et al.* (1996).

200. International Crisis Group (2002: 153).

201. Physicians for Human Rights (2004).

202. Human Rights Watch (2005c).

203. The *Daily Star* editorial is critical of the Arab League's silence on the destruction of Darfur, and attributes this silence to commercial interests in Sudan (*Daily Star* Editorial: Lebanon, May 25, 2004).

204. 'Arab Countries oppose Foreign Interference in Sudanese Internal Affairs.' Cairo: *Al-Ahram*, December 12, 2004: 3.

205. Eric Reeves, unpublished commentary distributed via list-serves. For more information, see Reeves' publication list on http://www.sudanreeves.org.

206. International Crisis Group (2004a).

207. Ibid.

208. Associated Press, 'Sudan Government, Rebels Peace talks break down in Chad.' AP December 16, 2003. Available at: http://www.ap.org.
209. Human Rights Watch (2005d).
210. Human Rights Watch (2005c).
211. Ibid.
212. See International Crisis Group (2005).
213. See Anderson (2004) and Brinkley (2005).
214. See the report by the International Crisis Group (2004a).
215. Editorial, 'Peace in Sudan,' *Washington Post*, January 13, 2005, page A 20.
216. See pages 87–88 of the Human Rights Watch (2005e) report of December 2005 for the full list of those indicted for the most gruesome of all human rights violations, the crimes of genocide and ethnic cleansing.
217. Human Rights Watch (2005e).
218. It is mentioned a great deal in Sudanese popular discourse and in my interviews that northerners are beginning to wonder if it might not be better to let go of the dissenting regions rather than continue the wars that have dragged down the whole country in the name of unity.
219. For example, this remark was made by al-Fatih Erwa, Sudan's head of mission to the United Nations in New York, at an event organized by the International Peace Academy in 2003.
220. Of course, the opposition armies that controlled some of the areas affected by drought were responsible for delayed warnings that could have alerted the world community to the disastrous food deficits. See *Africa News* (1998) 'Interview with Kerubino Kwanyin Bol,' Issue No. 29, August 1998.
221. Burr (1990).
222. It is important to note that mass relocation of IDPs is usually prompted by high-ranking members of the government after they have made investments in the area. For example, one IDP camp was ordered for demolition after a government minister, Ali al-Hajj, the man in charge of peace affairs before the NIF split, had built a multi-storey house for himself in the middle of the camp.
223. See the Christian Aid's report on massacres related to oil production in Upper Nile.
224. See the compilation of statistics of death and the scale of destruction in various commentaries and reports by Eric Reeves on his website, http://www.sudanreeves.org.
225. UN Integrated Regional Information Networks (2004).
226. Agence France-Presse (2004).
227. See International Crisis Group (2004b).

BIBLIOGRAPHY

Abd al-Rahim, Muddathir (1969) *Imperialism and Nationalism in Sudan: A Study in Constitutional and Political Development, 1899–1956.* Oxford: Clarendon Press.

Abdin, Hasan (1985) *Early Sudanese Nationalism, 1919–1925.* Khartoum: Khartoum University Press.

Africa News (1998) 'Interview with Kerubino Kwanyin Bol.' Issue No. 29, August.

Africa Watch (1990) *Denying the 'Honor of Living'. Sudan, A Human Rights Disaster.* New York and Washington, DC: Africa Watch.

African Rights (1991) *Destroying Ethnic Identity: The Secret War Against the Nuba.* London: African Rights.

African Rights (1995a) *Sudan's Invisible Citizens: The Policy of Abuse Against Displaced People in the North.* London: African Rights.

African Rights (1995b) *Facing Genocide: The Nuba of Sudan.* London: African Rights.

African Rights (1997) *Food and Power in Sudan: A Critique of Humanitarianism.* London: African Rights.

Agence France-Presse (2005) 'Sudanese Amry Begins to Absorb Southern Militia.' AFP, January 5.

Al-Affendi, Abd el-Wahab (1991) *Turabi's Revolution: Islam and Power in Sudan.* London: Grey Seal Islamic Studies.

Al-Agab, Ahmed al-Teraifi (1987) *Decentralization in Sudan.* Khartoum: Graduate College Publication No. 20, University of Khartoum.

al-Haj Hussein Adam (2003) 'The Arab Gathering and the attempt to cancel the other in Darfur.' Available at http://www.Sudanile.com.

Alier, Abel (1990) *Southern Sudan: Too Many Agreements Dishonored.* Exeter: Ithaca Press.

Al-Rai al-A'am (2005) 'President al-Bashir praises the Merowe Dam Project.' March 20.

Al-Safi, Mahasin abdel Gadir (1986) *The Role of Southern Sudanese People in the Building of the Modern Sudan.* Khartoum: Arrow Commercial Printing Press.

Al-Safi, Mahasin abdel Gadir (ed.) (1989) *The Nationalist Movement in the Sudan.* Khartoum: Institute of African and Asian Studies, University of Khartoum.

Amnesty International, May 3, 2000, *Sudan: The Human Price of Oil.* London: Amnesty International.

Anderson, Mary B. (1996) *Do No Harm: Supporting Local Capacities for Peace through Aid.* Cambridge, MA: Local Capacities for Peace Project: The Collaborative for Development Action, Inc.

Anderson, Scott (2004) 'How Did Darfur Happen?' *New York Times,* October 17.

Ayubi, Nazih (1993) *Political Islam: Religion and Politics in the Arab World.* London and New York: Routledge.

Barsella, Gina and Ayuso Guixot, Miguel A. (1998) *Struggling to be Heard: The Christian Voice in Independent Sudan, 1956–1996.* Nairobi: Paulines Publications Africa.

Bauman, G. (1987) *National Integration and Local Integrity: The Miri of the Nuba Mountains.* Oxford: Clarendon Press.

Bayart, J.-F. (1991) 'La Problematique de la Democratie en Afrique Noire. La Baule et puis après.' *Politique Africaine* 43 (October): 11–12.

Beinin, Joel and Joe Stork (1996) *Political Islam: Essays from Middle East Report (MERIP).* Berkeley, CA: University of California Press.

Beshr, M. O. (1968) *The Southern Sudan: Background to Conflict.* London: C. Hurst & Co.

Beshir, Muhammad Omer (1974) *Revolution and Nationalism in the Sudan.* London: Rex Collings.

Beshir, Muhammad Omer (1975) *The Southern Sudan: From Conflict to Peace.* London: C. Hurst and Co.

Beshir, Muhammad Omer (1979) *The Southern Sudan: Background to Conflict.* Khartoum: Khartoum University Press.

Bleuchot, Delmet and Derek Hopwood (eds) (1991) *Sudan: History, Identity, Ideology.* St. Antony's Middle East Monographs, No. 25. St. Antony's College.

Bosshard, P. and Hildyard, N. (2005) *A Critical Juncture for Peace, Democracy and the Environment: Sudan and the Merowe/Hamadab Dam Project. Report from a Visit to Sudan and a Fact-finding Mission to the Merowe Dam Project.* International Rivers Network.

Bowker, Geoffrey and Susan L. Star (2000) *Sorting Things Out: Classification and Its Consequences.* Cambridge, MA: MIT Press.

Brinkley, Joel, (2005) 'Surge in Violence in Sudan Erodes Hope.' *New York Times,* November 7.

Brusset, Emery (1998) *Sudan's Foreign Policy Environment: Some Implications for Humanitarian Assistance.* Munich, Germany: Conflict Prevention Network.

Burgat, François (2003) *Face to Face with Islam.* London: I. B. Tauris.

Burr, M. and R. Collins (1995) *Requiem for the Sudan: War, Drought and Disaster Relief on the Nile.* Boulder, CO: Westview Press.

Burr, Millard (1990) *Khartoum's Displaced Persons: A Decade of Despair.* US Committee for Refugees Issue Brief. Washington, DC.

Cater, Nick (1986) *Sudan: The Roots of Famine.* Oxford: Oxfam.

Christian Aid (2001) *The Scorched Earth: Oil and War in Sudan.* London: Christian Aid.

Collins, Robert (1971) *Land Beyond the Rivers: The Southern Sudan, 1898–1919.* New Haven, CT: Yale University Press.

Collins, Robert (1975) *The Southern Sudan in Historical Perspective.* Tel Aviv: Shiloah Center for Middle Eastern and African Studies.

Collins, Robert (1983) *Shadows in the Grass: the British in Southern Sudan, 1918–1956.* New Haven, CT: Yale University Press.

Collins, Robert (1992) 'Nilotic Slavery: Past and Present.' In *Human Commodity,* Elizabeth Savage (ed.). London: Frank Cass.

Collins, Robert (1999) 'Africans, Arabs, and Islamists: From the Conference Tables to the Battlefields in Sudan.' *African Studies Review* 42 (2): 105–23.

Crummey, Donald, Catherine Miller, François Ireton, Isabelle Dalmau (eds) (2006) *Land, Ethnicity and Political Legitimacy in Eastern Sudan.* Cairo: Centre d'Etude et de documentation économiques, juridiques et socials.

De Waal, Alex (1985) *Famine that Kills: Darfur, Sudan.* Oxford: Clarendon Press.

De Waal, Alex (1997) *Famine Crimes.* Oxford/Bloomington: James Currey/Indian University Press.

De Waal, Alex (2004) 'Counter-Insurgency on the Cheap.' *London Review of Books*, 26, 15.

Deng, Francis (1995) *War of Visions: Conflict of Identities in the Sudan.* Washington, DC: Brookings Institution.

Deng, Francis M. and Morrison, J. Stepent (2001) *US Policy to End Sudan's War: Report of the CSIS Task Force on United States-Sudan Policy.* Washington, DC: Center for Strategic and International Studies.

Deng, Luka Biong (1999) *Famine in Sudan: Causes, Preparedness and Response: A Political, Social and Economic Analysis of the 1998 Bahr el-Ghazal Famine.* Discussion Paper 369. Brighton: Institute for Development Studies.

Duffield, Mark (1994) 'The Political Economy of Internal Wars: Asset Transfer.' In *War and Hunger: Rethinking International Responses to Complex Emergencies.* J. Macrae and A. Zwi (eds), pp. 50–69. London: Zed Books.

ECHO Global Plan 8 (1999a) *ECHO Global Appeal for Sudan, April 1999–March 2000.* Brussels: European Commission Humanitarian Office.

ECHO Global Plan 8 (1999b) *The Unintended Consequences of Humanitarian Assistance: A Study into Causes of the 1998 Famine in Bahr el-Ghazal, Sudan.* Brussels: ECHO.

El-Bakri, Zeinab and el-Wathig M. Kameir (1983) 'Aspects of Women's Political Participation in Sudan.' *International Social Science Journal* 35, 4: 605–23.

Eltigani, E. (ed.) (1995) *War and Drought in Sudan: Essays on Population Displacement.* Gainesville, FL: University Press of Florida.

Eric (2001b) 'A War on Terrorism and the Betrayal of Southern Sudan.' *The Atlanta Journal and Constitution*, September 26.

Fadlalla, Mohamed H. (2004) *Short History of Sudan.* IUniverse.

Ferguson, James (2006) *Global Shadows: Africa in the Neoliberal World Order.* Durham, NC: Duke University Press, p. 213.

Flint, Julie and de Waal, Alex (2006) *Darfur: A Short History of a Long War.* New York: Zed Books.

Fluehr-Lobban, Carolyn (1990) *Islamic Law and Society in the Sudan.* Philadelphia, PA: University of Pennsylvania Press.

Garang, John (1987) *John Garang Speaks.* London: Kegan Paul International.

Gerges, Fawaz A. (1999) *America and Political Islam: Clash of Cultures or Clash of Interests?* Cambridge/New York: Cambridge University Press.

Hale, Sondra (1996) *Gender Politics in Sudan: Islamism, Socialism, and the State.* Boulder, CO: Westview Press.

Hannaford, Ivan (1996) *Race: The History of an Idea in the West.* Washington, DC: the Woodrow Wilson Center Press.

Harir, Sharif (1992) *Militarization of Conflict, Displacement and the Legitimacy of the State: A Case from Darfur, Western Sudan.* Bergen: Centre for Development Studies, University of Bergen, Norway.

Harir, Sharif (1993) 'Racism in Islamic Disguise: Retreating Nationalism and Upsurging Ethnicity in Dar Fur, Sudan.' In *Never Drink from the Same Cup*, Hanne Veber *et al.* (eds), pp. 291–311. Proceedings of the Conference on Indigenous Peoples in Africa, CDR-IWGIH Document No. 74. Tune: Denmark.

Harir, Sharif and T. Tvedt (eds) (1994) *Short-cut to Decay: the Case of the Sudan.* Uppsala: Nordiska Africaininstitutet.

Harker, John (2000) *Human Security in Sudan*: The Report of a Canadian Assessment Mission Prepared for the Minister of Foreign Affairs Ottawa (Part 1). Ottawa: Canadian Ministry of Foreign Affairs.

Hasan, Yusuf Fadl (1973) *The Arabs and the Sudan.* Khartoum: Khartoum University Press.

Hasan, Yusuf Fadl (ed.) (1971) *Sudan in Africa.* Khartoum: Khartoum University Press.

Hendrie, B. *et al.* (eds) (1996) *Operation Lifeline Sudan: A Review, July 1996.* Nairobi: OLS.

Holt, P. M. (1966) *Modern History of the Sudan.* New York: Praeger.

Human Rights Watch (1994a) *Civilian Devastation: Abuses by All Parties in the War in Southern Sudan.* New York: Human Rights Watch.

Human Rights Watch (1994b) *'In the Name of God:' Repression Continues in Northern Sudan.* New York: Human Rights Watch.

Human Rights Watch (1995) *Children in Sudan: Slaves, Street Children and Child Soldiers.* New York: Human Rights Watch.

Human Rights Watch (1996) *Behind the Red Line: Political Repression in Sudan.* New York: Human Rights Watch.

Human Rights Watch (1999) *World Report: Events of December 1997–November 1998.* Washington, DC: Human Rights Watch.

Human Rights Watch (2000) *Sudan: A Human Rights Report.* New York: Human Rights Watch.

Human Rights Watch (2003) *Sudan, Oil and Human Rights.* New York: Human Rights Watch.

Human Rights Watch (2004) *Destroyed Livelihoods: A Case Study of Furawiya Village, Darfur.* New York: Human Rights Watch.

Human Rights Watch (2005a) *UN: Put Sudan's Top Leaders on Sanctions List: ICC Should Investigate Darfur Officials.* New York: Human Rights Watch, December 12.

Human Rights Watch (2005b) *Darfur Women Raped Even after Seeking Refuge.* New York: Human Rights Watch.

Human Rights Watch (2005c) *Darfur: Arrest War Criminals, Not Aid Workers: Government Must End Harassment of Aid Agencies, Restrictions on Free Speech.* London: Human Rights Watch, May 31.

Human Rights Watch (2005d) *Expand African Union Mission in Darfur: A Letter to the African Union Peace and Security Council.* May 5.

Human Rights Watch (2005e) *Darfur: ICC Prosecutor Briefs Security Council Should Declare Support for Court's Investigation.* New York: Human Rights Watch, June 29.

Hutchinson, Sharon (1996) *Nuer Dilemmas: Coping with War, Money and the State.* Berkeley and Los Angeles, CA: University of California Press.

Hutchinson, Sharon (2001) 'A Curse from God? Religious and Political Dimensions of the Post-1991 Rise of Ethnic Violence in South Sudan.' *The Journal of Modern African Studies* 39 (2): 307–31.

Idris, Amir (2001) *Sudan's Civil War: Slavery, Race and Formational Identities.* Lewiston, NY: Edwin Mellen Press.

Inter-Governmental Agency for Development (1995) *Declaration of Principles for a Negotiated Settlement in Sudan.* Asmara: IGAD.

International Crisis Group (2002) *God, Oil and Country: Changing the Logic of War in Sudan.* Brussels: International Crisis Group.

International Crisis Group (2002) *Sudan's Best Chance for Peace: How not to Lose it.* Brussels: International Crisis Group.

International Crisis Group (2004) *Darfur Rising: Sudan's New Conflict.* Africa Report No. 76, March. Brussels: International Crisis Group.

International Crisis Group (2004a) *Darfur Rising: Sudan's New Crisis.* Nairobi/Brussels: International Crisis Group Africa Report No. 76, 21–24.

International Crisis Group (2004b) 'Sudan: Now or Never in Darfur.' Brussels: International Crisis Group, May 23.

International Crisis Group (2005) *Darfur Needs Bolder International Intervention.* Brussels: International Crisis Group, May 25.

Inter-regional Information Network (2001) 'Sudan: Oil Wells Burning?' IRIN News Agency, January 29.

Inter-Regional Information Network (2005) *Sudan: Darfur IDPs Unlikely to Return Home in the Near Future.* Nairobi: Office for the Coordination of Humanitarian Affairs, May 11.

Jaspers, Susanne (1999) *Targeting and Distribution of Food Aid in SPLA-Controlled Areas of South Sudan.* Nairobi: World Food Program.

Johnson, Douglas (1994) 'Destruction and Reconstruction in the Economy of the Southern Sudan.' In *Short-Cut to Decay: the Case of the Sudan,* S. Harir and T. Tvedt (eds). Uppsala: Nordiska Afrikainstitutet.

Johnson, Douglas (1998a) *The Sudan Conflict: Historical and Political Background: Analysis and Evaluation Paper.* Munich, Germany: Conflict Prevention Network.

Johnson, Douglas (1998b) 'The Sudan People's Liberation Army and the Problem of Factionalism.' In *African Guerrillas,* Christopher Clapham (ed.) Bloomington, IN: Indiana University Press and Oxford: James Currey.

Johnson, Douglas (2003) *The Root Causes of Sudan's Civil Wars.* Oxford: James Currey.

Jok, Jok Madut (1996) 'Information Exchange in the Disaster Zone: Interaction Between Aid Workers and Recipients in South Sudan.' *Disasters* 20, 3: 206–215.

Jok, Jok Madut (1998a) *Militarization, Gender and Reproductive Health in South Sudan.* New York: The Edwin Mellen Press.

Jok, Jok Madut (1999a) 'Militarism, Gender and Reproductive Suffering: the Case of Abortion in Western Dinka.' *Africa* 69, 2: 194–212.

Jok, Jok Madut (2001) *War and Slavery in Sudan.* Philadelphia, PA: University of Pennsylvania Press.

Jok, Jok Madut (2004) 'The Targeting of Civilians as a Military Tactic.' In Ann Lesch and Osman Fadl (eds) *Coping with Torture: Images from the Sudan.* Trenton, NJ and Asmara: the Red Sea Press, 2004.

Jok, Jok Madut and Sharon Hutchinson (1999) 'Sudan's Prolonged Second Civil War and The Militarization of Nuer and Dinka Ethnic Identities.' *African Studies Review* 42 (2): 125–145.

Jok, Madut Jok (1999b) 'Militarization and Gender Violence in South Sudan.' *Journal of Asian and African Studies* 34(4): 427.

Karim, Ataul *et al.* (1996) *Operation Lifeline Sudan: A Review.* Geneva: OLS.

Kebbede, Girma (1999) *Sudan's Predicament: Civil War, Dsiplacement and Ecological Degradation.* Brookfield, VM: Ashgate Publishing.

Keen, David (1994) *The Benefits of Famine: A Political Economy of Famine and Relief in Southwestern Sudan.* Princeton, NJ: Princeton University Press.

Keen, David (1998) *The Political Economy of War, with Special Reference to Sudan and Bahr el-Ghazal: Analysis and Evaluation Paper.* Munich, Germany: Conflict Prevention Network.

Khalid, Mansour (1990) *The Government they Deserve: the Role of the Elite in Sudan's Political Evolution.* London and New York: Kegan Paul International.

Kok, Peter Nyot (1992) 'Adding Fuel to the Conflict: Oil, War, and Peace in Sudan.' In *Beyond Conflict in the Horn: Prospects for Peace, Recovery, and Development in Ethiopia, Somalia, Eritrea and Sudan,* M. Doornbos *et al.* (eds), pp. 104–112. The Hague: Institute of Social Studies.

Kok, Peter Nyot (1996) 'Sudan: Between Radical Restructuring and Deconstruction of the State Systems.' *Review of African Politics and Economy,* 70: 560.

Lesch, Ann (1998) *The Sudan: Contested National Identities.* Oxford: James Currey.

Lesch, Ann and Fadl, Osman (eds) (2004) *Coping with Torture: Images From the Sudan.* Asmara and Trenton, NJ: The Red Sea Press, Inc.

Lewis, Bernard (2003) *The Crisis of Islam: Holy War and Unholy Terror.* New York: Random House, Inc.

Lienhardt, Godfrey (1961) *Divinity and Experience: The Religion of the Dinka.* Oxford: Oxford University Press.

Macaskill, Una (1998) *Humanitarian Assistance in Sudan in 1998: Analysis and Evaluation Paper.* Munich, Germany: Conflict Prevention Network.

MacMichael, Harold. A. (1967) *The Tribes of Northern and Central Kordofan.* London: Cass.

Majak, Damazo Dut (1990) *The Northern Bahr el-Ghazal: People, Alien Encroachment and Rule, 1856–1956.* Ph.D. dissertation, University of California, Santa Barbara.

Mallaby, S. (2000) 'Taking Foreign Policy Private'. *Washington Post,* May 29.

Malwal, Bona (1981) *People and Power in Sudan: The Struggle for National Stability.* London: Ithaca Press.

Malwal, Bona (2005) *Sudan's Latest Peace Agreement: An Accord that is Neither Fair nor Comprehensive.* Omdurman: A. K. Mirghani Cultural Center.

Mamdani, Mahmood (2001) *When Victims Become Killers: Colonialism, Nativism and the Genocide in Rwanda.* Princeton, NJ: Princeton University Press.

Manji, Irshad (2004) *The Trouble with Islam Today: A Muslim's Call for Reform in Her Faith.* New York: St. Martin's Griffin.

Meyer, Gabriel and James Nicholls (2005) *War and Faith in Sudan.* Grand Rapids, MI: Wm B. Eerdmans Publishing Company.

Minear, Larry (1991) *Humanitarianism Under Siege: A Critical Review of Operation Lifeline Sudan.* Trenton, NJ: Red Sea Press.

Munson, Harry (2004) 'Lifting the Veil: Understanding the Roots of Islamic Militancy.' *Harvard International Review,* 25 (4).

Nadel, S. F. (1947) *The Nuba.* Oxford: Oxford University Press.

Ntata, Pierson R. T. (1999) *Participation by the Affected Population in Relief Operations: A Review of the Experience of DEC Agencies During the Response to the 1998 Famine in South Sudan: A Report Prepared for the Active Learning Network on Accountability and Performance in Humanitarian Assistance.* Nairobi: OLS.

Nyaba, Peter Aduok (1997) *The Politics of Liberation in South Sudan: An Insider's View.* Kampala: Fountain Publishers.

O'balance E. (2000) *Sudan, Civil War and Terrorism, 1956–1999.* London: Macmillan Press Ltd.

O'Fahey, R. S. (1980) *State and Society in Dar Fur.* New York: St. Martin's Press.

O'Fahey, R. S. and M. I. Abu Salim (1983) *Land in Dar Fur: Charters and Related Documents from the Dar Fur Sultanate.* Cambridge: Cambridge University Press.

Omaar, Rakiya and Alex de Waal (1993) *Components of a Lasting Peace in Sudan: First Thoughts.* London: African Rights.

Omi, Michael and H. Winant (1994) *Racial Formation in the United States: From the 1960s to the 1990s.* New York and London: Routledge.

Patterson, Donald (1999) *Inside Sudan: Political Islam, Conflict, and Catastrophe.* Boulder, CO: Westview Press.

Physicians for Human Rights (2004) *Destroyed Livelihoods: A Case Study of Furawiya Village, Darfur.* Cambridge, MA: Physicians for Human Rights.

Physicians for Human Rights (2004) *The Use of Rape as a Weapon of War in the Conflict in Darfur, Sudan.* Boston, MA: Physicians for Human Rights.

Pipes, Daniel (2002) *In the Path of God: Islam and Political Power.* New Brunswick, NJ: Transaction Publishers.

Pipes, Daniel (2003) *Militant Islam Reaches America.* New York/London: W. W. Norton.

Polgreen, Lydia (2006) 'Refugee Crisis Grows as Darfur War Crosses a Border.' *New York Times,* February 28.

Prunier, Gérard (1996) *Identity Crisis and the Weak State: The Making of the Sudanese Civil War.* London: WRITENET.

Prunier, Gérard (2005) *Darfur: An Ambiguous Genocide.* Ithaca, NY: Cornell University Press.

Reeves, Eric (1999) 'Don't Let Oil Revenues in Sudan Fuel Genocide.' *The Globe and Mail* (Canada) May 4, 9.

Reeves, Eric (2001a) 'Rapacious Instincts in Sudan.' *The Nation,* June 4.

Reeves, Eric (2001c) 'Oil Development in Sudan.' *Bulletin of the Association of Concerned Africa Scholars,* December, 7–10.

Rethven, Malise (2002) *Fury for God: The Islamist Attack on America.* London: Granta Books.

Rolandsen, Øystein (2005) *Guerrilla Government: Political Changes in the Southern Sudan During the 1990s.* Uppsala: The Nordic Africa Institute.

Ruay, Deng Akol (1994) *The Politics of Two Sudans: The South and the North.* Uppsala: Nordiska Afrikaninstitutet.

Ryle, John (2004a) 'Mass Graves Old and New: A New Dam on the Nile, the Threat to Ancient Nubia and the Crisis of the Sudanese State.' *The Times Literary Supplement,* October 15.

Ryle, John (2004b) 'Disaster in Darfur.' *The New York Review of Books* 51 (13): 24–5.

Ryle, John and Georgette Gagnon (2003) *Report of an Investigation into Oil Development, Conflict and Displacement in Western Upper Nile, Sudan.* Ottawa: Canadian Sudan Inter-Agency Reference Group (SIARG).

Sagar, J. W. (1950) 'Notes on the History, Religion and Customs of the Nuba, *Sudan Notes and Records* 5.

Scandinavian Institute of African Studies (1994) *From the Mountains to the Plains: The Integration of the Lafofa Nuba into Sudanese Society.* Uppsala: SIAS.

Snow, D. (1996) *Uncivil Wars: International Security and the New Internal Conflicts.* London: Lynne Rienner.

Sommer, John (1968) *The Sudan: A Geographical Investigation of the Historical and Social Roots of Political Dissension.* Ph.D. dissertation, Boston University.

Stevenson, R. C. (1984) *The Nuba of Southern Kordofan: Ethnographic Survey.* Khartoum: Khartoum University Press.

Sudan Studies Association Newsletter. 24 (2): February 2006:6

Tibi, Bassam (2002) *The Challenge of Fundamentalism: Political Islam and the New World Disorder.* Berkeley, CA: University of California Press.

Tobin, I. N (1985) 'The Effects of Drought among the Zaghawa of Northern Darfur.' *Disasters* 9: 213–223.

Toulabor, Comi M. (1994) 'Political Satire Past and Present in Togo.' *Critique of Anthropology* 14 (1): 59–75.

UN Inter-regional Information Network (2004) 'Sudan: Armed and Angry – Sudan's Southern Militias Still a Threat to Peace.' IRIN News Agency, June 4.

United Nations (2005) *Sudan: Darfur Atrocities do not Amount to Genocide. Report of the Secretary General, February 2005.* New York: United Nations.

United Nations Commission on Human Rights (UNCHR) (1999) *Question of the Violation of Human Rights and Fundamental Freedoms in any Part of the World: Situation of Human Rights in the Sudan* (E/CN.4/1999/38/Add.1, 17 May). Geneva: UNHCR.

United Nations Commission on Human Rights (UNCHR) (2000) *Situation of Human Rights in the Sudan.* Document E/DEC/258. Geneva: UNHCR.

United Nations Commission on Human Rights (UNCHR) (2001) *Situation of Human Rights in the Sudan.* Document A/RES/55/116. Geneva: UNHCR.

United Nations Commissioner on Human Rights (1999) *Situation of Human Rights in the Sudan: Visit of the Special Rapporteur, Mr Leonardo Franco, to the Republic of Sudan.* Addendum to E/CN.4/1999/38 Geneva: UNHCR.

United Nations Commissioner on Human Rights (2000) *Situation of Human Rights in the Sudan.* Document E/DEC/258. Geneva: UNHCR.

United Nations Commissioner on Human Rights (2001) *Situation of Human Rights in the Sudan.* Document A/RES/55/116. Geneva: UNHCR.

United Nations General Assembly (UNGA) (2000) *Human Rights Questions: Human Rights Situations and Reports of Special Rapporteurs* and Representatives: Situation of Human Rights in the Sudan* (A/55/374, 11 September). Geneva: United Nations.

United Nations Human Rights Commissioner (2006) *Supplementary Appeal: Return and Reintegration of Sudan Refugees and IDPs to South Sudan and Protection of IDPs in Khartoum and Kassala States of Sudan.* Geneva: UNHCR.

United States Refugee Committee (1998) *Quantifying Genocide.* Washington, DC: US Refugee Committe.

Wai, Dunstan M. (1981) *The African-Arab Conflict in the Sudan.* New York: Africana Publishing Company.

Warburg, Gabriel (1992) *Historical Discord in the Nile Valley.* Evanston, IL: Northwestern University Press.

Warburg, Gabriel (2002) *Islam, Sectarianism and Politics in Sudan since the Mahdiyya.* Madison, WI: University of Wisconsin Press.

Wöndu, S. and Lesche, A. (2000) *Battle for Peace in Sudan: An Analysis of the Abuja Conferences, 1992–1993.* New York: University Press of America.

Woodward, P. (ed.) (1991) *Sudan After Nimeiri.* London: Routledge

Young, J. (2004) 'Sudan's Blue Nile Territory and the Struggle Against Marginalization.' In *States Within States: Incipient Political Entities in the Post-Cold War Era,* P. Kingston and I. S. Spears, pp. 67–80. New York: Palgrave MacMillan.

Zartman, I. W. *et al.* (1995) *Collapsed States: The Disintegration and Restoration of Legitimate Authority.* London: Lynne Rienner.

APPENDIX: MAPS

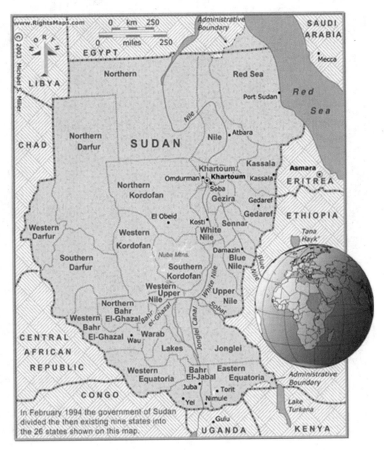

Map 1. Sudan in relation to Africa

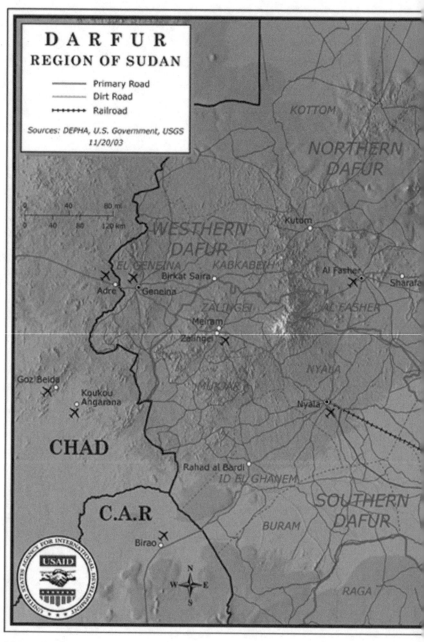

Map 2. Darfur

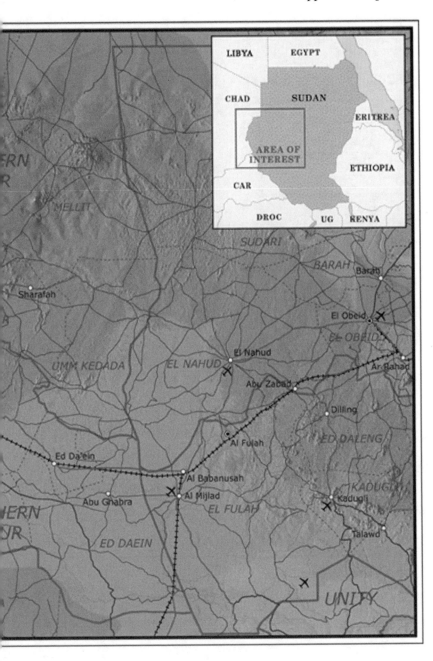

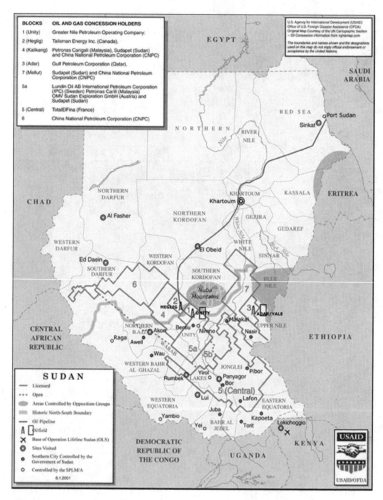

Map 3. Oil development in Sudan

INDEX